Praise for
THE BANDANA EXPRESS

"Virginia has its own version of *Friday Night Lights* in *The Bandana Express*, a tale of the grand-old single-wing offense of the Giles Spartans, by Jeremy Haymore, complete with a foreword by ESPN's Marty Smith, which in itself is worth the price of admission. But there's more, so much more. High school football in and around the banks of the New River has always been sort of a sacred thing to the folks of Southwest Virginia, especially in Giles. Haymore brings it all to life in a way that will matter to those who love the sport, no matter where they live. If you're weary of the sports world in the time of NIL, this story of a team more than four decades ago just might help cure what ails ya."

—Roland Lazenby, *New York Times* bestselling author of *Michael Jordan: The Life*

"The lessons learned and relationships forged on the dusty football fields of Southwest Virginia have sustained me for a lifetime. This true story will capture your heart, rally your soul, and reinforce what truly matters!"

—Frank Beamer, former head coach at Virginia Tech and member of the College Football Hall of Fame

"Between 1955 and 2012, almost seven decades, my life was consumed by the sport of football. I thought I had experienced every ounce of its passion and pain. I was wrong. Jeremy Haymore, in his brilliant book, *The Bandana Express*, forced me to suffer, celebrate, and laugh out loud as it wound to its unlikely conclusion. If you love football, read it. If you don't love football, read it anyway. You will love it, and it will make you a better person."

—Bill Curry, former NFL player, longtime coach, and ESPN analyst

"This book captures the heart, grit, and soul of what makes small-town football special. It's more than a story about wins and championships—it's about a community that came together, believed in something bigger, and built a legacy that still echoes today."

—Bud Foster, former defensive coordinator at Virginia Tech

"Coach Ragsdale is a legend in Virginia high school coaching. I have so much respect for him and the impact he's had on the New River Valley and all of Giles County."

—Shane Beamer, head coach at the University of South Carolina

"An inspirational story about what makes high school football so special. This is a must-read!"

—Darrin Donnelly, bestselling author of *Think Like a Warrior*

"Jeremy Haymore has captured the spirit of Steve Ragsdale's squad with superb imagery and detail. The story is a history lesson in the single-wing offense, wrapped in a tale that highlights the perseverance and triumph of a championship program. It is a great read for anyone who loves the game."

—Bucky Brooks, former NFL player and NFL Network analyst

"As a proud Giles alum and former trigonometry student

of Coach Steve Ragsdale, opening *The Bandana Express* felt like stepping into a time machine, bringing me right back home. I could hear the roar of the stadium under the lights in Pearisburg, the clashing of pads and helmets, and the bean-filled water bottles shaking in the stands. Jeremy Haymore brings the history, heart, and grit of small-town football to life in a way that makes you feel it. This isn't just a football story; it's a tribute to the tradition that raised so many of us."

—Lauren Sisler, ESPN sports reporter and Giles High School graduate

"Jeremy Haymore brilliantly pens a true story in *The Bandana Express* that takes the reader on a journey of history, struggle, and transformation, one that serves as a soaring testament to the sacred power of sports to heal, unite, and transform. The field becomes a sanctuary, the team a family, and the game a language of hope and heart in this masterful tribute and powerful reflection on belonging, survival, and promise. In the end, *The Bandana Express* reminds us that sports, at their best, don't just build character; they rebuild lives, restore community pride, and provide a pathway for personal redemption."

—Stephen Panus, author of *Walk On*, keynote speaker, and leadership-development coach

"Jeremy Haymore's *The Bandana Express* captures the spirit of the game with striking authenticity and care. Through painstaking research, heartfelt storytelling, and vivid detail, Haymore brings to life the overlooked corner of Southwest Virginia, where grit and loyalty define the culture and the football field is sacred ground. For anyone who ever dreamed under the lights on a Friday night, who grew up with mud on their cleats and ambition in their chest, or who wants to understand what football really means in Appalachia, this book is for you."

—DeLane Fitzgerald, head coach at Southern Utah University

"*The Bandana Express* is a journey back in time with a high school football team and community that evolve together into a family. The coaches, players, and people from 1980 come alive, making the reader feel as if they are part of the team. A book for young and old alike."

—Bill George, former head coach at the US Coast Guard Academy and author of *Home Fields*

"Jeremy Haymore's account of the 1980 Giles Spartans, *The Bandana Express*, carries the reader onto the fields of high school football games and into the heart of timeless rivalries that communities across our nation thrive on. Ex-players, coaches, and fans alike will enjoy this play-by-play of the football season that catapulted this underdog team into the state finals. This up-close-and-personal look at a coach who has the added weight of a family legacy to live up to, and how he inspired a group of young men to aspire to greatness against all odds, is a sports story for the ages!"

—Carey Henry Keefe, author of *A Tide of Dreams*

The Bandana Express:
The True Story of the 1980 Giles Spartans
by Jeremy Haymore

© Copyright 2025 Jeremy Haymore

ISBN 979-8-88824-769-3

All rights reserved. No part of this publication may be reproduced, stored in a retrieval system, or transmitted in any form or by any means—electronic, mechanical, photocopy, recording, or any other—except for brief quotations in printed reviews, without the prior written permission of the author.

Edited by Hannah Tonsor
Cover design by Catherine Herold

Published by

3705 Shore Drive
Virginia Beach, VA 23455
800-435-4811
www.koehlerbooks.com

THE BANDANA EXPRESS

THE TRUE STORY OF THE 1980 GILES SPARTANS

JEREMY HAYMORE

VIRGINIA BEACH
CAPE CHARLES

For my children—may my journey to bring this story to life be something they can always be proud of.

TABLE OF CONTENTS

Author's Note ... 1

Foreword ... 7

Prologue ... 10

Chapter 1: Mountain Roar ... 13

Chapter 2: Weak As Cat Pee ... 22

Chapter 3: Narz ... 30

Chapter 4: The Gold Standard ... 39

Chapter 5: Fight Cloud ... 48

Chapter 6: The Bandana Is Born ... 57

Chapter 7: Who Beat? ... 67

Chapter 8: We Are Family ... 75

Chapter 9: Crossing Big A Mountain ... 85

Chapter 10: Traveling Salesman ... 95

Chapter 11: Edgar Allan Mo ... 106

Chapter 12: Drive, Drive, Drive! ... 117

Chapter 13: Another One Bites The Dust ... 126

Chapter 14: Oh Sh*t! ... 138

Chapter 15: Interstate 77 ... 146

Chapter 16: The Bandana Expressway ... 158

Chapter 17: The Gambler ... 171

Chapter 18: Hullabaloo ... 185

Chapter 19: Tight As A Banjo String ... 194

Chapter 20: Resurgence ... 205

Chapter 21: Seesaw ... 213

Chapter 22: Tickled To Death ... 222

Notes ... 242

Bibliography ... 289

AUTHOR'S NOTE

STEVE RAGSDALE WON 255 GAMES over a thirty-year career at Giles High School. The program's consistency during his tenure exemplified tradition. After 1980, he led the Spartans to four more appearances in the state finals, with championships in 1993, 27–18 over Lunenburg Central, and in 2005, 35–34 over Manassas Park. In both instances, they defeated an opponent sporting a twenty-seven-game winning streak. Steve quietly retired following the 2007 season. His successor, Jeff Williams, won a state title in 2013 running the same single-wing offense. In 2008, the playing surface at Spartan Stadium was dedicated as Stephen C. Ragsdale Field, and six years later, he was inducted into the VHSL Hall of Fame. Despite his many accomplishments, Steve's peers invariably described him as down-to-earth and authentically humble.

This book took me almost fifteen years to complete. While it took much longer than anticipated, I often reminded myself that nothing worthwhile comes easy. High school football taught me that. Thus, I decided early on to give the project to God for completion in His time and for His glory, not my own. Over the past decade and a half, I have reviewed over one hundred newspapers nationwide, some with more than fifty years of primary-source material. In addition, I consulted scrapbooks, annuals, historical texts, websites, films, pictures, music, and other documents. Though I've included endnotes and a bibliography so the reader can track my research, the most rewarding part of the experience was meeting the many great people tied to this story. I conducted nearly 150 interviews, many of them face-to-face.

Not only was I able to speak with players from the various teams represented, including thirty-four members of the Bandana Express, but also with some of the greatest coaches ever to wear a whistle in the state of Virginia. A huge thank you to the following for so graciously offering their memories of the events in *The Bandana Express* and beyond:

Steve Ragsdale, Don Lowe, Vic Edwards, Rusty Kelley, Jerry Albert, David Chapman, Jeff Williams, Greg Mance, Charlie Mullins, Mike Ratcliffe, Steve Chafin, Barry Farmer, Chuck Stone, Timmy Psathas, Mark Chapman, Leon King, Greg King, Todd Dennis, Chris Woods, Don Sparks, Phillip Steele, Timmy Martin, Jamie Martin, Danny Huskey, Bobby Munsey, Kevin Tate, Alvin Martin, Rodney Freeman, Randy Martin, Anthony Shipman, Cecil Austin, Willie Riggs, Tim Wilson, Dan Cook, Rowdy Stump, Mike Mitchener, Gary Stump, Scott Hundley, Jeff Stevers, Glenn Smith, Curtis Woods, Robert Stump, Fonzie Austin, Billy McCroskey, Terry Freeman, David Martin, Brian Strader, Benny Hendricks, Babette Farmer Martin, Ronda Myers Penn, Bill Puckett, Gary Clark, Neal Andrews, Priscilla Morris, Joe Gollehon, Paul "Chappy" Baker, Mark Hubbard, Charles Fraley Jr., Margee Ragsdale, Jeff Huskey, Neal Mustard, Billy Cook, Allen McClaugherty, Ed Morris, Naomi Crabtree Morris, Richard Newton, Helen French, Carroll Dale, Dewey Lusk Jr., Dave Brown, Frank Beamer, Ruth Simmons, Gary Wake, Jerry Huffman, Dan Phlegar, Bobby Hale, Lucinda Brown Hale, Billy Neal, Lockard Conley, Bucky Lawson, Bill Graham, Burt Delap, Chris Rombow, Mark Perkins, Rick Franklin, Daniel Haymore, Ken Stickley, Fred Zirkle, Buddy Martin, Danny Surface, Eddie Evans, Roger Lovern, Gary Martin, David Carr, Doug Marrs, John O'Neal, Eddie Hall, Winfred Beale, Larry Bradley, Junior Coleman, Brad Mullins, Timmy Jones, Larry Jones, Steve McDaniel, Bill Patteson, Charles "Bubbie" Fraley III, Wayne Gautier, Dave Crist, Norman Lineburg, Buddy Shull, John Howlett, Danny Suthers, Phil Robbins, Dewey Lusk III, Curtis Burkett, Wade Lopez, Glen Styles, Edward Sanderson, David Huffman, Ed Scott, Pat Elliott, Mike Nunnally, Elmer Fox,

Allen Pinkett, Joe Boone, Chip Buckman, Todd Turner, Doug Houtz, Tim Veltman, Scott Lageman, Frank Hughlett, David Webster, Ken Sieber, Dave Bell, Mike Grammo, Mike Devaney, David Epperley, Tom Dolan, John Sieber, Dave Scarangella, Doug Doughty, Ed Racely, Mickey Thompson, Matt Griffis, and Brad Bradley.

My only wish is to have had the privilege of meeting Harry Ragsdale. Harry died on November 9, 1983, after a long illness, just two days before Giles traveled to Abingdon for the first round of the playoffs. After an emotional pep rally, the Spartans rallied behind their grieving coach and upset the top-seeded Falcons 27–0. "It was one of the greatest wins I've ever had," Steve said.

Nearly five hundred miles away, Allen Pinkett was in State College, Pennsylvania, preparing for Notre Dame's Saturday-afternoon matchup with Penn State. Pinkett carried thirty-six times for 217 yards and four touchdowns the following day, becoming just the third rusher in Fighting Irish history to go over a thousand yards in a season. Still, Notre Dame suffered a heartbreaking 34–30 loss to the Nittany Lions in the final seconds. Afterward, Pinkett told Penn State's student-run newspaper, the *Daily Collegian*: "I compare this game to the state championship when I was a high school junior. I gained [224] yards, had five touchdowns, and made one conversion. But when it counted, my conversion at the end of the game fell short." He told me it was the one play that haunted him throughout his career, from high school to the NFL.

Ironically enough, when Pinkett was being recruited following the 1981 season, Ed Scott sent every school interested a copy of the 1980 state championship. Reportedly, when it reached Penn State, Joe Paterno stopped the film and made his entire staff watch, telling them, "This is the greatest high school football game you'll ever see." From the first time I heard a recount of the contest, I was inclined to agree.

There are a few other sources so often referenced that I'd like to acknowledge them here as well. Rick Baker's website, FourSeasonsFootball.com, keeps meticulous records of high school football scores and records for Central Appalachia, and it proved invaluable for me throughout my writing. Vic Edwards's book, *Winging It: Spartan Football 1961–2001*, was another of these consistently referenced sources, as was Mark Perkins's *Football History of Narrows High School*, a videotaped overview of the Green Wave from 1931–1962. Hats off to these three individuals for their diligent research and commitment to high school football.

Thank you to John Koehler, Hannah Tonsor, Catherine Herold, and everyone at Koehler Books for the opportunity to share this story with the world. I appreciate your patience and wisdom as you shepherded me through the publication process.

I want to thank Marty Smith, one of sports media's greatest storytellers and a *New York Times* bestselling author, for writing the foreword. As a proud Giles alum and member of the 1993 Spartans, Marty attended the game as a youngster thirteen years prior. As soon as I discovered this, I knew his unique perspective would be ideal to introduce *The Bandana Express*.

Also, I would be remiss if I didn't mention the devoted friends and family who regularly held me accountable and provided honest feedback. With their support, I never went a day without making progress. When life was ever-changing, this project remained a certainty. The Lowlife defense always stopped Pinkett, and Harry was always proud.

Finally, this is a true story. Using research and reason, I endeavored to weave the circumstances, perspectives, and dialogue into a cohesive narrative. While I aspired to give a positive account that presented the best portrayal of all involved, the facts were not altered for dramatic effect. When memories conflicted, I considered as many sources as possible until a consensus was reached. Otherwise, this was precisely how the events were conveyed to me. Unfortunately, several individuals mentioned in this book have passed away since they were interviewed. I deeply regret it was not finished in time, but for their loved ones, I hope it rekindles memories of an era they all described as a wonderful time in their lives.

"Gas may be a buck a gallon, hamburger $1.50 a pound, and the economy heading straight to you-know-where, but for two hours on a weekend night, everything's forgotten as young men go to war to extend—or build—tradition."
—Bob Foley, *Bluefield Daily Telegraph*, September 2, 1979

FOREWORD

WHEN I WAS A LITTLE BOY, there was only one department store in my hometown, Pearisburg, Virginia, where *The Bandana Express* takes place. The store was called Leggett's, and it was located on Wenonah Avenue, a block up from the Giles County Courthouse. The marquee adorning its exterior included a long swooping capital "L," with an ornate circular design slapped onto the vertical side of the letter. For small-town country folk, that place was fancy. It was also the only place we could buy clothing ensembles in town, other than the Maxway over in the Food Lion shopping plaza, across the highway from the Dairy Queen.

Every year in the late summer months, my sweet momma, Joy Smith, took my sister and me down to Leggett's for some new school shoes and maybe some jeans if I'd grown last year's britches into high-waters or the knees were battered and holey from constant backyard basketball games and front-yard football games and neighborhood-wide games of "war" with plastic machine guns (bought at the Maxway).

Inside Leggett's was a wonderland. Crisp new shirts and pants and jackets and vests on well-curated racks for the season. A jewelry station. The smell of new shoes. And every fall, there was an entire section full of red bandanas. In the Leggett's. In the Maxway. In the Food Lion. Bandana prints painted on the windows of the Dairy Queen and the Pizza Hut and every plate-glass storefront on Main.

The mecca for Spartan gear was the Giles Shoe Center, a locally owned footwear retailer at which I got a pair of Chicago Bears–themed Walter Payton KangaROOS, the signature "Sweetness" high-top sneakers with Velcro pockets sewn into the tongue. *Nothing* was cooler than ripping open the top of your 'Roos after recess to unveil the quarter you stashed away for a milk or an ice cream later at school. Giles Shoe Center had Giles Spartan jerseys—big mesh, always no. 00. There were jackets, T-shirts, foam trucker hats. And more bandanas than the O.K. Corral.

Bandanas were *everywhere* in Giles County.

Because if you lived anywhere in Giles County east of Pearisburg, all the way to the Montgomery line, bandanas were *the* must-have accessory. We wore them on or around our heads. Tied them in our belt loops or around our wrists like wristbands. Draped them around our necks like the Cowboys gang in *Tombstone*. Ladies weaved them through their Aqua Net–infused hair as Spartan-themed headbands.

The bandana was our battle flag. Nearly half a century later, it still is.

The 1980 Giles Spartans, inspired by star running back Leon King, created a tradition that lives on to this day. King was the best player on the team that season and remains one of the greatest to ever wear a Spartan football jersey. So, when he donned a red bandana under his helmet that magical season, it became a unification tool for the entire team. For the entire community. And it became legend.

The Bandana Express.

In January 1980, my family moved to Pearisburg. I was three months shy of four years old. My dad, Leo Smith, *loved* football. He'd park me in front of the television on Saturdays and Sundays and teach me the game, and it tickled the hell out of him that I instantly loved it too. That fall, he started taking me to see the Spartans. I was mesmerized, as were most young boys my age, immersed in an experience that was truly sensory overload. The vibrant colors. The unbridled passion. The emotional release. An entire community pulling in the same direction.

Hope.

For kids like us, twenty-eight-year-old head coach Steve Ragsdale and his Spartan men were mythical creatures. Superheroes. Still are. If you've read Buzz Bissinger's book *Friday Night Lights*, or maybe seen Peter Berg's film or television adaptations, you have an idea what high school football can mean to a community. It creates an identity that permeates the people.

Jeremy Haymore captures all of that within the pages of *The Bandana Express*, with a deeply comprehensive, impeccably researched account of a magical season in which the Spartans won the first state championship in school history. And in doing so, injected a pride into Pearisburg that its residents had never known.

You'll learn about the culture Coach Ragsdale instilled and demanded. You'll learn about a legendary father's influence and careful tutelage. You'll learn about the greatest rivalry in the entire state of Virginia—Giles versus its hated crosstown nemesis, the Narrows Green Wave. And you'll learn how a bunch of country boys came together and leveraged an underdog mentality authentic to Appalachia to make history.

In the fall of 1993, when I was a senior, no team since the Bandana Express had delivered another football state championship to Giles County. While we had all-state talent at several positions, there were a lot of kids like me who filled in the gaps.

But we were a great team. And we, too, delivered a small-town dream.

It remains one of the greatest moments of my life.

Marty Smith, ESPN
Defensive Back, 1993 Giles Spartans
Group A, Div. II Virginia State Champions

PROLOGUE

December 11, 1993
Group A, Division II Championship
Giles vs. Lunenburg Central

SET AGAINST A BACKDROP of the Appalachian Mountains, the summit of Angel's Rest dominated the horizon above Pearisburg, Virginia. Regardless of frigid afternoon temperatures and a biting December wind, the Giles High School football stadium had been packed for hours, proud bandana flags popping in gusts upward of thirty miles per hour. Inside, forty-two-year-old Steve Ragsdale was poised to address his team in the hallowed hallway of the school's agriculture building. The Giles Spartans were minutes away from playing for a state championship, their second appearance in a title tilt, the first since 1980. Their opponents, the Chargers of Lunenburg Central, were the defending state champions and winners of twenty-seven games in a row. They were seeking their fifth state crown under Chippie Chappell, who had amassed a staggering 203–23–3 record in his eighteen seasons at the helm. It was a daunting task for Giles, but the kind upon which their program had been built.

The Spartans had defeated Haysi, 8–0, in a quagmire a week earlier, with Steve citing Vince Lombardi and the Green Bay Packers' muddy triumph in the 1965 NFL championship to rally the troops. He had used Lombardi as a reference many times over his sixteen-year career. This week, however, Steve had something unprecedented planned. The focus would be on his team's legacy and carrying the torch of those who came before. He paced back and forth to start, reviewing the game plan and key coaching points. He then reinforced their hard-nosed style of play, becoming increasingly animated. "Every play we run, you run it like it's the last one! Everything you've got in you! Get on that man, keep your feet moving—you ain't satisfied unless he's on his back. Nothing less is acceptable!"

Finally, he arrived at the brass tacks of his pregame remarks. "I was watching *Friday Football Extra* last night, some of you may have seen it, and they were comparing this game with our 1980 championship game and everything like that," Steve explained in a Southern cadence. In its tenth season on Roanoke's WDBJ Channel 7, *Friday Football Extra* was a weekly high school football show featuring scores and highlights from Central and Southwest Virginia. Four years before its creation, beloved WDBJ sports reporter Roy Stanley had covered the 1980 state finals. On that day, the warm weather in Pearisburg was a stark contrast to this raw and blustery afternoon. This was more reminiscent of the semifinals against Jefferson Forest, Steve remembered.

"You know, I was looking at that thing, and I was thinking . . . God, that was a great experience. And today is a great experience," he proclaimed. He wished his father, Harry, was there to share this day with him the way he had in 1980. He had left an indelible mark on his son's career. At the time, Steve had been so focused that he couldn't appreciate what was happening. Lunenburg Central would add another chapter, but the beginning would always be special. The Bandana Express had brought a community together. *It was a storybook deal*, he thought.

Steve continued. "They were showing Leon King running the football . . . and guys y'all have heard about your whole life and seen pictures of up on the wall in here—Leon King, Greg Mance, Greg King, [Leon's] brother, all of them, Mike Ratcliffe, Charlie Mullins." Each name gave his players chills, for they were the pioneers of "Spartan Football," the embodiment of a brotherhood they were about to represent. An identity. Their faces were immortalized in the varsity locker room, hanging alongside every all-region and all-state selection. There were nearly thirty of them now. Their distinct brand of single-wing football was widely recognized and gave their program identity, but the Spartan players had brought it to life.

"Well, boys, you've got the chance today to put your name in the same category as theirs," Steve added. For some, it was the last time they would ever wear the Giles uniform. These Spartans were finished running Fungo Mountain and driving the blocking sled. There would be no more one-on-ones. This opportunity came with a larger sense of purpose. "And these little kids that are down in the second grade now, or even three or four years old—one of these days they can be hearing about so-and-so who played on the 1993 Spartan football team," Steve concluded. They had been those kids thirteen years prior. They had grown up wearing red bandanas and dreaming of this moment. They had heard the tales of the state championship against Park View (Sterling) and former Notre Dame and NFL Houston Oilers running back Allen Pinkett. Those who witnessed it recalled the best high school football game they had ever seen. Now, it was their turn. That's what tradition meant to every one of them.

Steve dismissed his boys in a barrage of enthusiasm. It was game time. The click-clack of cleats accompanied the Spartans as they made their way to the field, and the Giles fans erupted at first sight of their team.

CHAPTER 1

MOUNTAIN ROAR

November 10, 1961
Narrows vs. Blacksburg

HIDDEN ALONG THE VIRGINIA–WEST VIRGINIA BORDER, a natural phenomenon has long captured the imagination of those who settled there. When the conditions are right, winds rushing inland from the Atlantic strike Peters Mountain with such force that as the current crosses the summit, it creates a sound unique to only two places on Earth. Pioneers likened this bellowing of the Appalachians to the roar of a lion. However, on this cold Friday night in the small community where Peters meets East River Mountain at "The Narrows" of the New River, the only roar of significance was the nearly seven thousand fans packed into the town's high school football stadium.

Despite the absence of postseason play in Virginia, interest in the contest between Narrows and Blacksburg was far-reaching. Heavy rain had forced a postponement three weeks earlier, but because both teams had finished the regular season undefeated, the scenario created an impromptu New River District championship game. With all but one of the remaining district teams having reached their season's end, the stage was set for the closest thing to a playoff game ever held in Giles County. In anticipation of a massive crowd, Narrows High School officials had acquired surplus bleachers from the inauguration of President John F. Kennedy and installed them on the visitors' side of Ragsdale Field. Fans were encouraged to arrive early, and those living within walking distance to leave their cars at home. Still, as the eight o'clock kickoff approached, it was apparent that, even with an increase in seating capacity, a sizable overflow of spectators would be left with just a standing view of the action.

The modest downtown district was silent. On Main Street, a large green-and-gold banner hung at Coburn's Department Store, the oldest business in town, declaring Narrows "Home of the Green Wave." Painted rocks on a nearby hillside urged the home squad to "Beat Blacksburg." Final arrivals pushing up Monroe Street could see the lights of the stadium shining on toward Wolf Creek and hear the school's fight song echoing off the surrounding mountains.

Media from throughout the region converged on the town of 2,500, once just a whistle-stop en route to the West Virginia coalfields. Eight different newspapers planned coverage, including the area's leading publication, *The Roanoke Times*, whose new sports editor, Bill Brill, had decided to cover the game himself. WNRV, the local AM radio station in Narrows, was also set to broadcast, but their daytime license meant the call would not air until the following morning. Nevertheless, the excitement surrounding the matchup had prompted station manager Bob Whitehead to procure Bob Gilmore and Frank Soden of the Virginia Tech radio network to provide play-by-play and analysis of the events.

Harry C. Ragsdale watched through the bespectacled eyes of a veteran grid mentor. In his thirty-second year at the high school, he had guided the Narrows football program since its infancy. At an overall record of 155–67–20, he had seen it all. Only Richlands's Ernie Hicks had held his post longer. Looking back, Harry could recall moments in his career with vivid clarity and full-color detail. Conversely, this scene would have been nothing short of a dream for the rawboned kid of twenty-three who arrived on a Norfolk & Western passenger train in the summer of 1930.

Now, standing at the door leading from the gymnasium down onto the field, Harry had perhaps his best team yet. In his usual fashion, he had tried to downplay his chances coming into the season, citing only three returning lettermen and telling anyone who would listen that his boys would be lucky to win two or three games. Yet, they were now seeking their twenty-third straight win and were the only Group I-B squad in the state with a perfect 8–0 record. A 247–12 scoring advantage made it clear the 1961 team had rarely been challenged.

Nonetheless, Harry had chewed his fingernails down to the quick, for he knew a win against the Indians of Blacksburg would not come easy. Even with their dominance of the New River District, newly formed in 1960 from the sprawling District Six, Narrows had managed just an 8–9–2 record against Blacksburg since the two first locked horns in 1936. Not to mention, they had won just three of the last twelve meetings.

Harry could remember facing Blacksburg in similar circumstances. In 1940, the Indians had stood in the way of a twenty-two-game winning streak as Narrows traveled to open their season against Blacksburg in Virginia Tech's Miles Stadium. Many of the same questions surrounded his young Narrows club with few returning players and, likewise, Harry was reportedly downcast about his team's prospects. On that afternoon more than two decades earlier, a late second-half touchdown by Frank McClaugherty had helped the Narrows Green Wave edge the Indians, 6–0. He knew this year's clash would be no less competitive.

Escorted by Duane Eddy's 1958 hit "Rebel Rouser," the players streamed out onto the field and assembled into a celebratory pile that had become a Narrows pregame tradition. They were greeted by a crowd the likes of which they had never seen. They were followed by assistant coaches Allen McClaugherty and Bill Patteson. A fresh-faced understudy, Patteson had played basketball, but not football, for Harry and was in his fifth year of teaching and coaching at Narrows. Finally, Harry strode toward the field, his quintessential sport coat and fedora-style hat accenting a sideline walk that was unmistakable.

On the opposing sideline, the visitors were led by twenty-seven-year-old Ken Stickley. An assistant at neighboring Christiansburg High School where he was hired in 1959, his first two teams had failed to break .500, so this year's unbeaten 7–0–2 campaign had caused quite a stir. Assisting Stickley was Bill Brown, a popular fixture on the Blacksburg coaching staff for over a decade. Their success had been delivered on the backs of three senior captains: Danny Surface, Steve Arrington, and Jim Breland. Surface and Arrington provided punch from the halfback positions in the full-house backfield, but the centerpiece was the 205-pound Breland, a college prospect and all-state candidate who made the move to fullback mid-season.

As the trio walked to midfield for the coin toss, Narrows public address announcer Herbert H. "Hub" Brown introduced their Narrows counterparts. "Cocaptain, number thirty-four . . . Danny Phlegar!" The crowd erupted with pride and devoted enthusiasm. Dan Phlegar stood six foot four, weighed 215 pounds, and was the most sought-after high school player in the entire state. He was a returning all-state end and was being recruited by nearly thirty schools, including Notre Dame, Alabama, and Tennessee. Coaches from the University of Virginia, Virginia Tech, and the Virginia Military Institute were in attendance. In Harry's opinion, he was the best high school player he had ever seen. His cocaptain, Bobby Hale, was just a tough-nut lineman who personified the bloody-your-nose mentality that made Harry's signature single-wing offense go.

Right from the opening kickoff, it was clear Blacksburg hadn't crossed Brush Mountain just to become another notch in the vaunted

Narrows winning streak. On the second play from scrimmage, Danny Surface took the handoff from quarterback Buddy Martin and slashed over center for eight yards on an inside counter trap. This was a favorite from Stickley's T-formation. Four plays later, Surface exploded into the secondary on the same play, this time for sixteen. As the blue-and-gold-clad visitors advanced into Green Wave territory, Stickley mixed the play calls but continued to pepper the middle of the Narrows defensive line. Within minutes, Jim Breland bulled his way for his second fourth-and-short conversion of the drive, and the Indians had a first down and goal-to-go. From there, Steve Arrington struck pay dirt on a five-yard run off the left side, carrying two defenders into the end zone. A methodical fourteen-play, sixty-yard march to open the game. Undeterred by a missed extra point, Blacksburg led 6–0.

Arrington had also scored the first touchdown the previous year, but Narrows still won easily, 30–6. This, however, felt different. These were the first points scored on their first-team defense all year, and the home side supporters had been silenced. Suddenly, the Blacksburg aggregation seemed more awe-inspiring than the Green Wave players initially regarded. Unfortunately, circumstances didn't improve for Narrows on their first possession, as they found moving the football nearly impossible against the Indians' defense and stalwarts like sophomore end Fred Zirkle. A quick three-and-out and Narrows was forced to punt.

This trend continued as Blacksburg controlled the ball and the clock for the remainder of the first half, piling up first downs into the double digits. On the other hand, the esteemed Narrows single wing was stagnant. The Green Wave remained without a first down and did their best just to beat back the Blacksburg threats, including a sixteen-play second-quarter drive. The Indians failed to extend their lead but headed to the locker room with high spirits, up 6–0 on the defending district champions. Coming off the field, Harry decided it was time to send his team a message.

He was more of a psychologist than a taskmaster when it came to his players, but on this night, Harry leaned heavily on the latter approach in an unforgettable halftime speech. He took his boys through the gym and into the auditorium, a departure from their regular routine. Once seated below him, Harry, flanked by Patteson and McClaugherty, unleashed a verbal tirade intended to shock and anger his players. His words were deliberate. His intensity was calculated. He felt they were playing hesitant, uncertain, and cautious—afraid to lose. They had become so consumed with the atmosphere that he needed to redirect their attention. He wanted to make each player personally mad at him, including Stanley, the elder of his two sons, a sophomore. No individual was spared. When Harry stopped to catch his breath, his assistants interjected with comparable ferocity.

Meanwhile, against a backdrop of homecoming festivities and marching band performances, Harry was being compared to the famous Amos Alonzo Stagg for would-be radio listeners. The "Grand Old Man of Football" had retired the previous fall at the age of 98. While his silver-haired appearance and long tenure likened him to Stagg, at this moment, Harry addressed his team with a youthful fire. As they returned to the field, he was confident he got their attention.

After Dan Phlegar returned the opening kickoff of the second half to the Narrows thirty-four, the Green Wave offense again took the field. The first play coming out of the break was to be "Spin 33," a wingback reverse from the deceptive full-spin series. Many players would recount how the series was always practiced but rarely used. During the previous two seasons, it just wasn't necessary. The straight and buck-lateral series had been enough to produce a nearly unstoppable attack.

"It's first-and-ten now for the Green Wave, and we'll see if the halftime session in the locker room has helped any," play-by-play announcer Bob Gilmore added prophetically on WNRV. The ball was snapped to fullback Bucky Lawson, who executed a 360-degree spin before handing off to wingback Billy Neal. Neal cut inside behind Phlegar, who had planted his man nearly ten yards downfield, and in the blink of an eye, all 125 pounds of Neal was in the open field and racing toward the Blacksburg end zone. The home crowd roared to life as Neal scampered all the way to the Indians' twenty-two-yard line, a run of forty-four yards to start the second half.

Harry knew they needed to capitalize on the shift in momentum. Neal and rotating tailbacks Jerry Huffman and Bob Davis combined to move the ball inside the ten, but when a third-down pass from Davis to Paul Richardson was upended short of the goal line, Narrows faced a fourth-and-goal at the Blacksburg two. Harry took a time-out in advance of the pivotal call. A success would draw the Green Wave even, but a Blacksburg stop would breathe new life into the Indians and their fans. He decided on "Weakside," a specially tagged fullback off-tackle play to the short side of the unbalanced formation, with Bucky Lawson on the decisive push. Lawson took the snap, gave a nod to the perimeter, and crashed inside, diving toward the goal line. Among the bodies, Lawson raised his head from the ground just in time to see the official's signal—touchdown!

The twin smokestacks of the Virginian Railway power plant watched in the distance as the raucous crowd boomed. The score was tied. Phlegar lined up to try the point-after but instead took the direct snap and ran around the right end, shaking a would-be tackler before ducking inside the right corner of the end zone for the extra point. As all conversions were worth one point, Narrows led 7–6. A sixty-six-yard drive in eight plays. Bob Gilmore confirmed the revival: "This is an entirely different Narrows ball club in this second half."

Early in the fourth quarter, just minutes after an eleven-yard run by Bob Davis on their bread-and-butter off-tackle play seemed to spark the Green Wave, Narrows was confronted with a second-and-fourteen from their own forty-five. Harry opted for the running pass, another single-wing staple akin to a sprint-out, and Davis looked to Dan Phlegar on the backside post, covered in the secondary by a substitute for an injured Danny Surface, who had left the game with what the Indian sideline feared was a broken collarbone. The tailback lofted a deep throw, and Phlegar, brushing aside an injured hand himself, went up and over the Blacksburg defender to snag the pass around the twenty-five-yard line. He shook off two potential tacklers and headed to the end zone for a fifty-five-yard touchdown. Ragsdale Field thundered again as the Green Wave extended their lead to 13–6 with the extra point upcoming. Just as passionate as the hometown faithful, an animated Harry sprinted down the sideline with Phlegar as he rumbled toward the goal line like the steam locomotives of yesteryear.

On the radio broadcast, Virginia Tech color commentator Frank Soden gushed over Phlegar. "If he was wearing a uniform at Blacksburg, for VPI (Virginia Polytechnic Institute), he'd fall in the same category as All-American Carroll Dale, to say the least." A wide receiver for the NFL's Los Angeles Rams, Dale had attended J.J. Kelly High School in Wise, Virginia, and went on to be an All-American at Virginia Tech. In the offseason, he sold sporting goods for Appalachian Athletic House out of Bristol, Tennessee, and called on many local schools. For these reasons, he was a favorite among many in Southwest Virginia.

Harry set his unbalanced formation to the left on the extra point, another tactic he rarely utilized. The ball started in that direction but was handed to wingback Norman Clevenger on the reverse pass. The fourteen-year-old freshman rolled to his right, then tossed a high floater into the end zone, and Dan Phlegar again went skyward to secure the conversion amid multiple defenders. It was a fitting climax to his high school career.

Ahead 14–6, an interception on the ensuing drive all but sealed it for the Green Wave. Harry began to melt the remaining time off the clock, pounding the middle with inside runs. The final whistle sounded with Narrows executing their single-wing offense in classic fashion. They had clawed their way back, battling with grit and determination, just as Harry's teams had done for more than a generation. The celebration of their twenty-third straight victory was underway. Harry's boys had heard his message at halftime. Thankful, they carried him off the field to a spectacular ovation. He had never been so proud of his players, his school, and his town. It was to be a moment etched in time for Harry Ragsdale.

The next morning, a ten-year-old boy switched on his small transistor radio and waited to hear the events of the previous night unfold. The youngster had grown up with the Green Wave. He had seen their games come alive every Sunday afternoon on the dining room wall through the flutter of a 16mm film projector. He could diagram every one of their plays. His face spoke of both anticipation and triumph. Finally, the radio crackled, and WNRV was on the air.

"Good morning, ladies and gentlemen. This is Bob Whitehead speaking to you from Ragsdale Field in Narrows, Virginia. The broadcast you are about to hear is a tape-recorded broadcast of the happenings that took place last night in Narrows," the voice on the radio said.

CHAPTER 2
WEAK AS CAT PEE

August 26, 1978
Giles vs. Graham (Scrimmage)

AS HIS EYES TRACED toward the evening sky above the city of Bluefield's Mitchell Stadium, Steve was quite sure his neck would be stiff in the morning. He felt like every time he turned around, he was watching one of Graham's extra points sail over his head and through the uprights. Another point-after, and the Graham G-Men now led the Giles Spartans 35–0. It was both teams' final preseason scrimmage. When Steve looked at Graham, he saw grown men, some with full beards. Nearly half the starters could bench press over 300 pounds, including lineman-turned-kicker John O'Neal, who could bench 365 himself. He knew they had the strength of a state contender. But when the thin, twenty-seven-year-old rookie head coach looked at his group, he drew quite the opposite conclusion.

Weak as cat pee, he thought.

Stephen C. Ragsdale had been named the head football coach at Giles High School just three months earlier, but while his tenure had just begun, his was a familiar name in Giles County. Ragsdale was synonymous with enduring leadership. Steve's father, legendary coach Harry Ragsdale, had led cross-county rival Narrows High School for thirty-three years, with his career on the gridiron spread across four different decades. His final season marked the culmination of a thirty-two-game winning streak. Even after he retired from coaching, he spent another decade in school administration, and more recently, he had been elected to a four-year term as the town's mayor. Known simply as "Coach" to so many, Harry Ragsdale was a pillar of the community and one of the county's most respected and revered citizens. He was in attendance that night, along with Steve's mother, the former Sarah Simmons, as they celebrated their thirty-ninth wedding anniversary. As the spitting image of Harry, many wondered how long it would be before Steve returned to Narrows to command the helm of the Green Wave.

Having grown up watching his father's successful teams, Steve knew the unbalanced single-wing offense. By the time he was ten years old, he could diagram every one of Harry's plays. In the county seat of Pearisburg, they also knew of the famed single wing used at Narrows, deployed so many times to run roughshod over the other county teams and later a consolidated Giles High School. Nonetheless, Steve decided coming into the season that perhaps he should modernize his offensive principles. After all, it was the 1970s. Opting to run a wing-T-based offense to start the year, Giles looked more like Narrows under current coach Bill Patteson than Harry Ragsdale. They had scrimmaged Grundy the previous week, and while that was an even contest, it in no way prepared the Spartans for the current onslaught.

Graham was coached by Glynn Carlock. After a poor performance in their first scrimmage, Carlock had decided to use the Giles exhibition to increase morale ahead of his team's opening-week border clash with Bluefield, formerly Beaver High School. The storied rivalry between the city's two high schools, each set in opposite states, was preparing for its fifty-second iteration. When Carlock arrived at Graham in 1973, the G-Men had not defeated their West Virginia counterpart in a decade.

Before his hiring, Carlock had served as assistant coach across town under Merrill Gainer and John Chmara. The former had coached him at Big Creek High School and brought him to Bluefield in 1964 following Carlock's tour in the US Marine Corps and graduation from Concord College. During Carlock's stint as an assistant, the Beavers won eighty games and two state championships, and they never lost to Graham. In fact, the Virginia-siders were shut out six times in the nine losses, including a combined score of 97–0 the previous two seasons. So when the G-Men blanked Bluefield in just his second year, 13–0, Carlock had his signature win, and his legacy at Graham was born.

This season, the G-Men were slated to be the away team against the Beavers at Mitchell Stadium, a venue both schools had shared since 1936, moving their games from Wade Field. Therefore, with his eyes set on the season opener against Bluefield, Coach Carlock dressed his squad to play Giles in the same road-white game uniforms they would wear the following week, an emotional appeal to their sense of pride and tradition dating back to the days of Pro Football Hall of Famer "Bullet" Bill Dudley. The visitors from Pearisburg wore shabby practice gear, further highlighting the disparity between the two programs.

Every game we're in, if we win, it'll be an upset. All Steve could do was watch, arms crossed, as another O'Neal extra point sailed over his head, the score now 42–0. Graham had scored on nearly every possession. The end of the first half was about the only thing that had stopped the G-Men. Third-year southpaw quarterback Bobby Carter had thrown a touchdown pass, and four different running backs had scored on the ground, including brothers Terry and Eddie Hall. The Hall brothers doubled as Graham's inside linebackers in Carlock's split-six defense and blitzed better than 80 percent of the time. They were intimidating and had nicknames to match. Alias "Son of Sam," Terry was one of ten seniors for Graham. Townspeople still talked about the hit he put on Blacksburg running back Sidney Snell, who was currently in the backfield at Virginia Tech, in the 1976 playoffs. Eddie was just a freshman but was already a budding man-child. His moniker was "Hitman." Both downright knocked the stuffing out of folks.

Graham High School had won a state title in football previously, in 1962 under Lawrence H. "Burrhead" Bradley. The G-Men were awarded a points-based crown that season, exclusive to Group I-A, Virginia's top classification. And heading into the 1978 season, talk of a state championship–caliber team was circulating once again. Graham was the favorite to win the Group AA Southwest District, a distinction typically reserved for Harry Fry's Gate City team. Gate City had won the district five times in the 1970s and state championships in 1970 and 1974. Regardless, Graham had been a unanimous selection among the other coaches as this year's district front-runner. Even Virgil L. "Stubby" Currence, the grizzled, often pro–Bluefield High School sportswriter for the *Bluefield Daily Telegraph*, had picked them as the team to beat. It was the veteran Currence who had coined the name "G-Men" over forty years prior.

Coach Carlock had done his best to temper this buzz, even going as far as telling the newspaper that he'd never seen a roster score a touchdown or make a tackle, adding, "Games aren't won on paper. They're won on the football field." He wouldn't even discuss the playoffs. Still, the G-Men returned eight starters on offense, including the entire backfield, and nine on defense, where Carlock placed his primary emphasis. Graham teams were known for their physicality, born on the practice field by Carlock's authoritarian coaching style, a product of his military background. He often told his players he wanted every opponent to know they had played Graham High School when they woke up the following day, to feel the evidence of a physical thrashing. This was sure to be the case against the shell-shocked Spartans and their wide-eyed head coach.

Even with his connection to his father, Steve remarkably never played football. He was, however, a fiercely competitive basketball player, cultivated by years of games against Harry growing up. After starring for Narrows, he received a full scholarship to play at Roanoke College, where he was a member of the 1972 College Division National Championship team under Charlie Moir. He also excelled academically, unshaken by the negative stereotypes of his Appalachian drawl. Following graduation, Steve attended Virginia Tech and earned his master's degree. Like his father, he was to be a mathematics teacher. He was able to do his student teaching at Giles High School and, upon completion, was hired full-time. In conjunction, Steve was also named the head basketball coach, taking over for Gary Clark. As was the custom, the head basketball coach was an assistant in football, usually for the junior varsity team. Clark had decided to remain as jayvee coach, so Steve took over duties as the eighth-grade head coach in the fall of 1975.

Steve was content with this scenario and, for three seasons, served under head varsity coach Roy Bayless as the eighth-grade head coach. When Bayless resigned after the 1977 season, having decided to leave education altogether, Steve pursued being the head coach in football and basketball. In truth, Bayless's departure was not uncommon. Since the school opened, the head football coaching position had been a revolving door, averaging a new coach every two years. The result was a lack of consistency. The program's best record was 7–3, but without the stability of long-standing routines and expectations, the program could not build on team accomplishments and sustain a culture of success. Steve knew his biggest challenge at the school of nearly one thousand students would be establishing a winning tradition.

This issue was only exacerbated by a deeply fractured school community. In 1961, Giles High School combined schools from Pearisburg, Pembroke, Eggleston, and Newport in grades eight through twelve. Gone were teams like the Pearisburg Red Devils and Pembroke Corncutters. But instead of unifying as Spartans, many formed cliques and held on to old rivalries. These factions were a breeding ground for mistrust and negativity, with each blaming failure on favoritism and attributing success to locale. In the seventeen seasons since consolidation, Giles averaged less than four wins per year. They were the New River District's proverbial doormat and an expected win on every opponent's schedule.

But Steve had worked hard to negate this with his former eighth-grade teams, which had continued to improve—and other schools in the district took notice. He developed an aggressive mentality that was unique to the players he coached. At the time, his eighth graders felt like their regimen was more demanding than even the varsity's and, after a while, took pride in it. On the hill overlooking practice, Steve would line his players up like soldiers at attention, wanting them to see that while *they* were in full gear and hitting at practice, their older equivalents were running around in shorts. "That's why you're going to win! You're going to be tough, physical, and do the little things right!" he told them. "Some boys . . . they get on the bus and go home, they get their RC Cola and MoonPie, and they just blow through here like a cool breeze . . . but you boys are special," he added decisively. The players that grew alongside Coach Ragsdale knew this mindset was integral to being part of his football team. Unfortunately, some decided this was not for them, and he was finding this out in real time as the varsity head coach. He had few seniors, the only class that had not played for him in the eighth grade.

At present, Steve felt these problems piling up as quarterback Curtis Poole was tackled by Graham's David Bailey for a nine-yard loss. Bailey and opposite bookend Tim Moore were prime collegiate prospects. The Spartans' wing-T had not earned a first down the entire scrimmage and had managed to gain just twenty-five yards through three quarters. It seemed every other play Steve saw one of his backs fumble or get tackled for a loss. He needed to get his team off the field and back to Pearisburg before the situation got worse. Not only were the Spartans weak, but they were soft as drugstore cotton, and he believed winning, even with talent, required physical and mental toughness. For Steve, that meant the willingness to hit and the fortitude to battle through adversity. It was the well-established reputation of Giles teams to give up when they got behind. This had to change, but to do so would require leadership. He would be forced to develop his young players and hope to retain them the following year.

If we have sophomores in there, we're going to get killed.

During his time at Giles, Steve had observed a troubling trend. Every year in the eighth-grade program, the athletes had improved, but as they moved through to varsity, they just didn't turn out. A fellow teacher once asked him, "I can understand why a kid would not want to play football. But what I can't understand is why we have more of them at Giles than everywhere else. Why don't they want to play here?" It hit him like a ton of bricks. The fact was that the best athletes didn't want to play for a perennial loser. In Steve's mind, the solution was simple: come out, play competitive, and begin to build a foundation. As best he could remember, his father never had to recruit kids to play. Boys in Narrows grew up thinking they were supposed to play football. It was important in the community and a rite of passage. The issue was never if they would get enough kids out, but instead, whether they would have enough uniforms to dress them all. Just the opposite at Giles. Here, standing around in the designated smoking area, nicknamed "The Pit," seemed a more popular pastime than playing football for the Spartans.

Just weeks before, he had gone into a local drugstore to solicit an advertisement for the football program when the clerk made an offhand comment: "What difference is it going to make if they buy an ad and support the football team? We're just going to lose anyway." The words still echoed in his head, a brazen example of the cynicism that characterized the community's defeatist attitude. Changing this collective outlook would be difficult, but Steve felt they would respond if the Spartans could produce some visible success, as hidden behind this way of thinking, they were hungry for a winner. He just needed a way to unite them all behind the commonality of Giles football. He needed a symbol of hope.

Finally, the scrimmage was over. While Giles did manage a fourth-quarter score on the Graham reserves, the result was still an embarrassing 48–8 drubbing—in conventional scrimmage scorekeeping, an astounding seven touchdowns to one. A promising freshman back named Leon King had been allowed to watch but was itching to play. Steve had decided he would start the year on the junior varsity team. His brother, sophomore Greg King, would have to play in the varsity backfield. He had taken a pounding and wanted to quit. Terry Hall blasted him on a sweep in the second quarter like he was shot out of a cannon, and Greg could still feel it. Both were Pembroke boys and part of a small group of Black players on the Giles team.

Worse yet, afterward, as the team started east to Giles County, the bus broke down. Utterly discouraged, they had no choice but to sit on the outskirts of Bluefield, at the foot of East River Mountain, and wait for another bus to arrive from Pearisburg to pick them up. On the side of US Route 460, there was a lot of time to think. The mountain, like the shadow of Harry, stretched all the way back to Narrows. The Ragsdale legacy was a double-edged sword. In the darkness, Steve could feel the weight of his circumstances as he lamented in introspection. *What a great start to your coaching career*, he sarcastically told himself.

Resolute, he adjusted the ball cap on his head of dark hair and pulled up his white crew socks. As an intense competitor, Steve was determined to persevere, and he had come to a significant conclusion. Even though his team had yet to play a regular-season game, an immediate change was necessary. He was going to run his father's offense.

CHAPTER 3

NARZ

September 15, 1978
Giles vs. Narrows

BY THE TIME HARRY RAGSDALE RETIRED following the 1962 season, his steadfast use of the single wing had become synonymous with Narrows football. So much so that coaches from other localities would joke that even the buildings in Narrows leaned heavily to one side, giving a nod to the Green Wave's unbalanced line version of the offense. A masterpiece of old-fashioned power and timely deception, Harry's refined strategy combined the fierceness of the lion with the cunning of the fox. It was the perfect synergy: the strength of brute-force line bucks and off-tackle smashes mixed with the trickery of reverses, spins, and laterals. It was poetry in motion. On the contrary, when he organized his first team in the fall of 1931, the blueprint was much more rudimentary.

The 1906 brainchild of Glenn S. "Pop" Warner, the single wing was initially developed and identified as a specific formation. Later, however, it became associated with multiple variations of a direct-snap offensive system, one that nearly every team in America was running by the late 1920s. In his 1927 book, *Football for Coaches and Players*, Warner documented what he called Formation A, the unbalanced single-wing formation, and recommended it for use in the high school game. His philosophy focused on simplicity, strength, and the perfection of fundamentals and techniques. The rugged nature of the kids in Narrows naturally suited them for this style of play, and thus, Harry patterned his early offense after Pop Warner's unbalanced single wing. Bruising backfields and devastating blocking characterized the Narrows single wing from 1931 to 1941. Like Warner, Harry dabbled with sleight of hand, but at the heart of his Narrows teams was always a precisely executed power game. This formula resulted in a record of 67–17–8, including two undefeated seasons and a 35–3–1 mark in his final four seasons before World War II.

Following an almost four-year military hiatus, Harry returned from the Panama Canal Zone as a lieutenant commander and found a much different game than when he left for Naval active duty in 1942. Usage of the single wing began to decline in favor of the novel T-formation. He remained loyal to his offensive beliefs, but the game was changing. Then in 1951, Charlie Caldwell, head coach at Princeton University, published a book titled *Modern Single Wing Football*. It detailed the offense of the 1950 Princeton team led by tailback Dick Kazmaier that finished unbeaten and ranked sixth in the final Associated Press poll. Caldwell had adapted his system to utilize many of the same innovations made fashionable by the T while maintaining the integrity of the original unbalanced line, double-tight-end structure. It was just what Harry was looking for.

The single wing of the 1930s, content with the raw power of the straight series, was instead supplanted by a scheme that included more deceptive sequences like the buck lateral and full spin. It was an attack, not of short-yardage scrums, but multifaceted scoring potential. He particularly liked Caldwell's buck-lateral series and even corresponded with him on occasion. The literary work would become Harry's football bible, and Narrows ran the Princeton offense to Caldwell's exact specifications. This was the version Steve learned growing up as he watched the Green Wave rule the New River District in Harry's final three seasons.

I'm going to run what I know, and what I know is the single wing.

Nevertheless, by the latter half of the 1970s, recollections of its triumphs had faded into legend and, for many, evoked little more than antiquated imagery of leather helmets and rugby-like balls. From Pop to Princeton to Pearisburg, the lineage notwithstanding, Steve was skeptical of how the change would be received as he transitioned from the wing-T to the unbalanced single wing the week of the Spartans' opening game. While some Giles players may have been confused, others seemed less concerned that their offense now operated without a quarterback and more about simply surviving practice. This was especially true for a group of sophomores that included Timmy Martin and Barry Farmer, a Pearisburg and Eggleston boy, respectively.

Even with the quick turnaround, Giles debuted against the Fort Chiswell Pioneers with a 22–6 victory. Junior speedster George "Fonzie" Austin rushed for 156 yards, and Steve had won his first game as a head coach. Fort Chiswell, on the contrary, was a Group A opponent from the Mountain Empire District and, he knew, a far cry from the competition the Spartans would face in the Group AA New River District. This was confirmed the next week, as the Spartans were shut out 16–0 by Floyd County. To compound a dismal offensive performance, the Buffaloes were among the weakest teams on their district slate. Disappointed, Steve was forced to confront the inevitable—his return to Narrows and a clash with the resurgent Green Wave on Ragsdale Field.

The setting felt surreal as Steve led his team onto the field named in his father's honor. It had been a fixture in the community since well before he was born. Now in its third location, the stadium had changed dramatically, from a field without seating to one that could accommodate over seven thousand spectators. When multitiered concrete bleachers were added in the early 1940s, the student body felt the project should be named for their coach. Thus, by the time

Harry was commissioned into military service, the stadium was already using the name "Ragsdale Field." Over time, improvements were made, including lights and fencing, as the field was shared with a Minor League Baseball team. More recently, a press box was added, completed just two years prior by students at the county vocational school.

Even so, as the home team took the field and joined in their pregame pileup, it was evident that it was not additions or upgrades that made the place so memorable. It was those who bled for the pride of Narrows that gave the sacred ground life. Those like Hub Brown, who had played on Harry's District Seven championship team of 1935 and was still the voice of the Green Wave, just as he had been when Steve was a kid. Legend and lore such as this had painted Steve's youth green and gold. Ironically, the colors of his adult return weren't those of the Green Wave but the Columbia blue, white, and scarlet red of their bitter rival, the Giles Spartans.

To complicate the situation, Steve was also facing his high school basketball coach, Bill Patteson. An Emory & Henry College graduate, the forty-six-year-old Patteson had led Narrows to nearly three hundred wins on the hardwood and was in his second year of double duty as the Green Wave's head grid boss. Consistent with the traditions of his role, he had served as the junior varsity football coach for much of his twenty-year hoops career in Narrows. Still, until events dictated otherwise, he never planned to lead both varsity programs. Stuart Justus resigned the previous summer after just one season, a 3–7 campaign, and the program was left without a head mentor. Patteson, also the athletic director, thought a successor had been found, but unforeseen circumstances left the position vacant with the 1977 season rapidly approaching. He was set to go on his family beach vacation but told Narrows officials that he would take the job himself if a suitable replacement was not found. The phone rang a few days later, and Patteson accepted the post less than two weeks before practice began. By happenstance, this precedent paved the way for Steve to become a dual-sport head coach just one year later.

The community was familiar with Patteson, a staunch disciplinarian dubbed "Wild Bill." In the fourteen seasons and four head coaches since Harry retired, many former players remembered the impact of their jayvee coach. He consistently produced winning junior varsity teams and directed the recreation department for the town of Narrows. He had a proven track record, so they were not surprised when the Green Wave finished 7–2–1 in just his first year. It was a football renaissance in Narrows, and Patteson won multiple Coach of the Year honors. A 56–74–1 record from 1963 to 1976 reflected the struggle to fill the massive shoes left by Harry Ragsdale, but by 1978, the smallest Group AA school in the state had a forty-six-man squad and was poised to challenge for a district title once again.

The atmosphere inside the stadium was foreboding. For Steve, it was like playing a member of his family, and he and assistant Don Lowe, who also went to Narrows, were taking every stomach medication imaginable. Harry admitted to his close friends, including Coach Patteson, that he worried about what Steve might encounter if he took the job at Giles. The rivalry was not for the faint of heart. Profoundly personal to so many, Steve's mother, Sarah, herself a Narrows graduate, couldn't bring herself to attend the game. After all, Harry had coached the fathers of a number of the Narrows players. It was apparent that some in the Green Wave fan base would not approve of Harry's support of Giles football, even if the new head coach was his son. In their minds, nothing trumped loyalty to the green and gold.

Harry could remember his first experience with the rivalry. The history between the two localities ran deep, and the precursor to the Narrows–Giles conflict was the Green Wave's feud with Pearisburg High School, later the location of the consolidated Giles High School. In October of 1930, the two schools faced off on the outdoor, dirt-floor basketball court at Narrows. Since the county did not yet have organized football, basketball was played in the fall season. As soon as the game began, a brawl broke out between players from each team. Not much had changed in the near half century since.

In 1960, Harry capped a 19–7–1 advantage in football over the Pearisburg Red Devils with a 28–6 win. Some outside of Narrows, including several regional sportswriters, predicted a possible decline in the Green Wave's superiority with the opening of Giles High School. While Harry never lost to the Spartans, in the years after he retired, the Green Wave struggled with mediocrity and held just an 8–6–1 edge over Giles. In the first game of the 1963 season, the Spartans stopped the renowned Narrows winning streak at thirty-two games, tying them 7–7. Of course, Green Wave backers explained it away as Pearisburg needing the "whole county" to help them do it, in reference to the school consolidation. A single whisper of such a merger between Narrows and Giles would light a fire under loyalists from both sides. Subsequently, the annual storylines remained bound by mutual disdain and underscored by controversial hits, angry mobs, and death threats.

While the Giles Spartans had fared better in the 1970s, the Narrows faithful, empowered with Patteson now at their helm, believed the Green Wave would return to their former glory and rightful dominance over the Spartans. The expectation of victory breathed new life into Green Wave pride. An embodiment of this attitude was Russell "Hot Rod" Dennis. Hot Rod had purchased an icebox-style service station and garage on US Route 460 at the beginning of the season and renamed it "Hot Rod's Green Wave Exxon." His tow truck was painted green and gold, and on Friday nights, he would blare the siren at crucial moments, which to a visiting player was ominous and intimidating. Anticipation for the season was already high, but with the Green Wave 2–0 and Giles coming to town, it had reached a fever pitch, to say the least.

A passionate Narrows supporter had even confronted new Giles assistant Rusty Kelley in his front yard a few weeks prior, declaring: "Giles boys aren't tough. Mark it down—they'll never beat Narrows again. Ever." As much as this bothered Steve, it looked more like reality than prognostication early in the first quarter. After a three-and-out by the Spartans, the home squad drove right down the field for the opening score, a one-yard run by fullback Andy Metro. On their next possession, junior tailback Rusty Cook broke free for a fifty-six-yard scoring jaunt, and before the Spartans could catch their breath, the Green Wave led 13–0.

The previous year's team had utilized quickness, but the 1978 edition lined up and ran right at opposing defenses with potent inside runners like Metro and Cook. The workhorse was Cook, who had already amassed 365 yards and six touchdowns coming into the game, averaging a whopping 15.9 yards per carry on his twenty-three attempts. Giles players had been trying unsuccessfully to tackle him since youth league. Some swore his legs were made of steel.

One player already feeling the effects of this early assault was another sophomore, Mike Ratcliffe. Known to most in Giles as "Mo," Ratcliffe had been moved up from the junior varsity and was now in action against one of the most formidable teams in the area. Tasked with starting at linebacker in place of junior Robert Stump, who had been injured in a motorcycle accident, Mo had never played linebacker and was suddenly getting mauled by the Narrows offensive line, chiefly guard Chucky Williams, arguably the best in the district. Like generations before him, Mo detested "Narz." While many did pronounce the town's name in one syllable, rhyming it with the word "cares," for him, the epithet was voiced like "cars" and was a term of contempt. He fought back the urge to slug one of them. Clearly, frustration was mounting fast for the Pearisburg boy.

I don't want to start another sophomore unless I have to, Steve had told himself.

Like the Graham scrimmage, fellow sophomore Greg King

continued to take a physical beating. Even with a notable offense led by Cook, the Green Wave's calling card was still their stingy, hard-hitting defense. They had not allowed a point in their first two games, a 34–0 shutout of Alleghany and a 24–0 blanking of George Wythe. Backed up in his own territory and desperate to give his offense a spark, Steve called a screen pass to King. But the play call did not fool the Narrows defense. Waiting was Green Wave defensive end Tony Robertson, who intercepted the pass and returned it twelve yards for the touchdown. The home crowd celebrated the pick-six, and the rout was on. Following the point-after, the Green Wave led 20–0, with the game still in the first quarter.

"Don't ever let me call a screen pass inside my own damn twenty-yard line again," Steve told Don Lowe as he passed him on the sideline.

In the second quarter, Narrows quarterback Steve Thornton threw a twenty-two-yard touchdown pass to Marty Fleeman, and Rusty Cook ripped off another long run, finding pay dirt from fifty yards away. By the time the first half was complete, the Green Wave had taken a commanding 34–0 lead.

Coach Patteson considered his options for the second half. He had dreaded the possibility of a blowout scenario with such a disparity between the two teams. He did not want to run up the score, but he had an entire roster of his own players to consider.

For Giles, after being pelted with rocks and other debris on their way to the visitors' locker room, located behind the old high school on the home side of the stadium, Steve posed a poignant question: "Boys, y'all just want to load up on the bus and go on home?" His stunned players sat in silence.

The Green Wave added two more scores in the third quarter, pushing their lead to 48–0. The Spartans' best scoring opportunity came late in the fourth when they drove to the Narrows six-yard line, but a Green Wave interception preserved the shutout. Narrows had still not allowed a point through three games, outscoring their opponents 106–0. Tailback Rusty Cook outgained the entire Spartan team, rushing for 156 yards on just eleven carries, as Narrows nearly tripled the Giles output, and the single wing was held scoreless for the second week in a row.

Broken and demoralized, the Spartans climbed aboard the bus and headed back toward Pearisburg. They were ready to get home, but as they eased out of Narrows, Steve noticed a sound that instantly stoked a visceral reaction. With the windows down, he could hear the inflammatory jeering coming from the Green Wave fans as they walked along the sidewalk of Monroe to Main. They were mocking him and his team. In contrast to the silence of self-reflection after the Graham scrimmage, he knew he must respond. He was unsure if his boys could handle this level of emotional challenge, but it was time to stand tall or risk further damage to team morale. Steve ordered the bus to stop, dead in the middle of the street. He rose to his feet and addressed his team.

"Listen to them! *Listen to them!* They're laughing at you!"

The players listened as the passersby taunted them, adding insult to injury. Lineman Barry Farmer had tears in his eyes, the result of a severely dislocated shoulder during the game. Timmy Martin and Mike Ratcliffe, who had grown up together, just looked at each other. Greg King sat thinking how awful it all was. They had all played for Steve in the eighth grade but never experienced anything like this.

"I want you to remember this!"

Steve knew his group of sophomores was not ready to be in this position, especially against a team the caliber of Narrows, but he didn't have time to coddle his young players. It was a pivotal part of their journey, and the defending state champions awaited the following Friday night.

"You sophomores: We'll be back down here in two years . . . and they won't be laughing then!"

CHAPTER 4

THE GOLD STANDARD

September 22, 1978
Giles vs. Blacksburg

AFTER THE EMOTIONAL LOSS to Narrows, the New River District slate didn't get any easier for Steve and the Spartans. Even with the hype surrounding the Green Wave, the gold standard in the commonwealth was still the Blacksburg Indians, the 1977 Group AA state champions. The Virginia High School League (VHSL) had used several alphanumeric systems to organize schools by enrollment. Current designations were implemented in 1970 alongside playoffs for two of the state's three classifications, A and AA, with AAA following one year later. As Steve had sat quietly on the bus leaving Pearisburg, he'd searched his mind for optimism. *I just don't want to get beat to death.*

Still, he was glad the Narrows game was behind him. He had challenged his team afterward, but it was unclear if they would answer the call. They had been battered at the hands of the Green Wave, physically and mentally, particularly that group of sophomores. A week later, they were on the road again and facing another monumental task. His game plan was to minimize further damage at the hands of the defending state champs. *We're just going to try to hold the score down tonight. We aren't going to throw it—I don't care what happens.* An abysmal 0–8 passing and three interceptions against Narrows only gave the Green Wave added opportunities. Steve intended to keep the clock running to shorten the game.

The coach opposite Steve was thirty-one-year-old Dave Crist, who was no stranger to success in his young career. Before coming to Blacksburg High School in 1975, the Luray native had been an assistant at Madison County, a Group A high school located in the northern Piedmont region of Central Virginia. Under head coach Eddie Dean, the Mountaineers made the state finals in three of the four years of his apprenticeship, posting a 47–3 record and winning the state's small-school crown in 1973. Following the 1974 season, a series of coaching changes at Blacksburg left the door open for Crist's return to the New River Valley, the home of his alma mater, Virginia Tech, and he was hired less than three weeks before practice began.

Now entering his fourth season, the unassuming Crist had an impressive 30–5 mark at Blacksburg. In his first year, the Indians equaled their 1974 output, going 8–2 but missing the playoffs. He took a neighboring coach's advice and put beloved assistant Bill Brown in charge of his defense. Known as "Brownie" to his early players, he was the cornerstone of Blacksburg football. He had served as the head coach himself in 1951 but was best known for his role as the school's top assistant, dating back to his arrival from East Tennessee State College in 1949. Crist immediately recognized the value of his expertise. Blacksburg finished 11–1 the next fall behind the strong running of Sidney Snell, losing only to eventual runner-up Martinsville, 6–3, in the state semifinals.

When the 1977 season began, hopes of another playoff run were in doubt, as they dropped their season opener to the Radford Bobcats, 6–0. Undaunted, they won out in district play, and just a few days before their final contest, Crist realized they could potentially out-point Radford with a win against William Byrd and a Bobcats loss to Narrows. Unbeaten Radford was a heavy favorite, but Narrows pulled the upset in shocking fashion, 32–6, sending the Indians to postseason play. Set to face Gate City's "Cannonball Express" in the opening round, Crist knew very little about the two-time state champs. Ironically, help arrived from two unlikely sources: opposing head coaches Phil Robbins at Christiansburg and Norm Lineburg at just-eliminated Radford. Robbins had coached in the Southwest District at John Battle High School for six seasons, and Lineburg's Radford teams had faced Gate City three times in the playoffs since their inception. The two coaches graciously offered to share resources to aid in preparation, and their assistance helped Blacksburg defeat the Blue Devils, 20–7. It was a gesture of goodwill Crist hoped to someday return. Two weeks later, in seventeen-degree cold, they slipped past Covington in the final minutes, 7–6. To complete their improbable run to the state title, the Indians rallied behind the return of injured lineman John Skelly and defeated Southampton, 16–7, the following week. After the win, the Blacksburg players carried a joyous Bill Brown off the field in celebration.

Bill Brown talked about Harry Ragsdale often, reminiscing about great battles between Narrows and Blacksburg, most of which were decided by a touchdown or less. So when Steve was hired as the head coach at Giles the following spring, Brown told Crist, "Harry is coming back! Get ready—single wing is coming!" His prediction was well founded. The single wing was back, and so was Harry, to a degree.

One area—besides the single wing—where Steve learned to emulate his father was adept psychological motivation, and his preparation for Blacksburg was no exception. Harry always had an angle to play, a way to tug at an emotional thread that would appeal to his players. For Steve, games against Blacksburg (and, at times, adjacent Christiansburg) were always about the country versus the city.

Where the Giles–Narrows rivalry may have been more akin to a backyard brawl between brothers, the Giles–Blacksburg game was a culture war of sorts. Blacksburg was the antithesis of Giles. Thematically, it was the haves versus the have-nots, and Steve repeatedly touched on the fortune of wealthy Blacksburg residents. It was the sons of farmers and factory workers against those of doctors, lawyers, and college professors. Blacksburg was the home of Virginia Polytechnic Institute and State University, commonly referred to as Virginia Tech. The town itself had grown very fast in the 1970s, from a population of under ten thousand to one approaching thirty thousand. The players knew they had to go to Blacksburg for certain goods and services, which Steve leveraged to underscore the perceived inequality. Without fail, these distinctions were presented daily as motivation.

Entering the season, the Tech-towners returned the feature back from their championship run, Mark Dymock. Dymock had gained over fifteen hundred yards as the tailback in Dave Crist's two-tight-end, I-formation offense in 1977 after serving as the fullback to Sidney Snell as a sophomore. However, this season, without a true blocking fullback, Crist decided to move to the full-house T-formation and hoped that with Dymock at fullback, he could find more diverse ways to get the senior the ball.

For the Indian coaching staff, the most challenging aspect of the Giles game was keeping their players' minds off the following week's contest with Narrows. They had been high emotionally for their first three games, wins against Group AAA Salem and rivals Christiansburg and Radford. It was easy for the Indians to overlook Giles, as they had beaten them 56–0 and 40–0 the previous two seasons. With a win, Blacksburg was sure to join Southampton as the top two teams in the state when the first Group AA state poll of the year was released the following week.

This worried Crist, but it was magnified by his team's increasingly depleted roster heading into the game. He learned early in the week that Dymock would be forced to watch with a leg injury he suffered in the win over Radford the week before. Quarterback Gary Weddle was also out with a damaged thumb, and by Friday, seven starters were sidelined with influenza, including several along the offensive and defensive lines. These gaps were in addition to three players lost to injury in the preseason. Crist feared his team might panic.

Giles had a good start to their opening possession, gaining two quick first downs, but for the remainder of the first quarter, neither team could get anything going offensively. Crist remarked how hard the Spartans were playing, unconcerned with being the underdog. Steve was pleased with his team's effort, but it had garnered no points, and the Blacksburg defense continued to keep them backed up in their own territory. He felt there were only two people around who knew how to defend the single wing: Bill Patteson and Bill Brown. The Indians recovered a fumble in Spartan territory but quickly faced a fourth down at the Giles thirteen-yard line early in the second. From there, a nervous Mike Coleman, not their usual placekicker, booted a thirty-yard field goal, and Blacksburg led 3–0, a score that would remain until halftime.

Steve was thrilled to be in this position but still had to temper his enthusiasm. Regardless, this was what his team needed. He knew Blacksburg was missing several key players, but that was irrelevant to his team's morale. In the home locker room, Coach Crist had decided to make some adjustments. Mark Dymock's replacement, Tony McGuyer, was bothered by a hip pointer in the first half, and Crist chose to replace him with halfback Mike Coleman, who could provide more speed at fullback. The junior had moved back to Blacksburg from Texas before the season in hopes that Crist's switch to the T-formation would give him a better opportunity at playing time, even with Dymock returning.

Coming out for the second half, Coleman ran harder than he had all season. He and halfback Eddie Bowyer helped Blacksburg dominate the time of possession. All the same, the Indians still could not find the end zone, as they were plagued by turnovers and penalties. The game moved to the final stanza with Crist's squad clinging to a meager 3–0 lead, and Giles continuing to play inspired in the face of scant offensive output.

Finally, late in the game, the Spartans were given their opportunity and a momentary glimpse at glory. With the Indians deep in Giles territory, backup Indian quarterback Billy Myers fumbled an exchange with a returning Tony McGuyer, and the ball was scooped up by Giles sophomore defensive back Timmy Martin. For a split second, Timmy was all alone, with an unabated path to the end zone, and Steve saw victory flash before his eyes. But it was not to be, as he stumbled and was cut off by Myers. The beleaguered Giles single wing, which produced only six first downs and forty-six yards rushing for the game, again could not capitalize, and the Spartans were forced to punt from their own end zone.

With field position at the Giles twenty-six-yard line, it took Blacksburg just five plays to add to their lead. With a nine-yard touchdown run off-tackle, Mike Coleman capped a 103-yard rushing performance, including eighty-two in the second half. The PAT was good, and Blacksburg pushed their advantage to ten. Unfortunately for the Spartans, this score would go final just over two minutes later. Nonetheless, Steve was elated about the close game. *We gave them a darn fit!* he thought.

Only losing 10–0 to Blacksburg was a moral victory for Giles, especially after the embarrassing Narrows blowout. The Spartan players didn't care about holes in the Indians lineup. All that mattered was they had been competitive against one of the best teams in the state. Steve had to focus on the positive, that his team had rebounded from the Narrows game and grown against Blacksburg, not the reality that his fledgling offense had gone scoreless the last three games and been shut down entirely by Bill Brown's defense. He hoped that the remainder of the season would bring further progress.

Steve's father also hoped to see the Spartans improve. The elder Ragsdale attended Spartan football practice nearly every day. Under any other circumstances, he wouldn't have set foot on the Giles High School grounds except to attend a Narrows–Giles sporting event, but he put aside their bitter rivalry to support his son.

Harry would arrive on campus in the early afternoon and visit Principal Bill Puckett. Puckett valued Harry's administrative guidance. Then, as the school day ended, he would trek to the practice field with his lawn chair in hand. The players knew that wherever Harry's lawn chair was located, that's where the hitting would occur that day. Even at seventy-one years of age, he loved the physicality of the game. Wearing his signature fedora hat, he would be seen excitedly moving about in his lawn chair, animated with each bit of aggressive contact. He enjoyed the basics of blocking and tackling: one-on-one drills and live scrimmaging. But, above all, he observed everything that transpired to later mentor Steve.

At the same time, Harry never interfered or advised his son publicly. He was present and visible but made sure the leadership line was drawn clearly and definitively. Harry rarely spoke to players within the context of practice. Even during the installation of the single wing, he gave Steve the space to bring the offense to life with his own personality. Conversely, the two spoke privately by phone nearly every night. On occasion, as the players conditioned to close practice, Steve would consult his father, but it was always outside of his players' earshot. They never knew what the father and son discussed.

Afterward, Harry would come to the coaches' office and spend time with the staff, often leaving them mesmerized with tales from his life and fabled career. Born in 1907 to Thomas and Tabitha Ragsdale, Harry grew up just south of Kenbridge, a tobacco-farming community in Lunenburg County. With a distinct voice born of his Southeastern Virginia roots, Harry would sometimes chronicle his youth, of attending the local Non-Intervention and Lochleven schools and later Lynchburg College, where he was president of the student body his senior year and an undersized but gutsy lineman for the Hornets and their head coach, Edward L. Wright. It was there that Harry first learned the game and the single wing.

Other times, his rich baritone would detail his tumultuous beginnings teaching at Narrows: "Then he said, 'This is the meanest and roughest bunch of boys in the world down here. They ran the last man off. You just ball up your fist and knock the first one down!'" These were the words of John Fox, a prominent community member and engineer at the Virginian Railway power plant, who had requested a man-to-man talk upon his arrival in 1930. Harry had taken the job sight unseen for $115 a month after his post at the Chesapeake & Potomac Telephone Company fell through due to the economic downturn earlier that year. "I was scared to death the first day of school," he continued, his listeners hanging on every word. "I had never seen this part of the state before, and I didn't like it at first. I almost left the next year to take a job in Rock Hill, South Carolina," he revealed, but he was convinced to stay when the county agreed to officially start football.

Some evenings, Harry would recount tales of his first team. "In the first game we played at Narrows in 1931, Brooks Johnson returned the opening kickoff ninety yards for a touchdown after taking a lateral from John Tiller," he told of the 27–0 win over Eggleston. Johnson and Hunter Hale were his inaugural cocaptains. On other occasions, Harry would speak of the triumphs that led Narrows football out of the Great Depression. District titles in 1935 and the undefeated seasons of 1938 and 1939, which also produced "claimed" Class C state championships. These games, not recognized by the then–Virginia High School Literary and Athletic League, were informal arrangements made by top-ranked teams, as only Class A, the state's top classification, was officially sanctioned. The winner declared themselves champions, even for a refusal to play. "In 1938, Culpeper wouldn't play us. Their coach told me he had seen us and didn't want any part of us," he pointed out.

Harry would light up with the mention of names like Jess Johnson, Allen McClaugherty, Kenneth French, and many others. He would smile as he told of the numerous coaches he had encountered along the way. With aliases like old Hollywood mobsters, Harry had faced the likes of Shorty, Nap, Stretch, Ringie, Boodie, Tex, Moe, Itchy, and

Smokey. He had battled his college teammates and former players. He had matched wits with one-time college stars, a former All-American, and a past NFL player. There were coaches with stadiums and fields named after them—even a team without a coach. His biography was its own colorful journey, a kaleidoscope of memories woven into a patchwork of stories and lessons.

In some instances, Harry would use his Rolodex of experience to give Steve immediate feedback and advice. The assistant coaches would note how, like many sons, Steve would initially dismiss his father's ideas, only to return to them a few days later.

Harry could remember a time when he, like Steve now, had faced a scoring slump. The 1946 Narrows Green Wave was not only winless but failed to score a point the entire season. The highs of prewar prosperity were nowhere to be found. The 1947 season was not much better, as the Green Wave did not win until the seventh game, defeating Bob Lawson's Christiansburg club, 34–6, and ending a fourteen-game drought. The win had provided Harry with his first taste of gridiron victory since 1941, a span of almost six years.

Just as he had, Harry believed Steve would see brighter days ahead.

CHAPTER 5

FIGHT CLOUD

August 24, 1979
Giles vs. Graham (Scrimmage)

I HOPE THIS SCRIMMAGE gets rained out. I don't want to face Graham again. They just thrashed us last year. Steve's outlook was as dismal as the showers that fell over Roanoke that morning. Returning from a minor outpatient procedure at Roanoke Memorial Hospital, he couldn't shake his thoughts of that night's rematch. Even with an increased turnout, Steve unconsciously linked his new team's potential to his first-year woes. *How are we going to win a game this season?* He fully expected the area newspapers to predict the Spartans to finish last of nine schools in the New River District when picks were released later that weekend, primarily because they failed to win a district game the previous year. The darkness was not without its silver lining, though. As he arrived back in Pearisburg, the rain subsided, and he knew the contest with Graham would remain as scheduled. Through the gloom of 1978, some much-needed rays of sunshine began to appear, none brighter than sophomore tailback Leon King.

The first time Steve saw Leon play, he knew he was going to be something special. He immediately took notice of Leon's agile moves, smooth and shifty. He accelerated down the sideline full speed, hit a 360-degree spin on a would-be tackler, and continued without breaking stride. It was late October 1976, and Steve and Harry had decided to attend the youth league championship game under the lights at Giles High School. A seventh grader, Leon dazzled his opponents, weaving his way to four touchdowns, and the Pembroke Trojans trounced the Narrows Jaycees 52–0. His teammates felt like they were playing with Chicago Bears running back Walter Payton. "Sweetness" was one of Harry's favorite NFL players, and looking on, he and Steve could hardly disagree with the comparison.

Upon entering high school, which at Giles began in the eighth grade, Leon and fellow Pembroke boys Greg Mance, Chris Woods, and Mark Chapman boldly told their teachers they would win a state championship by the time they graduated. Bolstering their conviction was Steve's final eighth-grade squad, which lost but a single game, a 22–20 thriller to Blacksburg, and Leon was a catalyst for much of the team's success. During August that season, junior varsity coach Jerry Albert told Steve that Leon had asked to get some extra reps with the jayvees following eighth-grade practice. Fearing he may grow cocky, Steve agreed.

That'll take a little wind out of Leon's sails—keep his feet on the ground. He suspected a few knocks from the older crew would serve as an enlightening baptism by fire for the young running back. Leon was a scrappy live wire, and his reputation had preceded his arrival at Giles High School. Officials at both Pembroke Elementary and King Johnston School had informed Steve about his more spirited attributes. Coach Albert saw Steve smile at him as Leon jogged into the huddle, and he knew the lesson he wished to convey. Much to Steve's surprise, Leon proceeded to run all over the jayvees. They couldn't lay a hand on him. Play after play, it was apparent that the older players were no more successful at containing the elusive youngster than his eighth-grade counterparts. At barely 145 pounds, Leon was feisty, brimming with football moxie, and tough as nails. Steve could only grin now with anticipation. He loved Leon's competitive fire, as the two shared a lionhearted will to win.

To begin his freshman year, and Steve's first year atop the varsity program, his coach had decided to leave Leon on jayvee. Having already annexed multiple sophomores to varsity, he hoped that's where he would remain. Even so, several games into the season, Steve began to toy with the idea of moving up his talented freshman. Coming into the Christiansburg game, Leon had dressed out with the varsity team, but Steve had yet to place him in the lineup.

In the weeks following the Blacksburg loss Leon's freshman year, the Spartans had fallen to Radford, 32–14, and George Wythe, 26–6, but Christiansburg offered a more favorable matchup with both teams sitting at 1–5 for the year. Still, Blue Demons back Phillip Oliver ran wild early, slicing through the Giles defense like a hot knife through butter and scoring two first-half touchdowns. Steve looked down the sideline at Leon. He didn't want to undermine the junior varsity, who were currently 4–1 with one game remaining, but he saw possibility in him, and the varsity team was in the midst of a five-game losing streak. Down 12–0 after another scoreless half, Steve was ready to make a move. Walking off the field, he called Leon over.

"What do you think, Leon? You ready to play?"

"Yeah, man." He was seething.

Once gathered, Steve took his team to task. "Hell's bells, boys!" he squalled, the volume and pitch of his voice suddenly increasing as the locker room door closed behind him.

Nonetheless, the Spartans did little to stem the tide in the second half, save a lone touchdown in the waning minutes. A single stat line cited a one-yard run by Leon King. While a quiet contribution, the sixty-five-yard drive, spearheaded by the ardent freshman, heralded his move to varsity. The impact of Leon's tenacity was undeniable, albeit an investment in the future.

Harry could remember his first Christiansburg game and the play of another promising freshman. It was October 1932, and with the score knotted 6–6 late, Jess Johnson returned an interception sixty yards for the decisive touchdown in an 18–6 victory. He would lead all Narrows scoring through 1935. Adding to the triumph, Christiansburg was coached by one of Harry's Lynchburg College teammates, Robert Gerald, whose great-great-grandfather was Captain George Pearis, after whom Pearisburg was named. Gerald had previously guided the 1927 squad to the Class B state finals, losing 7–0 to Lane High School of Charlottesville. Harry, of course, painted it as a rivalry, which the 1933 *Narrosonian* confirmed "inspired the boys to fight harder."

The 1978 season had been a tough one. Even with a 26–6 win over non-district foe Lord Botetourt, the excitement was short-lived. District rushing leader Kim Gillespie had a field day for Carroll County a week later, running for four touchdowns in a 41–6 trouncing over Giles. The final humbling experience came during the last week when they traveled to Galax. That same night, Narrows was playing Radford to decide the New River District championship and Region IV playoff picture. The Green Wave had shocked the Bobcats a year earlier, keeping them out of the playoffs and sending Blacksburg on their championship run. This year, Narrows was undefeated, and an overflow crowd was expected at Radford.

Meanwhile, Steve had looked in their stands at Galax and struggled counting to ten. To make matters worse, his statistician didn't even show up, deciding to attend the Narrows–Radford game instead. The Galax Maroon Tide had little trouble dispatching the Spartans 34–14.

Steve had been hopeful his team would continue to progress after Blacksburg but found few moments to celebrate. The Spartans limped to the finish line, decimated by attrition. Nearly every week was a physical and mental beating, and with limited success, the positives began to fade, and low morale led to discouragement. After the Southampton Indians claimed their third state title of the decade that December, Steve broke down how the Spartans compared in a mythical matchup with Group AA's best. Southampton had beaten Gate City, 56–6, Gate City had defeated Narrows, 21–7, and Narrows had destroyed Giles, 48–0. *If we had played Southampton, they would have beat us 112–0!*

It was to be a long winter for Steve. After a 2–8 campaign ended with barely twenty-five players dressed, a conversation with assistant coach Vic Edwards served as a dose of reality. Steve had decided to move Edwards, who had led the eighth-grade troops, and Don Lowe to the varsity staff to replace the departing David Chapman and Jack Williams. He now felt comfortable leaving the eighth graders under the charge of assistant Rusty Kelley. Determined to be straightforward, Edwards asserted, "You better be doing some things to get the kids out—it's not going to just happen!" Growing up in some of Harry's most successful years, Steve had witnessed an idyllic scenario. He felt that if kids wanted to play, they would readily show up, with no need to inquire otherwise. Edwards's frank honesty about the situation at Giles convinced him he needed to rethink his philosophy and work to increase participation.

Steve read books on excellence in coaching and leadership, particularly about Vince Lombardi. Among his favorites was *Vince Lombardi on Football*. He wanted to soak up everything he could about the culture Lombardi had created with the Packers. Having worn the green and gold, being a Green Bay Packers fan was almost a matter of course for Steve. Furthermore, his favorite player growing up, Carroll Dale, played for the Packers from 1965 to 1972, which included Super Bowl I and II championship teams. Steve especially admired how Lombardi emphasized the extraordinary nature of the entire organization, creating confidence and pride associated with the Packers' name. Steve wanted to recreate the cultural identity of

"Packer Football" with his Giles program and introduced the concept of "Spartan Football." He believed no sport demanded more of its athletes than football. Therefore, he needed to convey that football players were exceptional and should be associated with success. By branding Spartan Football as a social status, involvement would be appealing to new prospects.

To make this tangible, Steve decided that no third-party apparel, whether sold or gifted, would display the phrasing "Spartan Football." That term was reserved for a select group. The only way to get a Spartan Football T-shirt was to earn it by playing varsity football, with the exclusivity intended to reward retention and completion. Steve wanted it to be valuable, and the only currency he accepted was blood, sweat, and tears. Otherwise, Spartan Football was not for sale.

You can't buy tradition.

To complement this decision, Steve worked with the school administration to reorganize the once-defunct booster club, focusing on advocacy and support rather than financial assistance. He also mulled a possible change in color prominence, from the dominant Columbia blue to scarlet red, previously used only for trim. He felt a fresh look and an aggressive color could help the Spartans begin anew, and, as this trend would be unique to football, it could add to his team's identity.

That spring, Steve began to target the top fifteen to twenty prospective football players in each class, grades eight through twelve. The physical education teachers helped him identify recruits, and then he circled their pictures in the yearbook to put a face with a name. Steve found there were potential players whose rural parents had never played sports, and they had never considered playing football. All they needed was a nudge.

Steve also attended a coaching clinic at Virginia Tech, where he heard head coach Bill Dooley speak on the "50 Eagle Defense." Dooley was entering his second year atop the Hokies program and was a proponent of the scheme, a 5–2 alignment with a strong safety, which he had used formerly at the University of North Carolina. Steve had used the 6–2 defense he learned from Harry but found the system, designed initially to oppose compact offenses, outmoded and limited in flexibility against developing formations intended to spread the field. After listening to Dooley, he decided to adapt the package and call it their "Spartan Five." In staying with his new theme, the strong safety, known to some as a "monster," would be styled the "Spartan."

"Playing football is like climbing a mountain. There are no easy ways to do it. If you're looking for an easy way to get to the top, there aren't any," Steve told his squad when practice began. Entering the 1979 season, every class on varsity had played for him in the eighth grade and knew his expectations. Numbers had also swelled to forty, exceeding his goal of a thirty-five-man varsity roster. Steve had plenty to be upbeat about. Not to mention, he had recently started dating a young woman named Patti Watson of Moneta, Virginia. "The girl I went out with on a date last night was pretty, but not as beautiful as that girl right there," he remembered saying the first time he saw her. Still, he couldn't let go of the past year's preoccupation.

During his career, Harry remained cautious with each coming season and often used coach-speak to understate his team's potential. Like his father, Steve felt it was to his team's advantage to be overlooked. But Steve's words, on the other hand, were bordering on pessimism. The *Roanoke Times & World-News* quoted his outlook for the Spartans as "anywhere from mediocre to poor," while he told the *Blacksburg Sun* that he felt like he was "just treading water." When Giles faced Grundy, Steve was shocked when, after an evenly contested first scrimmage, Golden Wave coach Larry Bradley told him: "I won't be surprised when this is all over if we don't see y'all in the playoffs this season."

Man, you must be crazy.

Glynn Carlock's Graham club was young but still talent laden as they arrived in Pearisburg for their scrimmage with the Spartans. Although they had gone 8–2 in 1978, disappointing losses down the stretch kept them out of the playoffs. This year's group had battled a top-notch Narrows team to a stalemate a week earlier, and Carlock was optimistic. He told the *Bluefield Daily Telegraph* and sports editor Bob Foley: "I feel we're as strong physically as last year, but just not as experienced." Steve knew they were still one of the top programs in the Southwest District, which included all Group AA schools west of Interstate 77.

After an exchange of punts to start, Giles began their second possession on their own twenty-three-yard line. After just a few plays, Steve noticed a difference in the Spartans against Eddie Hall and the Graham defense. Leon was running inside like a man possessed, twisting and turning for extra yardage. Steve likened it to a cartoon fight cloud, a dust plume with arms and legs sticking out in various directions. Leon would disappear into a swarm of bodies, Hitman and the gang hitting him from every angle, only for him to inexplicably spurt out and continue running down the field.

Numbering from the outside in, Giles ran two power plays to the long side of the unbalanced formation from the straight series, a wider off-tackle play denoted as "44" and a tighter trap variation designated as "46." These two plays were bread-and-butter runs for the tailback, one of two deep backs that could receive the snap. Alongside the fullback, the two were set left to right, respectively, for Giles. Leon continued to make hay on 46 ("four" back through the "six" hole), carrying the ball four consecutive times for twenty-four yards.

While the Spartans had a larger group of upperclassmen, the question remained if they would rally around a sophomore upstart. But Leon was thriving. Wearing jersey no. 43, he played with a confident swagger but was never showy. Instead, he let his love of contact do the talking, and his teammates took notice. On the next play, Leon handed off to senior wingback Fonzie Austin, who broke free on the reverse for a blazing fast fifty-four-yard touchdown. Austin, the district's hundred-yard dash champion, alternated at wingback with Terry Freeman, the two running in plays from the sideline. Suddenly,

Giles led 6–0, or in standard scrimmage scoring, 1–0.

Graham responded on their next possession with a twelve-play, sixty-five-yard drive that culminated in a seventeen-yard touchdown pass from freshman quarterback Eddie Neel to fullback Eddie Hall, and the score was even. The G-Men added another after halftime, and the exhibition moved to the fourth with Giles down 12–6.

With just minutes remaining, Leon took control of the offensive huddle, declaring, "I didn't come out here tonight to lose! Get off your rear end and block somebody up there!" He was in his element. Kids play football for different reasons, but he played because he loved it. It didn't matter if it was played in a parking lot. Steve could see that the other boys respected Leon. They knew he wasn't afraid to knuckle up. He had the charisma and passion for leadership, and his teammates responded. Leon slipped past as many as four Graham defenders on the next play, sidestepping and spinning his way to a twenty-yard gain, and the home sideline launched into impassioned vigor. For junior Mo Ratcliffe, it was the first time he knew this group would not quit when they got behind, like so many Giles teams before them. The single wing tallied the final touchdown a few plays later, and the scrimmage concluded 12–12, or two scores each.

Giles had gone the distance with Graham, a significant source of confidence for Steve and the Spartan players alike. Watching Leon lead his teammates through adversity, Steve knew he had found the glimmer of light they had lacked. Now, he just needed to galvanize the support of the community. As the second-year head coach contemplated his messaging in the days to come, he thought of Harry, who had greeted him on the field. Someone had once asked of the legendary Green Wave mentor: "Coach, when you go out to practice on Monday after a big win on Friday night, what do you tell your team?" Steve knew his father's response. He had heard the answer countless times.

"I tell them the same damn thing I told them last Monday," Harry replied.

CHAPTER 6

THE BANDANA IS BORN

September 22, 1979
Giles vs. Narrows

BEFORE THE TURN of the twentieth century, the earth rumbled with such force emanating from Pearisburg, Virginia, that the impact was felt in twelve states. On May 31, 1897, an estimated 5.9 magnitude earthquake shook the eastern seaboard, which was not accustomed to seismic activity. Locals reported that Angel's Rest, the peak of Pearis Mountain that overlooked town, was cracked. It was one of the most significant moments ever recorded in Giles County, founded in 1806. Even so, by comparison, the community of the county seat was no more prepared for the earth-shaking events that were about to occur than those of the distant past.

The 1979 Orange Bowl featured the Oklahoma Sooners and the Nebraska Cornhuskers in a Big Eight Conference rematch on New Year's Day. Dick Enberg and Merlin Olsen called the game in prime time for NBC. In Giles, the broadcast aired on WSLS Channel 10 out of Roanoke, one of just three channels viewable with a set of rabbit ears and the right amount of aluminum foil. Watching, Leon was already thinking about next season. The Barry Switzer–coached Sooners were masters of the wishbone offense, orchestrated to near perfection by quarterback Thomas Lott. A three-year starter, Lott had gained publicity for the array of colorful bandanas he wore under his helmet as he and his backfield, including Heisman Trophy–winner Billy Sims, captured the national spotlight. Lott wore a bandana to protect his Afro hairstyle from indentations, but his signature style was also trendsetting. Leon had worn one to cover his cornrow braids, but watching Lott lead the Sooners to a 31–24 victory over Nebraska on national television, he decided to make the bandana his trademark as well. Like Lott, Leon was unaware of the stir it would cause among detractors.

When the season finally arrived, Leon quietly donned a blue bandana, unbeknownst to Steve. By the time he had led the Spartans against Graham and to wins over Fort Chiswell, 33–8, and Floyd County, 46–6, the county was abuzz. Giles rarely started 2–0, and with the next bout coming against Narrows, everyone was talking about sophomore Leon King against senior Rusty Cook and the mighty Green Wave.

In 1978, winning their first New River District crown since Harry retired, Cook rushed for 1,401 yards, the defense had six shutouts, and Narrows went 11–1. While graduation claimed over twenty roster spots from the defending champs, the Big Green Machine of 1979 was still loaded with talent. In his calculated preseason tone, Steve told Giles County's local newspaper, the *Virginian Leader*: "Narrows is big, real big. They've got Cook, and that's enough right there. He's hard to bring down. I hope he doesn't hurt too many of our boys when we play them."

On a typical in-season afternoon, the Spartan players would exit the locker room, pass the smoking pit, and gather behind the baseball backstop to receive directives from Steve before proceeding to the practice field, located atop the hill behind the visitors' bleachers. Steve used these short meetings to establish the mindset for practice. On Mondays, his message was consistent: "Boys, it all boils down to two things: blocking and tackling. Whoever works the hardest and practices the best will win on Friday night. All right?" It was the repeated reinforcement of core beliefs.

However, on this particular Monday, something else was circulating among his players. Sparked from interactions between Giles and Narrows students at the county vocational school, word had arrived that Narrows planned to take Leon's bandana from him during the game, and by whatever means necessary. The direct source of the statement seemed to be unknown, but rumors were rampant. Several players heard a bounty had been placed on Leon's head, with a cash reward for obtaining his bandana, and some wondered if Hot Rod Dennis was involved. Another understood the threat from Narz to include a racial slur directed at the bandana-clad sophomore. Others told of threatening letters sent to the school, photographs of burning bandanas shared in the community, and even a funeral wreath sent to express their condolences for the impending demise of the Spartans. Reality and fiction were becoming increasingly hard to determine.

After a players-only discussion, it was decided. Robert Stump, a senior captain who wore a mohawk, complete with a large "G" on each side similar to the Packer-like logo on their white headgear, spoke up. "We're all going to wear them," he announced. In solidarity with Leon, everyone would wear a bandana under their helmet. It would be a collective push. There was just one problem—while the Spartan players were determined to stand up for their teammate, they were worried their visual display would raise the ire of their coach.

Steve Ragsdale was an intimidating disciplinarian. When he stepped between the lines, he expected complete focus and had zero tolerance for horseplay, which he defined as "grab-assing." Though just twenty-eight years of age, he commanded a larger-than-life presence, and while they had great respect for him, many of his players were also deathly afraid of provoking his wrath. A rebuke, or "ass chewing," from Steve was an intimate encounter. He would often develop a white froth in the corners of his mouth when he became incredibly animated and sometimes inadvertently spit as he screamed, leaving spatter on the face mask of the unfortunate player. For this reason, they gave him a wide berth, and some traveled well out of their way to avoid him altogether.

Steve had not yet heard the chatter coming out of Narrows, but he had noticed something as he walked through the locker room after school that day. In front of the mirror, Leon was putting on his bandana. At first glance, he didn't like the optics, but he didn't say anything at the time, and the team continued on to practice. The next day, several other Spartan players wore a bandana, and even more were visible by Wednesday, primarily red in color. At first, red was simply more abundant and readily available at stores in town and surrounding areas, but it became the color of choice when, by midweek, Leon switched from his original blue bandana to a red one. By now, almost the entire team was wearing one.

What in the world is going on out here with all these bandanas? Steve thought.

Steve called his assistant coaches, Don Lowe and Vic Edwards, into the coaches' office and told them to investigate. He wanted to get the story behind his players' actions and felt they would willingly confide in the staff. After practice, they told Steve the story of Thomas Lott at Oklahoma, Leon's bandana, and the threats coming from Narrows. *I've got a problem here. I've got to do something.* In essence, the players' fears were justified.

Steve typically disapproved of any kind of flamboyance or ostentatious display of individualism. This was not just a preference but a way of life. He cared little about being fashionable. He often donned mismatched or makeshift clothing and was notoriously thrifty. He was no-frills to the core. This situation, on the other hand, seemed different. The bandanas appeared to be uniting his players ahead of their annual clash with their bitter rival. Steve knew he had a decision to make.

On Thursday, Giles held their final prep for the Narrows game. Thursday sessions were held in full game dress, as Steve wanted their uniforms slightly dirty on game day to prevent them from worrying about how they looked. After practice, Steve called his players in to talk to them as a group. *Timing is everything.* By now, all the Giles players were wearing bandanas. Steve addressed his team: "OK, boys, what's the deal with the bandanas?"

Silence.

His players looked around sheepishly, expecting their no-nonsense leader to end their symbolic show of support. Then he dropped a bombshell.

"Well, if they're going to take it off one of us, then by God, they're going to have to take it off all of us." Steve reached into his back pocket and pulled out his own red bandana. "You see this bandana right here? If we whip Narrows's ass tomorrow night, I'll take this bandana over and tell them exactly what they can do with it!"

Seeing their otherwise uncompromising coach join their player-led campaign released a flood of raw emotion, and the Spartan players went totally berserk, erupting into a frenzied celebration. Harry's mentorship had provided the invaluable wisdom of a master psychologist. Of course, Steve would never disrespect Coach Patteson or his dad in such a manner, but his players didn't know that. For the first time, these players felt they were going to beat Narrows.

Harry could remember harnessing the passion of his players as well, particularly the McClaugherty brothers: Harry, Allen, and Frank. When motivated to tears, they had been almost unbeatable. Harry McClaugherty went on to play at the University of Virginia and Allen at Virginia Tech. Allen eventually returned to his alma mater, where he served as an assistant alongside his former coach. Starring consecutively in the Narrows backfield, the Depression-era trio inspired the saying: "When you come down Wolf Creek, watch out for the snakes and the McClaughertys."

The boys from Wolf Creek were considered exceptionally rugged. Nearly four decades later, T-shirts in the hallways of Narrows High School proclaiming "100% Wolf Creek" still echoed the sentiment. School spirit reflected community pride, and the Green Wave supporters were fanatical. At 2–0, they were already writing daily letters to the *Roanoke Times & World-News* complaining of poor coverage. The front window of Hot Rod's Green Wave Exxon was painted with the name of every Narrows player, coach, and cheerleader. WNRV had even added a segment for Hot Rod to predict area games. Personally, Dennis had eighteen hundred dollars riding on a Green Wave victory.

Tensions neared a boiling point, even more so at area stomping grounds. A Narrows player did not come to the Tastee Freez in Pearisburg unless he expected a fight, and a Giles player didn't go to Johnny's Tall Boy in Narrows unless he expected the same. One primary turf was the county's largest employer, the Celanese plant. Located along the New River between Narrows and Pearisburg, the Celanese Corporation of America began producing cellulose acetate, used commonly as a synthetic filament, yarn, and fabric, at their Celco plant in 1939. The manufacturing complex transformed the once-agrarian county into a regional center of industry, and for the plant's nearly twenty-two hundred employees, a mixture of residents from across the county, the upcoming Giles–Narrows game represented a year's worth of bragging rights. In some cases, this fueled large stakes, as rumors circulated of entire paychecks being wagered.

Even with downpours in the forecast for game day, nothing could dampen the intensity of the white-hot rivalry. Everyone in the school system was involved. Even the most rigid traditionalists on both sides couldn't help but get caught up in the feeling of camaraderie. Robert Farmer, the father of Barry and cheerleader Babette, was the machine-shop teacher at the vocational school. A former head football coach at Giles himself, he had led the Spartans to their first winning record in 1964 and joined the vocational school when it opened four years later. Like most schools, hats and head coverings were against the rules. Farmer was physically imposing at six foot four and decidedly strict with his students. Yet, on Friday, he demonstrated a memorable act of leniency, permitting the Giles vocational students to wear their bandanas in class. Despite objections from the Narrows aggregation, Farmer sat in the back of the room and smiled.

Several inches of rain had fallen in the region by late afternoon, postponing the game until Saturday night. Though frustrating to those who had traded shifts at the Celanese, the move did little to quell enthusiasm. If anything, it amplified it, as the entire Giles community seemed to have a bandana by game time, some traveling as far as Blacksburg and Bluefield to find one.

In what was becoming their pregame ritual, Steve gathered his players in the hallway of the Giles High School agriculture building. He would talk to them collectively and individually, and they would relax on the floor, silently reflecting on the game plan and their assignments. Harry had done the same with his players, lying on the gymnasium floor at the old Narrows High School. On this night, the Spartan players could already hear the distant roars, as even amidst the lingering drizzle, the crowd was decidedly rowdy, cheering the back-and-forth antics between the two sides.

The players could feel the energy in the stadium as the eight o'clock start time approached. For the Spartans, it was unlike any they had felt before. There were bandanas everywhere. Giles suddenly had their own version of the "Terrible Towel," the rally towel tradition of the Pittsburgh Steelers that had debuted just a few years prior. As they took the field, Leon became aware of a sign in the visitors' stands. Usually, he never noticed anything in the crowd, but this caught his attention. It read, "2 Wrongs Don't Make a Right, 2 Kings Don't Make a Cook," referring to brothers Leon and Greg King against Rusty Cook and his brother Ricky, a junior linebacker for the Green Wave. His feet sank inauspiciously into the soggy turf as Giles was set to receive.

Unnerved, Leon was unable to secure the opening kickoff and, after picking up the loose ball, was brought down on his own six-yard line. The Green Wave limited the Spartans to a three-and-out and, following a short punt, started with excellent field position at the Giles thirty-one. This was not the start Steve had hoped for.

Narrows drove to the doorstep almost immediately on runs by Cook and fullback Terry Sparks, but the Spartan defense held and forced a fourth-and-goal from the three-yard line. With Giles expecting another run, Narrows converted on a backside pop pass from quarterback Junior Simpkins to end Steve "Punkin" Frazier for the touchdown. Frazier added the point-after, and Narrows took the early lead, 7–0, with 5:33 left in the first quarter.

On the Spartans' next possession, Rusty Cook, a corner on defense, intercepted Leon's pass and returned it thirty-four yards for another score. Even with a missed extra point, the Spartans found themselves quickly in a hole, 13–0. Nevertheless, they were determined to battle back.

Early in the second quarter, the Spartans were in business at the Green Wave twenty-five-yard line following a Narrows fumble. Senior blocking back Mike Davidson then made a spectacular diving catch on a twenty-three-yard throwback pass from Leon, and the home crowd surged to life. Davidson left the game with a knee injury and was replaced by Timmy Martin. Greg King finished the drive with a two-yard scoring run, Eddie Carr kicked the extra point, and the Narrows lead was cut to six. Giles was back in the game, and so were the Spartan fans, who were madly waving bandanas at their opponents. Neither team would budge on their subsequent possessions, and the 13–7 score remained until intermission.

Steve addressed mistakes at the break, most notably in their buck-lateral series. In this misdirection-based sequence, the fullback threatened the interior of the defense before either keeping or handing to the blocking back, who pitched to the tailback heading wide on a sweep to the long side of the formation. They had trouble in the first half on "42 Buck," the pitchout, or lateral, to the tailback. Among the missteps, senior pulling lineman Benny Hendricks had been unsuccessful in blocking the cornerback. As Giles only set their unbalanced line to the right, he was repeatedly tasked with the same defender, Rusty Cook. Despite Hendricks's explanation, Steve uncorked with deliberate hyperbole: "I don't give a damn if he's over on the sideline—you hit him!"

The Spartan defense stiffened to start the second half after two Rusty Cook runs and a penalty moved the ball into Giles territory. Defensive lineman David Martin dropped Narrows fullback Terry Sparks for a loss, one of twelve tackles for the senior, and the Green Wave drive stalled. Just the same, three plays later, the Spartans faced a fourth down deep in their own territory when Narrows senior Todd Oney came off the edge, blocked the ensuing punt, and returned it twelve yards for a Green Wave touchdown. Cook barreled over for the two-point conversion, and in the blink of an eye, Narrows was on top 21–7 midway through the third frame.

Needing to answer, the Spartans responded with a fifty-five-yard drive behind the running of Leon King, Fonzie Austin, and fullbacks Greg King and Charlie Mullins. A Pearisburg boy, Charlie was already a defensive starter but had also become an additional backfield contributor as a junior, even with his left arm currently in a shoulder harness. In the Giles version of the single wing, the fullback was a forceful inside runner and provided the primary draw for the buck-lateral series. Though they had trouble with it in the first half, Steve returned to 42 Buck, and this time, puller Benny Hendricks foiled the corner, Rusty Cook, springing Leon to the Green Wave five. After Greg King moved the ball to the two, Charlie plowed straight ahead for the touchdown, and the Spartans had countered. The extra point was off the mark, but Giles was back within a score at 21–13.

The Giles fans could sense an emotional shift as the contest moved to the final stanza. Homemade bandana flags waved tirelessly in hopes of a come-from-behind victory. The Spartan defense bottled up Rusty Cook on the following series, and Narrows was forced to punt, but regardless of Steve's best effort to alert his team of a short kick, the rain-soaked ball hit a Giles player, and the Green Wave recovered. Narrows capitalized off the turnover and recaptured momentum on the next play when Cook broke off a forty-nine-yard run down to the Spartans two. The Narrows back showed why he was being recruited by Virginia Tech, Virginia, and North Carolina, breaking three tackles and converting another fourth-and-goal just minutes later. Another Punkin Frazier kick added to their tally, and the Green Wave were on top for good, 28–13.

The rain came more heavily as the final minutes ticked off the clock. The two teams finished statistically even, but five Spartan turnovers were the difference. Steve was disappointed in the loss, but he realized this rallying cry could be more significant than any single game. After all, Leon still had his bandana, and now, so did everyone else.

The earthquake of 1897 shook Pearisburg and, with it, Angel's Rest. While reports of a large fissure opening in the mountaintop were later proven amiss, the story survived. Years later, a legendary divide would again spark local lore, but this time, it was the tale of two schools, a seismic rivalry, and the birth of the Bandana Express.

CHAPTER 7

WHO BEAT?

October 5, 1979
Giles vs. Radford

"**A TIE IS LIKE KISSING** your sister," or so goes the classic coaching expression, and for Steve Ragsdale, there was indeed little satisfaction in his team's 6–6 tie with Blacksburg the following Saturday night. To make matters worse, Leon had taken a hit while passing, and local physician Dr. Erma McGuire, affectionately titled "Dr. Erma," determined he had suffered a concussion. Steve would be forced to make plans to replace the district's third-leading rusher as the Spartans began preparations for their next week's opponent, the Radford Bobcats.

He was pleased with the Spartans' defensive effort against Blacksburg. He told Bob Foley of the *Bluefield Daily Telegraph*: "Our defense . . . has gone beyond my expectations . . . Things right now are going better than I really thought they would." He went a step further in the *Virginian Leader*, adding, "They played with a lot of determination and pride," mentioning Curtis Woods, David Martin, Chuck Stone, and Mike Ratcliffe, among others.

Senior safetyman Curtis Woods saved multiple touchdowns and had an interception, and defensive lineman David Martin, a year removed from a season-ending knee injury against Blacksburg, blocked the decisive extra point. Steve's defensive ends also played well: Chuck Stone, who, because of his father's military service, had just moved back to Giles from out of state for his junior year, and the colorful, curly-haired Mo Ratcliffe, a two-way starter. Mo was growing into a catalyst for the Spartans' collective spirit. Based on his praise of Queen's new album *Live Killers*, his teammates were convinced he wanted to be a rock star. He exuded charismatic flair, reveled in wild abandon, and never shied away from a fight. While in seventh grade, the two defensive ends, now friends, had an epic donnybrook, students and teachers alike hanging out the windows to watch.

With the tie, the Spartans were 2–1–1 as the season approached the halfway point. *We should have won*, Steve thought. The *Blacksburg Sun* called the 6–6 stalemate a "shocker," while the *Roanoke Times & World-News* declared that Giles "almost pulled off the upset of the New River District." In truth, playing Blacksburg to an even draw was considered an accomplishment in the community, especially when combined with the growing bandana phenomenon. Still, it was a hurdle uncrossed for Steve. "We gave Narrows two touchdowns, and on two occasions, they had to go four times inside the five to score. I feel we should have beaten Blacksburg, and I'm hoping we get the same kind of effort against Radford," he told the *Bluefield Daily Telegraph*.

Steve's players knew he was not content. After all, they had been trained, some since the eighth grade, in the ways of Vince Lombardi. They were taught to always chase perfection. Steve found a reminder of this principle in the simplest of places: the wisdom of the family matriarch. His maternal grandmother, Daisy Hale Simmons, was nearly eighty-eight years old, and the only question she ever asked about his games was, "Who beat?" In her charming Appalachian vernacular, she only wanted to know one thing: whether they won or lost. This made an impression on Steve. There were no follow-up questions. She was not interested in moral victories, and neither was he. Not anymore. Winning was the only desired result, and Steve carried this on with him as part of his coaching philosophy.

Apart from the disappointment, there was a turning point of

lasting significance against the Indians. Steve had ordered new red jerseys and decided to reveal them against Blacksburg. Once again focused on establishing tradition, he felt they would create a distinct look for the football program. Steve was still the varsity basketball coach but knew that to entice the best athletes in school to play the physical game of football, he had to continue building an appealing culture. Steve also included an homage to Lombardi and the Packers, adding Green Bay–style white-and-Columbia-blue stripes on the sleeves, along with solid-white numbers.

As a boy, Steve witnessed his father use a singular set of jerseys during the final three years of his career. When the Green Wave entered the newly formed New River District in 1960 and began rolling up win after win wearing gold jerseys, Harry refused to switch. He was so superstitious that Narrows played every game in the same tops for the next three seasons. Not just the same color scheme but the same exact *jerseys*. He had other uniform combinations, but because white was not yet required of the visiting team, they never saw the field, and the Green Wave never lost. Coupled with the concept of Spartan Football, Steve hoped the red jerseys were part of laying that kind of foundation at Giles. Within a week, David J. Bisset, sports editor of Radford's newspaper, the *News-Journal*, had penned the headline, "Bobcats Entertain Red, Bandana Spartans."

Head coach Norman Lineburg woke up every morning to the sound of the Radford High School fight song. He would blare it as loud as possible in preparation for the day and immediately be filled with Bobcat pride. He repeatedly told his players it was the number one song in the country. Indeed, Lineburg and their football program had plenty of tradition to be proud of.

Harry could remember the early days of Radford football and the first time he had faced the Bobcats. It was November of 1934, just one year after cocaptain Kenneth Hall had first suggested the name "Bobcats," and Radford was coached by Arthur R. "Ott" Giesen. The defining play on the opposition's gridiron that day was a thirty-five-yard touchdown run by Narrows fullback Bob Bonham. A rare combination of speed and power, Bonham had started in each of Harry's first four seasons and was captain of the 1934 eleven. He had even received interest from the University of South Carolina. Narrows prevailed 18–6, the first of four straight wins against Radford in the prewar period.

In later years, Harry would tussle with the likes of coaches Fred McCoy and Jimmy Painter on that same field, infamously branded the "Dust Bowl." With the help of the Radford community, a new stadium opened in 1967, ushering in a new era for the black, white, and old gold. Lineburg became the head coach in 1970, taking over for Harold Absher, the new superintendent of Giles County Public Schools. Since Lineburg's hire, the Bobcats had been a powerhouse in Group AA. They owned a thirty-three-game winning streak from 1970 to 1973 and back-to-back state championships in 1971 and 1972.

The 1971 staff included an up-and-coming coach named Frank Beamer. A local product, Beamer had played quarterback for Tommy Thompson at Hillsville High School, now Carroll County. Thompson helped revolutionize the passing game in Southwest Virginia after visiting the Baltimore Colts' training camp in the early 1960s and was a close personal friend of both Lineburg and Harry Ragsdale. Beamer left Radford after the 1971 season to become a graduate assistant at Maryland and was currently in his first season as the defensive coordinator under Mike Gottfried at Murray State.

By the conclusion of the 1978 season, Lineburg had an 83–12–3 record at Radford and an overall mark of 116–54–5, including previous head-coaching stops at William Byrd and Fieldale-Collinsville. The Bobcats had another solid year, posting an 8–2 record, blemished only by losses to Blacksburg and district champion Narrows. After the season, he was rumored for the head-coaching vacancy at Salem, the newest member of the Group AAA Roanoke Valley District, but Lineburg turned the job down. It was a near-perfect situation at Radford.

However, in the spring of 1979, tragedy struck. Lineburg, also the head track and field coach, had to endure the death of one of his athletes, junior Todd Spillman. It was the most traumatic experience of his twenty-year career. Spillman, a beloved student and the son of a local pediatrician, was killed in a pole-vaulting accident during a routine practice. Lineburg was devastated. He was not only his coach but a family friend. By football season, he had not recovered. In fact, the entire community struggled to heal. He felt his heart wasn't in it yet and didn't know if he was ready to return. He questioned if he would ever approach the game the way he wanted to again.

He trudged on, and by week five, the Bobcats were fortunate to be 2–2 following a come-from-behind victory over Carroll County, 19–15. The Bobcats had the fewest returning starters in the league, but a .500 record was significant because Radford had not had a losing season since Lineburg arrived. With that said, Giles had only beaten Radford once in school history, a 14–12 win in the final game of the Bobcats' 0–10 season of 1962. Many had forgotten it even occurred, for, in the seventeen years since, they had rarely been competitive.

By Friday, Steve had decided that, with Leon sidelined, the backfield would operate by committee. Greg King and Fonzie Austin would split duties at tailback, while Fonzie would continue to alternate with Terry Freeman at wingback and Greg with Charlie Mullins at fullback. Timmy Martin would again start at blocking back for the injured Mike Davidson, out since the Narrows game. On defense, Steve emphasized readiness, as Norm Lineburg's offense was imaginative and challenging to prepare for. He told free safety

Curtis Woods to be alert for the Bobcats to test the Spartan secondary through the air, even as early as the first play from scrimmage.

The Radford public address announcer recognized Harry over the loudspeaker before the game. Behind the microphone was Bucky Lawson, Narrows's all-state back of 1961 and part of a long lineage of single-wing fullbacks that began with Bob Bonham and continued through his predecessor Danny Caldwell. The Bobcats then ceremoniously entered the stadium through the H-frame goalposts, one of their many traditions, but Steve had prepared his team in advance of the possible distraction.

Right from the opening series, everything went right for the Spartans. David Martin, known as "David June" after his middle name, slashed into the backfield from his defensive-tackle spot and hit Radford tailback Scott Williams almost as soon as he took the handoff. The tackle for loss set the tone defensively. David's younger brother, Randy, a reserve on the offensive line, watched in admiration from the sideline. After a seven-play drive, Lineburg settled on a punt from the Giles forty-nine. The seven downs would be the most in a single possession all night for the Bobcats.

The Spartans took control deep in their own territory. After two plays garnered little, Greg King passed to wingback Fonzie Austin on third-and-nine for a gain of twenty-seven, and the single wing was on the move. Minutes later, Greg capped the eighty-eight-yard march with a six-yard run, and following an Eddie Carr extra point, Giles took an early lead, 7–0.

On the first day of practice in August, Coach Lineburg and defensive coordinator Buddy Shull, a head coach himself at Floyd County for five seasons before coming to Radford in 1975, had shown their team the single wing. It was as if they could see the rise of the Giles program. Shull viewed his leader as a tremendous motivator, but Lineburg was not a screamer. He, on the other hand, was much more vociferous. Both coaches felt they complemented each other well.

The Spartans again applied pressure on the Bobcats' next

possession, as Howlett fumbled while being sacked for what would have been a six-yard loss. It was clear Radford was having trouble with the Spartans' quickness. Adjusting his glasses, Lineburg searched his oversized clipboard, loaded with information. He was renowned as an on-the-field coach, remarkable at making adjustments, but at the moment, he had no answer for the Giles defense.

The Spartans added to their lead just before the half when Greg King scored his second touchdown, this time a four-yard run. The point-after failed, but the boys in bandanas led 13–0 with less than a minute left in the second quarter. For those that had made the trek over from Giles, a number that rivaled the home crowd, the anticipation was palpable.

In the third quarter, Steve began to pound the middle of the Radford defense, running behind offensive linemen Benny Hendricks and junior Don Sparks, a solid newcomer up front and another Pearisburg boy. Using the fullback wedge and split variations learned from Harry, Steve turned the offense into a meat grinder up the gut. The clock continued to run, allowing the Spartans to protect a two-score lead.

For Radford, things began to unravel. Six second-half turnovers, including three John Howlett interceptions, two by Curtis Woods, plagued the Bobcats as they desperately tried to get back into the game. The Spartan offense continued to churn out tough yardage and ultimately capitalized on the Radford miscues. Fourth-quarter touchdown runs by Fonzie Austin and Charlie Mullins closed out the scoring, and Giles had a monumental victory, 27–0.

It was the first time Radford had been blanked on their home field in a decade and the first shutout loss since 1965. The Bobcats ran just twenty-six offensive plays for eighty-one total yards and only crossed midfield twice. Meanwhile, the Spartans more than tripled Radford's offensive output, even without Leon. It had been a difficult year for Norm Lineburg. After the game, his wife, Joann, and their four sons, Robert, Mark, Paul, and Wayne, met him on the field, just as they always did. Following their show of support, Lineburg exited Bobcat Stadium the same way he had entered, through the H-frame goalposts.

The Spartans were greeted with the praise of administrators, community members, and former players, all with words like "winning season" and "playoffs" falling from their lips now that the toughest part of their schedule was behind them. Later, Coach Lineburg brought his four captains, Steve King, Scott Williams, Tim Semones, and Timmy Saul, to the Giles locker room to congratulate Steve and the Spartans, a first-class act of respect that caused the Giles players to swell with pride.

Even amid the celebration, Steve was cautious. *We've got so far to go. From now on, we're going to have to play our best to beat anyone.* Nevertheless, he allowed himself to quietly enjoy the moment. They'd worked for it. Next week would come soon enough.

CHAPTER 8

WE ARE FAMILY

October 12, 1979
Giles vs. George Wythe

THIS IS THE MOST EXCITEMENT *I've ever seen around here*, Steve thought as he read the day's paper in advance of the Spartans' sojourn to Wytheville to meet the Maroons of George Wythe High School. "Giles is this year's surprise team in the New River District, and the Spartans have the three league biggies—Narrows, Blacksburg, and Radford—behind them," proclaimed the *Bluefield Daily Telegraph*. In three games, the Spartans had gone 1–1–1, but following the signature win over Radford, school spirit was at an all-time high, and the community was rabid with bandana fever. *The enthusiasm has been unbelievable.*

At long last, there was freedom from the past for long-suffering Giles fans. Their boys had stood toe to toe with the district heavyweights and emerged with a chance to make the playoffs. Their thirst for success was finally being quenched, which provided genuine catharsis. Feelings of discouragement and shame were replaced with pride and undiluted joy. Spartan Football personified the community, and the bandana was emblematic of its deliverance. In the style of famous railway lines, especially those chugging toward an ultimate destination with few stops, they had taken to calling their team the "Bandana Express."

As Steve drove to school in the mornings, he would pass King Johnston, or "KJ," the de facto middle school, and see nearly every kid wearing a red bandana, many with them tied all over, tied together, even tied so long they dragged on the ground behind them. At the high school, Thursday-night bonfires led to passionate pep rallies every Friday, and class battles for the spirit stick were becoming fiercely competitive. Junior varsity player Chris Woods, Curtis Woods's younger brother, was instrumental in the genesis of a growing fixture at these pep rallies. A few weeks earlier, as he and his buddies watched the Baltimore Orioles in their run for Major League Baseball's American League pennant, they were captivated by superfan "Wild Bill" Hagy, whose "O-R-I-O-L-E-S" chants electrified the crowds at Memorial Stadium. Chris suggested friend Neal Andrews, nicknamed "Maggie," perform this same cheer at school pep rallies but as "G-I-L-E-S." He agreed, and Chris coined the persona "Wild Neal Maggie." Andrews tried it at the next pep rally, and it caught on immediately. Likewise, King Johnston School had its own weekly pep rally, and energy had even reached the elementary schools as students began writing letters of support to their varsity heroes.

After their offseason conversations, Steve delegated aspects of program promotion to assistant coach Vic Edwards. He led the design of bulletin boards, picture collages, and themed decorations, to name a few. At the same time, Steve oversaw the sale of approved spirit wear, excluding the phrase "Spartan Football," of course. For example, the staff sold red varsity jackets, lightweight Pla-Jac style, with a simple "Giles" on the back in script lettering, with an underlining swash-tail flourish. They sold like hotcakes, over six hundred of them. An onlooker couldn't go anywhere without seeing those red jackets, as they were second only to the bandanas themselves.

Leon was still experiencing symptoms of the concussion he had sustained two weeks before, and Dr. Erma advised that he wait another week before returning to play. As a competitor, Leon was aggravated. Playing hurt was as much a part of football for him as his trademark bandana. He could tolerate pain, but he was embarrassed to be injured. There was no such thing in his vocabulary. Leon was tough as woodpecker lips—by his logic, if he was breathing, he was playing. Steve finally had to intervene and tell Leon he was definitively not playing against George Wythe. Leon was so upset he wouldn't even speak to him. His absence complicated things, but the Spartans had played well against Radford without him, and Steve hoped for the same output on Friday night.

On Thursday, the *Roanoke Times & World-News* sports section was headlined by coverage of the World Series, in which the Baltimore Orioles had defeated the Pittsburgh Pirates 5–4, to take a 1–0 series lead. While Baltimore had Will Bill Hagy and his O-R-I-O-L-E-S chants, Pittsburgh had Willie "Pops" Stargell and "We Are Family," a hit earlier that year by Sister Sledge that the Pirates had adopted as their theme song. Among the pages, the newspaper also printed a feature by a young sportswriter named Dave Scarangella, now in his second year at the publication, titled "Giles Resurgence Surprises Coach." Previously, while a student at Virginia Tech, he had worked at the *Blacksburg Sun*, where he had covered Blacksburg High School's 1977 championship run.

The article focused on the program's growth and the stunning rout of Radford. Steve found irony in the word "resurgence" because they had never had a winning tradition to restore. While the attention was positive, the Spartans had not had a great week of practice. *I don't think we could do it again if we met them this week.* At times, he sensed his squad was going through the motions and worried they were getting complacent. "I know this week will be the first time we'll be the favorite," Steve acknowledged, the final paragraph outlining his angst. "Up until now, we've gone into games with the attitude we have nothing to lose and everything to gain. This time the shoe will be on the other foot. I don't know how we'll do," he disclosed.

Steve's concerns continued to play out in print on Friday morning, as Giles had broken into the Timesland Top 10, a ranking of the top teams in the *Roanoke Times & World-News* coverage area regardless of classification. At number nine, the Spartans' ranking was the talk of the school. Again, while he was proud of his team's accomplishment, he was guarded. They had a real shot at making the playoffs, but at 3–1–1, they would most likely need to win their five remaining games. He needed to find a way to keep his team hungry and focused. They weren't going to sneak up on anyone now. He stressed the importance of learning to handle success, but he wasn't sure his team was listening.

Charlie Mullins was beginning to think he was somebody. Against Radford, the junior carried seventeen times for eighty-three yards and a touchdown, his best outing at fullback, and had an interception on defense. Playing strong safety, or Spartan, he acted as a third linebacker in many situations, and Charlie felt he was becoming one of the best in the district. With Leon missing his second consecutive start, Charlie would need to replicate his performance against the Maroons. Yet, he was slowly ignoring Steve's direction, even more so with every pat on the back.

Another variable on Friday was the weather forecast. It appeared it would rain through kickoff, and as the day wore on, it was evident the school officials in Wytheville were not interested in postponing the contest. Steve only hoped his team would play better in the elements than they had against Narrows, where they suffered five turnovers and had a punt blocked.

Conditions had not changed by game time, and the Spartans took Pendleton Field as George Wythe's 1979 homecoming opponent, a pushover invite they had received many times through the years. Home games had been moved from Withers Field just a year earlier, and the new stadium, featured in Wythe County's newspaper, the *Southwest Virginia Enterprise*, was hailed as one of the finest in the state. Nonetheless, on this night, it was a rainy mess.

While a 5–4–1 campaign in 1978 seemed lackluster, 6–0 and 21–20 losses to Blacksburg and Radford, respectively, were all that had prevented the Maroons from making the playoffs. This year, they were battling depth issues and were currently 3–3 for third-year head coach Bill Kidd and his staff, which included emerging assistant Donnie Pruitt. The defense was solid, but they had struggled offensively, having been shut out in all three defeats. Gone was hard-charging running back Harvey Woods, who ran for a school-record 240 yards against Giles the previous year. Still, the Maroons were at home and had a good nucleus of returning starters.

Steve regarded George Wythe as consistently talented, even as far back as the 1930s when his father first encountered what was then known as Wytheville High School. Head coach Chet Brown had already won two District Seven championships with the Maroons before they first met Narrows in 1937. Les Parson arrived from Hopewell in 1946 and, with assistant Roy Irvin, added two District Six titles before his retirement in 1960. Along the way, the school changed its name when the new George Wythe High School was built in 1951. Steve knew the Maroons would play inspired, but his team seemed too nonchalant.

If you're gonna play a football game, you got to be ready before it starts, Steve always thought, and the game could not have started worse for Giles. Their first possession proved to be a portent of things to come. On the third play from scrimmage, Steve called 23 Reverse, a straight series complementary play. The ball was snapped to the tailback moving toward the long side, a la power plays 44 and 46, then handed inside to the wingback ("two" back) coming across to the short-side off-tackle hole. It had been a primary threat for the Spartans throughout the season, but on this occasion, George Wythe defensive end Danny Suthers hit Fonzie Austin for a seven-yard loss, setting up a Giles three-and-out.

Suthers was a three-year starter considered by his coach to be excellent against misdirection, and he proved equally savvy in the kicking game. The senior blocked the resulting Giles punt, his second of the year, and it was recovered at the Spartans twenty-nine-yard line. The special teams blunder caused Steve to reexamine his approach. *I ain't getting any more punts blocked*, he resolved.

With the aid of two penalties, the Maroons found themselves on the Giles two-yard line in just three plays. From there, junior tailback George Houston powered into the end zone. Suthers finished what he started by kicking the extra point, and George Wythe led 7–0 less than four minutes into the first quarter. *Things like that happen when you're not ready to play*, Steve thought.

The rain continued to fall for the remainder of the first half, and both teams found moving the ball difficult. Giles was able to mount a drive in the second quarter to the George Wythe twenty-one, but a Charlie Mullins fumble ended the scoring threat. The first half ended with an M.G. Harmon sack of tailback Greg King, and George Wythe carried their 7–0 lead to the break.

It seemed momentum may have changed on the first series of the second half, as the Spartans recovered a George Wythe fumble at the Maroon thirty-one. However, the drive ended four plays later with a second Charlie Mullins fumble, this one inside the five-yard line.

With a defensive stop and a sixteen-yard punt return, Giles would get it right back at the George Wythe twenty-four. This time, the Spartans capitalized, as senior wingback Terry Freeman hauled in a twenty-three-yard touchdown reception from Greg King, and Giles was within a point.

Greg had matured since his sophomore year. He was soft-spoken but set a good example, fighting through various ankle injuries as Steve asked more of him in Leon's absence. This was amplified against the Maroons as backfield mate Fonzie Austin was ill and nearly missed the trip.

Steve elected to go for two and put the ball in his tailback's hands on the perimeter, and the visitors held their collective breath as Greg was hit right at the goal line by George Wythe's Marc Moquin. The Giles sideline thought he was in, but the officials ruled him inches short, and the score remained 7–6.

It was a defensive struggle into the fourth quarter, as senior linebackers Robert Stump and Rob Oakes gobbled up tackles for the

Spartans, and Curtis Woods had another interception. Finally, with two minutes to go, Giles made one final attempt to push over the winning score. Four plays moved the ball across midfield before Greg King connected with right end Curtis Woods to advance the Spartans to the Maroon twenty-six with under a minute remaining. Giles was out of time outs and needed to hurry. As time ticked down, King again found Woods in dramatic fashion, but a game-saving tackle by Lee Willis at the eleven-yard line left only enough time for one final play. Unable to stop the clock, a field goal was not an option. Giles snapped the ball before the end of regulation, but George Wythe senior linebacker Robbie DuPuis, who finished with twelve tackles, batted down Greg King's pass at the goal line as time expired. The Spartans had lost 7–6, and their would-be playoff aspirations were crushed.

We just gave that game away. The Giles players knew it as well. The Maroons were without a first down in the second half and gained just four yards. The Spartans outgained their opponent threefold but were plagued by mistakes, including two fumbles by Charlie Mullins deep in George Wythe territory. Steve was fit to be tied and determined to get his team's attention come Monday. "This was a case of our kids not ever being in a position of winning before," Steve told the *Virginian Leader* after the game. "Hopefully, this will pay off for us in the future."

Usually, when Steve showed his players film of their previous game, they never watched the entire body of work. They would only analyze a few clips, with him replaying them repeatedly, harping on fundamental coaching points. To prevent the reinforcement of bad habits, he only showed them excerpts in which their performance directly impacted the result, either proper execution leading to a positive outcome or vice versa. In the latter instance, Steve was not one to spare an individual's feelings and had no problem calling a player out in front of the team. However, after the loss to George Wythe, Steve started Monday's practice by letting the entire game film run from start to finish. He never said a word, and nothing was corrected or critiqued. The players knew this abnormal behavior was not a good sign.

Their dread was only amplified when Steve gave no prepractice directives or remarks and sent them straight to the practice field. Once there, they proceeded to do their calisthenics. Their apprehension sharpened their awareness, so every exercise and stretch was completed to perfection. Not a single player was out of sync, for they knew it was nothing for Steve to send them back to the locker room to start practice over. Next, the entire team headed to the blocking sled. Likewise, every player gave exemplary effort, and their technique was flawless. It felt like hitting a brick wall, but they popped the ancient steel sled with each shoulder in unison and drove until the whistle blew.

Following the sled came one-on-ones, a hallmark of the Ragsdale brand of single-wing football. During one-on-ones, players were paired up and, from their offensive stance, simultaneously shoulder blocked on command until the whistle granted a reprieve. Ordinarily used to end practice, they were brutal, and with the coaches circling in constant observation, there was no place to hide. Each repetition was a ceaseless stream of contact, like a fight to the death, even more so after the George Wythe debacle. On a better day, an epic duel would attract Steve's attention, and he would become animated, circling the whole team around to highlight the effort of the combatants. But this departure from routine was without precedent.

Harry could remember a crossroads of similar significance. It was early October 1959, and the Green Wave had suffered a 39–14 loss to Dublin across Cloyd's Mountain in Pulaski County. The Dukes were coached by Dave Brown, who had been hired earlier that year from Blacksburg, where he and Harry had battled for most of the decade. The following Monday, Harry put his troops through a rugged and arduous workout, drilling the fundamentals endlessly until nightfall. When they thought it was over, he directed assistant Allen McClaugherty to turn the stadium lights on, and they labored for another hour. Sophomore Dan Phlegar, who only lived four blocks away, struggled to make the walk home afterward. A test of resilience, it ultimately achieved its purpose. Phlegar was selected as a high school All-American by *The Sporting News* and *Scholastic* magazines in 1961, and Harry never lost again.

As a kid, Steve had watched Phlegar lock horns with Lockard Conley, a well-built lineman from Wolf Creek, during one-on-ones. Witnesses remarked that when the two had finished, it looked like they had plowed the ground, and that was Steve's expectation presently. Harry looked on from his lawn chair as his son stopped the drill and addressed his team: "Boys, I know you're scared to death right now. But I'm only going to keep you out here, maybe, forty-five minutes. That's all." Many players breathed a naive sigh of relief. Then he finished his thought. "Because I don't think the human body can withstand what you're going to go through for more than that!"

The remaining time was filled with nothing but one-on-ones, grueling conditioning, and Steve's relentless barking. "That ain't worth a continental damn!" he thundered. "Step it up, or you can join the boys down in The Pit!" The typical offensive practice could be held for another day, as Steve's objective was simple: humble his players. Christiansburg was coming to town on Friday night, but the foremost obstacle was not the Blue Demons. It was the demons of years gone by. It was the history of folding the tents and quitting when confronted with adversity. Conversely, it was the immaturity of letting the first taste of success distract from the focus of chasing perfection. Before dismissing his players, Steve hammered home one final message: "If I've only got ten boys left out here, I don't care! We'll go to war with ten! *We'll go to war!*" And with that, practice concluded.

Afterward, Harry met his son coming off the field in his usual manner, and as the two walked back to the coaches' office, Steve's frustration was palpable. He was rarely satisfied, but the 7–6 loss to George Wythe left him utterly disappointed.

Once the other coaches had left for the evening, Harry addressed the turmoil. "Steve, I don't want you to get down on them," he said. "This team right here is gonna win six or seven games."

Harry knew Steve was peering through the lens of a two-week span, during which the Spartans appeared to take one step forward and two steps back. He, on the other hand, could see the bigger picture as an experienced mentor and, more importantly, father.

"Don't get down on them," he added, "because next year . . ." As he paused, Steve looked into his eyes and found the necessary perspective. "Next year, you're gonna win them all," Harry declared.

CHAPTER 9
CROSSING BIG A MOUNTAIN

August 20, 1980
Giles vs. Grundy (Scrimmage)

BY ITS THIRD SEASON, *The Dukes of Hazzard* had become one of the most popular shows on television. Airing on Friday nights between *The Incredible Hulk* and *Dallas* on CBS, the series followed the adventures of two fun-loving and rabble-rousing "good ol' boys." So when Waylon Jennings released the show's theme song in August of 1980, it didn't take long for it to ascend up the country music and Billboard Hot 100 charts. For the Spartan players, the tune might as well have been about buddies Mike Ratcliffe and Charlie Mullins.

Mo and Charlie were red-blooded, all-American country boys, each rough as a cob. Like most in Giles County, they loved the outdoors, particularly Charlie. Hunting, fishing, and frequenting the New River, one of the oldest in the world, were among his favorite pastimes. It was nothing to see one of them pop a grasshopper in his mouth, and they had eaten everything from worms to live crawdads to satisfy various dares. On the field, they were gritty, calloused, and hard-nosed. They never wore an arm or elbow pad and made fun of those who did. The more knots, bruises, and scars they had, the better. If they were bleeding, they laughed about it. Steve liked to say they were tough as pine knots. Mo and Charlie wallowed in their unsophistication and freely fashioned themselves as outlaws.

The Spartans' locker room did not have traditional lockers but rather racks suspended from the ceiling, similar to large coat hangers, to hold their equipment. After practice, Mo and Charlie would routinely leave their sweaty gear, including their clothing, on the equipment racks. The next day, their uniforms, which were bulky and did nothing to draw away moisture, would be damp and musty. Their socks would be stiff as a board. Nonetheless, they would put them on as usual and begin the cycle anew. Washing their practice clothes never crossed their minds.

At just 155 pounds, Charlie was not physically imposing, but he had a relentless motor and nasty disposition, perfect for a move to inside linebacker. His teammates compared him to Pittsburgh Steelers linebacker Jack Lambert. While missing Lambert's iconic toothless snarl, he dipped Copenhagen-brand snuff so it looked as though he had black pepper perpetually sprinkled all over his surly grin. Mo was not much heavier, only 165 pounds, and both stood less than six feet tall. In truth, an unremarkable athletic build was a common attribute among the Spartans. Most appeared inconspicuously average.

Steve knew Mo and Charlie's personality traits, while advantageous between the lines, left them susceptible to negative influences off the field. The duo loved to party, cuss, and raise general hell. "Boys, you mess with shit, and you're gonna get it on you," Steve repeatedly asserted, always drawing a contrast between the football players, of whom excellence was expected, and those emblematic of more wayward behavior, especially the idlers who loitered around the high school's smoking pit. Nevertheless, by the spring, Charlie was no longer listening, even to Steve's idiomatic teachings. After all, he had been named honorable mention all-district linebacker, even though he had played strong safety. In his hubris, he regarded himself to be untouchable.

Steve decided he needed to address the situation face-to-face. "Charlie... you should just go ahead and join the boys down in The Pit," he suggested tersely. The prospect of the Spartans moving on without him shocked and deflated the rising senior, but Steve was determined to make an impact. He could not allow this attitude to persist.

Charlie felt this was unwarranted and, in turn, bad-mouthed Steve, telling everyone, "I'm not playing my senior year for that SOB." In reality, his coach's move was another psychological play. While Charlie was more hellion than altar boy, he still had a stable upbringing and supportive parents. His father, John, was a member of the reorganized booster club and attended practice regularly. At the same time, his saint of a mother, Karen, approved of football but was oblivious to its inner workings. Her only concern was if her "Little Charlie" led the team in prayer when they huddled before each play. He never told her any different.

Steve thought that Charlie, at his core, was a good kid and believed his parents' support would be a factor in his redemption. It was not in his nature to walk away from a passionate and fiery challenge. This materialized by midsummer, as Charlie had decided to play, but it was not without umbrage. He primarily wanted to prove to Steve that he was an upstanding young man, not a redneck punk.

Despite their imperfections, Steve knew Charlie and Mo were the team's backbone, along with Leon. In many ways, their unpolished features were also their finest attributes. Their charisma and fighting spirit separated them as leaders, and, above all, their teammates trusted them. As Leon was still a junior, Steve promoted Mo, Charlie, and Greg King, the classic leader by example, to captain for the 1980 season.

Preparations for the season began on August 6 at seven o'clock in the morning. The usual apprehension of Coach Ragsdale's long and strenuous practices accompanied the start of two-a-days, but the Spartan players were confident. After all, this was their year. Giles had finished 6–3–1 in 1979, the second-best record in school history. Leon returned after the George Wythe collapse, and the Spartans rebounded with wins against Christiansburg, 28–6, Lord Botetourt, 6–0, and, later, Galax, 48–20, in a rout that saw Leon and Greg King combine for five touchdowns and the former go over a thousand yards for the season. The lone setback, a 13–0 loss to Carroll County, was again played amid muddy field conditions. Steve was named New River District Coach of the Year. Benny Hendricks was an All-Region IV pick at guard, and Curtis Woods made All-Group AA at defensive back. Steve decided to start a wall of fame to recognize future all-region and all-state selections. The objective was to celebrate tradition, and Hendricks and Woods's pictures were hung in the locker room as the first two honorees.

Playing alongside a competitor as dynamic as Leon spawned optimism. For the Pembroke boys, it began in youth league, but it had grown at every level. Even with Leon on varsity his entire sophomore year, the junior varsity team had completed an undefeated season, and many of the key players were now poised to join him. The intangibles of team chemistry together with the unifying symbol of the Bandana Express created one cohesive atmosphere—and the Giles Spartans were ready to tackle the 1980 season.

Steve, on the other hand, realized trials and tribulations were always near. The Spartans had unproven talent across both the offensive and defensive lines. On offense, they returned just two up front, Mo Ratcliffe at ten-man and Donald Sparks, nicknamed "Duck," at eight-man. In keeping with the Princeton system outlined in Caldwell's *Modern Single Wing Football*, the interior linemen in Giles's unbalanced formation were numbered in lieu of traditional position names. From left to right, the personnel designations were left end, ten-man, center, nine-man, eight-man, seven-man, and right end.

Steve had planned for Duck Sparks to replace Benny Hendricks as the primary puller on power plays and sweeps to the long side of the formation. Hendricks had played nine-man, but with the return of Barry Farmer, Steve had decided to pull the eight-man instead. Barry was among the group pressed into duty as a sophomore in Steve's first year but did not play his junior year due to a severe shoulder injury in 1978. He was slightly heavier at 210 pounds, but Duck was the more suitable all-around lineman. Furthermore, this was how Harry had taught the scheme. Steve's belief in the offense had grown each year, and with it, his realization that his father knew best. He told his peers, "Dad told me you can't date the single wing. You have to marry it." The figure of speech was appropriate, given Steve's summer, as he and Patti were married on July 12, 1980.

On the first day of full contact, the team split into offensive groups. Steve stayed with the backfield while Don Lowe took the linemen to the other end of the field. Within ten minutes, Steve was alerted that Duck was injured. Coach Lowe had pitted the two-hundred-pound Sparks against backup Gary Stump in a one-on-one drill, and while Duck was one of their stockiest linemen, Gary outweighed him by more than a hundred pounds. When the two hit, Duck misjudged contact, buckled backward, and landed with Gary on top of him. Embarrassed, Duck realized his right leg was bent awkwardly beneath him. After seeing several doctors, the diagnosis was a sprained knee. While there weren't any torn ligaments, he was still out indefinitely. Steve's concerns over the offensive line only deepened with his return uncertain. *We may be without our best lineman for the entire season*, he thought.

The rest of two-a-days crawled along. Some players floated lazily on the New River between practices, occasionally skipping rocks, telling lies, or hunting snakes with Charlie. Others hung out at Peel Epperly's Texaco, a two-tier service station in Pembroke with a game room on the upper level. Pac-Man was released earlier that year, but Peel's was lucky to have a pinball machine and some foosball tables. Regardless, they all dreaded returning to the sunbaked practice field each afternoon. A splash of water from a garden hose was as good as it got.

As they had the previous two seasons, Giles was slated to open with a scrimmage against the Golden Wave of Grundy Senior High School. This year, though, it was part of a three-team jamboree, including the Haysi Tigers. Graham had joined Bluefield's Grid-O-Rama at Mitchell Stadium, and the Spartans were set to open the regular season a week early, so Grundy would be their only exhibition. Steve planned to send the reserves against Group A Haysi.

Buchanan County's newspaper, the *Virginia Mountaineer*, reported that because Grundy's stadium was behind on renovations, school officials were concerned it may not be ready to host the season opener against Lebanon. Thus, it was decided that the tri-scrimmage would be held at Sandlick Elementary School, where Haysi played their home games, about twenty-five miles southwest of Grundy in neighboring Dickenson County.

Instead of traversing the more conventional way to Haysi, continuing on the well-traveled US Route 460, assistant Vic Edwards insisted that he knew a shortcut, having attended nearby Garden High School. He convinced Steve to try the alternate route over Big A Mountain. The nearly three-hour trek proved to be quite the fiasco, as the curves through the mountain took their toll. One curve was so sharp that the bus couldn't make the turn and had to back up several times, taking up both sides of the road, before continuing. The coaches joked that if they made it to Haysi alive, they were going to kill Coach Edwards.

Meanwhile, Steve addressed the possibility of racial slurs being directed at Leon, Greg, and others, including Mark Chapman, Cecil Austin, Anthony Shipman, Rodney Freeman, and Melvin Anderson. Giles first welcomed Black players following integration in 1964, among them former assistant coach David Chapman. "Boys, if they get you on the ground, they're probably going to call you some names. Don't say a word to them. Get back in the huddle, and next play, just knock the hell out of them!" he exclaimed.

Once the team finally arrived, it was like they were in another world entirely. Drained and nauseous from the bus ride, the Spartans faced stifling temperatures in the nineties. The foreign soil at Sandlick was rough and rocky, and it was only marked off in ten-yard increments with no pylons. Many had never been that far into Southwest Virginia and had no idea where Haysi was located, only that it was back in the coalfields somewhere, almost to Kentucky. The closest they had come to experiencing this region were television advertisements for the movie *Coal Miner's Daughter*, out earlier that year. Haysi may as well have been an alien land in *Star Wars*.

Buchanan and Dickenson counties were in the heart of Virginia coal country. As the Spartans took the field, they were greeted by coal miners fresh out of the mines. It was a new sight for many and left them unsettled. The faces staring back at them were covered in black coal dust, and the Giles players quietly compared them to zombies, a pop culture phenomenon of recent years.

Steve exchanged pleasantries with his counterpart, third-year head coach Larry Bradley. Both had been hired for their first head job in 1978, and like him, Larry was a second-generation football coach. His father, Lawrence H. "Burrhead" Bradley, retired in 1974 with an overall record of 145–91–15. While Burrhead was often seen with a cigar, Larry invariably had a mouthful of Levi Garrett–brand chewing tobacco and his spit cup in hand. He sported a thick black mustache and was rumored to have pulled out a hatchet mid-sentence to kill a snake on the floor of the coaches' office without a flinch.

Larry was more laid back than his father, whom he had played for at Graham, but was on his way to finding similar success, including in other sports. Larry had coached Grundy to their first state championship in wrestling in 1978, whereas Burrhead had guided the G-Men to a basketball title in 1956, six years before their gridiron crown. Looking on was Larry's seven-year-old son, Brad, who dreamed of one day following in his father and grandfather's footsteps.

Harry could remember when the school's football coach led every sport. In 1933, his baseball team finished as the state runner-up, losing to Clover High School of Halifax County in the finals, 6–2. The Narrows track program, under Harry's direction, was the best in the area in 1936. He had fond memories of four-sport star Jess

Johnson's contributions to both. Likewise, his 1951 Green Wave basketball squad finished third in the state, losing only to eventual champion Clintwood 52–39 in the state semifinals, and featured the multitalented David Foltz. Overall, it was estimated that, between all sports, Harry had won upward of five hundred contests.

After Bradley's first two years at Grundy showed marked improvement, senior captain Mark Van Meter informed his coach that their motto for the 1980 season was "The Year of the Wave." Among twenty-five returning lettermen, Bradley planned to rely on Van Meter and fellow senior Mike Bailey for leadership and stability in the upcoming season. They were both three-year starters at the guard positions and anchored the offensive line, vital to Bradley's two-tight end, power-I formation.

Grundy was mountainous on offense. While Giles only had one expected regular over 200 pounds, the Golden Wave had four up front that size or larger, including two over the 250-pound mark. Running behind them was powerful tailback Ralph Coleman, better known as "Junior." At six feet tall and 190 pounds, he was larger than most of the Giles linemen. Being a Golden Wave running back was in his blood, as Ralph Sr. had also toted the mail for Grundy. Just days after Junior was born in 1963, his father scored two touchdowns in a 31–6 romp over Virginia High of Bristol en route to an 8–1–1 season for head coach Brownie Cummins.

From the onset, the Southwest District club delivered an old-fashioned whipping. It was as though they didn't know of the hype surrounding the Bandana Express and didn't care. Steve stood behind the Giles defense, and, to him, the Golden Wave offense resembled a steamroller, with little finesse but plenty of brute strength. *They're ramming the ball right down our throat*, he thought, and the Spartan defensive line in particular.

The Spartan defense was an integral part of their breakthrough a year prior, and this new unit would need to find its own identity to replicate that success. Gone were defensive-tackle mainstays David Martin and Benny Hendricks, two of seven defensive starters lost to graduation. Junior Cecil Austin, Fonzie's younger brother, returned at nose guard, but the tackle spots were expected to be filled by two seniors forced to miss the 1979 season due to injury, Barry Farmer and Alvin Martin.

Hailed as "Turd," the 170-pound Martin missed his junior year after separating his shoulder in the preseason, requiring surgery. The Pembroke boy had gone by Turd since the fourth grade, and most of his friends had never heard him called Alvin unless it was by a teacher or coach. In fact, the Spartans were decorated with a host of creative nicknames. In addition to Mo, Duck, and Turd, there was Diesel, Fudd, Knot-head, and Jackrabbit, to name a few. Not to mention other variations like Weenie-head, Mull-head, and Psath-head.

The Golden Wave continued their ground assault behind Van Meter and Bailey until a thunderstorm rolled through the area, causing a lightning delay. Coming off the field, several unseemly old ladies yelled obscenities and heckled the Spartans as they sought shelter in Sandlick Elementary School. Coach Lowe shouted directions: "Keep running, boys! Don't say a word—just keep running! We're in another world down here!" All the same, Steve was displeased with the result thus far. *Grundy supplied plenty of thunder of their own.*

The delay did little to slow the Golden Wave. Junior Coleman continued to run exceedingly hard inside as Bradley mixed off-tackle, isolation, and trap plays. "Passing is a dirty word around here," he had stated publicly. Grundy only pushed over two touchdowns, but it seemed worse. There weren't any shenanigans—it was a physical, grind-it-out, bring-it-at-you type of deal. At one point, Charlie was hit so hard that he finished the play peering out the earhole of his helmet, chin strap broken. Free safety and blocking back Timmy Martin dislocated his shoulder but continued to play through the pain. When he tried to use this as an excuse for a poor block, Steve responded in frustration, "You've got two, right?" Still, Timmy later suffered a hand injury, and the coaching staff feared a break.

Offensively, the Giles single wing had trouble sustaining drives and was limited to a single tally. Leon was bottled up by the massive Grundy defense. Bradley's bunch boasted two three-hundred-pounders who rotated in the middle and two others over 250. Steve marveled as one of the behemoths didn't even bother to get down in a stance but rather just hunkered down like a sumo wrestler. The Golden Wave's dominance in the trenches left questions regarding the Giles offensive and defensive lines unanswered heading into the season opener.

A potential game-tying screen pass from Greg King to Leon fell short of the goal line on the day's final play. While the end result was just two scores to one, everyone involved felt like Grundy had hammered them from pillar to post. It was a sobering experience for the Spartans. Steve began to wonder if they were going to have a good football team. *We looked awful,* he thought. As they loaded the bus to head home, he overheard Mo and Charlie echo his doubts. Seated behind him, Charlie remarked, "I thought we were supposed to be better than this." Steely-eyed, Steve resolved to make this scrimmage the best thing that could have happened to the Spartans. It was time to get to work, and the bus fell ominously silent as it rumbled back toward Pearisburg.

CHAPTER 10
TRAVELING SALESMAN

August 29, 1980
Giles vs. Parry McCluer

AT THE END OF THE 1979 SEASON, with help from the booster club, Steve chartered a bus to take the returning Spartan players to watch the Group A and AA state championship games played at the University of Virginia in Charlottesville. Seeing the commonwealth's best on the artificial turf at Scott Stadium fascinated the country kids from Giles. Charlie Mullins and an ailing Mike Ratcliffe thought they looked like college teams, their execution nearly flawless. Mo had been to a Foreigner concert in Roanoke the night before and was severely hungover. "Here's what it looks like to get to the big time," Steve explained, aiming to motivate. Yet, even at his most optimistic, this felt far from their scope of possibility.

In Group AA, the Spartans watched perennial power Southampton defeat Jefferson Forest 14–0. It was the Indians' eighth straight appearance and fourth title under Wayne Cosby. The coat-and-tie-clad mentor retired following the season with a fourteen-year record of 137–27–1, including sixty-nine consecutive regular-season victories from 1972 to 1979. In the Group A final, the Fighting Blues of Parry McCluer won their second state crown in three years, beating Washington & Lee (Montross) 20–6. As fate would have it, Parry

McCluer would be Giles's first opponent in 1980, and as the season neared, the Spartans knew their late-August matchup would serve as an ideal measuring stick of how good they could be.

Nonetheless, after the head-to-head with Grundy, the Spartans' potential was not the main topic of discussion. "Y'all thought you were good . . . then you went down there and got embarrassed!" Steve trumpeted at the baseball backstop, white froth collecting in the corners of his mouth. Positioning himself as the common adversary would help his team continue to bond. "We only had one player who showed up to play, and that was Mark Chapman," he resumed. The hard-hitting junior, alias "Diesel," had excelled on junior varsity and recently began to attract the coaches' attention in practice. Steve liked the Pembroke boy's aggressiveness from the free safety position, and with Timmy Martin now sidelined with a broken hand, Diesel was ready to make the most of his opportunity.

While Chapman, Steve Chafin, and Anthony Shipman rounded out an entirely recast secondary, Steve's main concern ahead of the Labor Day–weekend clash with Parry McCluer was still line play, particularly on offense, as the single wing was the source of much of his team's identity. "Right now, it's blocking, blocking, blocking that concerns us," Steve told the *Blacksburg Sun*. With only one scrimmage, progress would have to be made on the practice field, which meant one-on-ones, double-team drills, and the sled. *Our season depends on blocking.*

A host of new starters were already set to debut on offense: Randy Martin at center, Barry Farmer at nine-man, Chris Woods at right end, and Greg Mance at wingback. But Steve also had to shuffle personnel to compensate for injuries. With Duck Sparks out of the lineup, Turd Martin and Rodney Freeman would play eight-man and seven-man, respectively, rather than their anticipated roles of carrying in plays from the sideline on a rotating basis. Also, Paul McGuire, son of Dr.

Erma, would replace Timmy Martin at blocking back. Nevertheless, Steve was bold, turning the focus to the Blues: "Now, we're going to go down there and play them—we don't care if they're the defending state champions!"

Meanwhile, school started, and the parking lot at Giles High School was alive again with muscle cars and rebellious teens blaring the likes of Pink Floyd's "Another Brick in the Wall." Mo Ratcliffe was assuredly somewhere among them. By midweek, Steve was looking to finalize his preparation and circle the wagons for the more than two-hour trip up Interstate 81 when Harry approached him with a timely message. "When Parry McCluer gets you down there on their home field, they don't expect just to beat you—they expect to hurt you," his father explained, stating that he had spoken to someone directly from Buena Vista.

Harry could remember many times he had used so-called bulletin board material as an emotional appeal. In some cases, a messenger would emerge with a statement of forthcoming defeat for the Green Wave directly from the community of their opponent. Often that was Harold Chafin, a local supporter who would detail how he had personally received the disparaging remarks while visiting that locality. It resonated with Harry's players and never ceased to ignite an impassioned response. The well-informed would joke with Chafin that he must have been a traveling salesman, as he always happened to be in whatever town Narrows played that week. But Harold Chafin worked at the Celanese.

Chafin was now the president of the First National Exchange Bank in Pearisburg and the host of the "Spartan Spot," a weekly radio show on WNRV. His son, Steve, was a junior preparing to start at cornerback for Giles. After the Grundy scrimmage, Harry assumed the role of traveling salesman himself, and it was just the call to arms the Spartans needed. Steve immediately informed his players of the discourse. An inferior team, like the one he had in 1978, would have been intimidated by this type of foreboding threat, but he knew this outfit, with characters like Mo, Charlie, and Leon, would respond to this type of challenge.

The *Roanoke Times & World-News* had picked Giles to finish third in the New River District, a spot Steve felt was advantageous. He knew his players would read the newspaper and accept it as truth. A selection near the bottom would hurt morale, whereas one at the top could risk overconfidence. Being picked third gave them hope but kept them under the radar. It also allowed him to use the angle of disrespect as motivation, which was precisely the tactic he chose. Steve goaded his team for the remainder of the week: "Hell's bells, boys! They're not just going to beat you—they're going to hurt your hind ends! I don't know if we'll have enough to get back on the bus to come home!" The *Bluefield Daily Telegraph* piled on, adding the Spartans would need a "heroic effort" to thwart the "bully boys of small schools."

The tradition of the Parry McCluer football program and its connection to the area reminded Steve of Narrows. An independent city in Rockbridge County, Buena Vista was a blue-collar community of 6,700 located between the Maury River and the Blue Ridge Mountains in the Shenandoah Valley. For the loyal and hardworking people who lived there, many of whom worked in manufacturing, it was less a place and more a state of mind. Ravaged by flooding following Hurricane Camille in 1969, the community regrouped, finding solace and kinship in their devotion to the Fighting Blues. Sports had shepherded them through hardship, and Buena Vista was categorically a football town.

The Blues were coached by forty-year-old Bobby Williams. A 1958 Parry McCluer graduate, Williams returned to his alma mater in 1974 after a decade under legendary coach Pete Brewbaker at neighboring Lexington High School. Since then, the stern-faced mentor had accumulated a 63–10–2 record, including state titles in 1977 and 1979. His stoic and no-nonsense demeanor commanded authority but required few words. Instead, he had assistants like line coach Dave Ellison to act as his taskmaster. Plays were also minimal in Williams's T-formation, but like Steve, he was a stickler for details, and his offense hummed with the precision of a well-oiled machine.

At the same time, the 1980 edition of the Fighting Blues was less experienced than their previous year's counterparts. Twenty-one lettermen had departed, including three all-staters, linemen Phil Radick and David Foshay, and running back Timmy Jones, who had rushed for 266 yards on twenty-four carries in the state finals. They were also smaller, which would provide a better matchup for the Spartans, but aggressive and quick, which Williams felt would be a key to their success.

The Giles booster club again helped charter a bus in anticipation of another long trip. Once they arrived in Buena Vista, the Spartans dressed at the high school but took the bus across town to Municipal Field for the game. They gazed at the wealth of trophies in the school's display case, and the Parry McCluer football tradition was evident. Unaffected by the summer heat, a large assembly had already gathered when they reached the field. The high humidity would continue into the evening, and the coaching staff worried leg cramps could become a factor. The Giles fans had traveled well, and the big-game atmosphere was impressive for a season-opening contest. Of course, that was the expectation in Buena Vista when the Blues played at Municipal Field.

On the banks of the Maury River, Municipal Field was not a state-of-the-art venue. On the contrary, it was somewhat dilapidated, with battered bleachers and a harsh playing surface. Even the Parry McCluer players, who practiced there twice a week, deemed the field rough and rocky. But none of that mattered on Friday nights. It was theirs, and the community made it come alive. A single wire cable hung around the field's perimeter as a makeshift fence, and fans stood three and four deep around it for games like this, bringing spectators right to the corner of each end zone. Not to mention, the hometown fanatics were spirited, vocal, and rowdy. It was as formidable a place to play for opposing teams as there was anywhere. In fact, the Fighting Blues had not lost on Municipal Field since 1976.

"Your opportunity is right in front of you," Steve told the Spartans before the game, and indeed it was. Municipal Field public address announcer Clayton Camden, a former principal at the school, boomed into the microphone, "HERE COME THE BLUES!" and Parry McCluer took the field in their traditional navy-blue uniforms and white helmets.

After an exchange of punts, the Blues began their second possession on their own forty-seven-yard line under the direction of senior quarterback Neal Mohler. Behind the strong running of fullback Greg Thurman, the Blues promptly marched down the field in nine plays and looked like the defending state champs. Bobby Williams paced the sidelines with his ever-present clipboard, which he kept shoved in the front waistband of his nylon coaching shorts. The better the run by one of his backs, the farther he pushed the clipboard. From the seventeen, the six-foot-three Mohler, a towering presence at quarterback, handed off to reserve halfback Steve McDaniel, who slashed off the left side, spun away from a defender, and crashed into the end zone for the touchdown. It was a drive reminiscent of the physical pounding administered by Grundy, and the hostile Municipal Field crowd let the Spartans know it. The scoring scamper was the first carry for the 125-pound McDaniel, commonly called "Speedy" by announcer Clayton Camden. While he did have a decisive interception in the state finals against Washington & Lee, he had not played offense as a junior and had expected to see limited action against Giles. Ricky Maybush kicked the extra point, and with 3:17 remaining in the first quarter, Parry McCluer led 7–0.

The ensuing kickoff bounded deep into Giles territory, and after a short return by Leon King, the Spartans took over at their own nineteen-yard line. The first two plays garnered little, but on third-and-seven, Leon connected with junior wingback Greg Mance for fifteen yards and a first down. Mance was understandably nervous—it was his first varsity football game, and he was afraid of falling short of Steve's expectations. The lanky 145-pound Pembroke boy had played quarterback before the program's switch to the single wing and quietly hoped he would not be moved to blocking back, likewise responsible for controlling the huddle and calling the cadence. On the contrary, his speed had improved, and Steve felt he had a broad skill set, ideal for the wingback position. Four plays later, a fifteen-yard face mask penalty helped the Spartans move the chains again, and on the final snap of the first quarter, Leon gained twelve to the Blues nineteen.

Run plays to the short side and up the middle had been ineffective thus far, and Steve noticed the slanting of the Blues' interior linemen was giving his fledgling offensive line problems. Parry McCluer's base defense was a 5–2 Monster, and while Giles ran a similar defense, they shaded their defensive linemen and had not faced anybody who utilized the angle technique like the Fighting Blues. The Spartans continued to chip away off the right side until finally, on the thirteenth play of the drive, Greg King bowled over from one yard out. Leon, who had seven rushes on the eighty-one-yard march, added the two-point conversion, and Giles forged ahead, 8–7.

The lead was short-lived, though. On the first play of the next drive, Coach Williams set his left halfback as a wing, a variation they used periodically. The Blues were a run-heavy team, but they also ran a sprint-out pass toward the wingback, looking to get the ball quickly into the flats. On this occasion, Mohler sprinted left but pulled up and pitched the ball far downfield to Steve McDaniel, who had wheeled out of the backfield from the right side on a throwback route. Giles senior cornerback Anthony Shipman lost sight of McDaniel and, by the time he realized he was beaten, could not recover. The home side erupted as McDaniel caught the pass along the far sideline at the Giles thirty-five and outran the Spartans to the end zone for a sixty-yard touchdown. Although the conversion run failed, the Fighting Blues were back on top, 13–8, with 9:13 left until halftime.

The rest of the first half was nip and tuck. Giles returned to the field, and Steve zeroed in on the strong safety, or monster, who had walked up on the right end and created a six-man line. To keep him guessing, Steve pounded the off-tackle area, alternating between 44 and 46. The drive lasted twelve plays and consumed much of the second quarter but stalled in Parry McCluer territory. Coming off the field, Steve stopped Greg Mance and advised him, "You're in at defensive halfback," replacing Anthony Shipman.

Stirred by the disruption of nose guard Cecil Austin, the Spartans limited the Blues to a three-and-out on their next possession. A Pearisburg boy, Cecil rode his bike everywhere, resulting in huge thighs and lightning quickness at 170 pounds. He reminded his teammates of Dallas Cowboys fullback Robert Newhouse. Following a turnover, the Giles defense held again when Steve Chafin picked off a Neal Mohler pass with time running down, and Parry McCluer retained a 13–8 edge at intermission.

At halftime, the officials approached Steve about his players wearing bandanas and asked that they be removed. New guidelines had been released in response to the increased wear of items under the helmet, but the Spartans took it as a personal attack on their symbol of unity. Steve, of course, wasn't going to tell them any different. The players decided to maintain visibility by tying them on their belt loops or tucking them in their pants, which would have to remain the trend for the rest of the season.

Steve knew that to beat a quality team like Parry McCluer, he had to stay with what was successful, even if it meant Leon would have to shoulder the burden of a high volume of carries. Leon loved to hit and would have helped in the secondary, but Steve believed the single-wing tailback should only play offense for nights like this. *If I have a horse who can carry the football, he is going to carry it.*

A short kickoff to the Giles forty-two and the Spartans began the second half on offense. Right out of the gate, Steve returned to the power plays. Leon hammered the long side with five straight runs on 46, the double-team of Rodney Freeman and Chris Woods, both Pembroke boys, providing a substantial push. At the same time, Greg Mance repeatedly delivered effective blocks on junior linebacker and all-state candidate Greg Thurman as the Spartans gained chunks of yardage. The Giles sideline could feel Leon's energy and conviction with each carry. He craved the ball in these situations. On the next play, Steve returned to 44, and Leon bulleted into the secondary, sidestepped a defender, and scored just inside the pylon on a twelve-yard burst. In less than three minutes, the Spartans had moved fifty-eight yards in six plays. Leon tossed to Greg Mance for the two-point conversion, and Giles was back on top, 16–13.

The Fighting Blues attempted to answer on their next possession and reached midfield after two back-to-back runs by Greg Thurman netted nineteen yards. However, the Spartans' defense stiffened, led by linebackers Charlie Mullins and Greg King and new strong safety Todd Dennis, a Pearisburg boy and go-getter who Steve planned to use multiple ways schematically as a senior. Parry McCluer elected to punt, and Leon called for a fair catch at his own sixteen-yard line.

Between series, Bobby Williams decided to switch his defensive ends, Neal Mohler and Dirk Wilhelm, putting Mohler, another all-state candidate, outside the Giles wingback. Nonetheless, Steve again turned to Leon, who, on this drive, carried the ball eight consecutive times, almost exclusively on 44 and 46. The Spartans advanced just forty-three yards but managed to eat seven minutes of clock, nearly all of the remaining time in the third quarter. That said, the muggy conditions were beginning to take their toll after fourteen straight hauls. Just as Steve had feared, Leon was experiencing severe leg cramps.

The Blues again went three-and-out as the game moved into the final period, but a fifty-yard punt by Steve Clark was downed at the Giles one-yard line, and they appeared to have the break they needed.

Leon was still cramping and not ready to return, and his absence could not have come at a worse time. The Spartans failed to get a first down and were forced to punt from the shadow of their own goal line. Announcer Clayton Camden offered support for punt returner Steve McDaniel, asserting over the loudspeaker, "Come on, Speedy!" Recognizing the risk of a blocked punt or favorable field position, Steve opted to have his punter, Steve Chafin, intentionally down the ball in the end zone for a safety. The choice reflected his faith in his defense, and with 8:50 left in the game, Giles now clung to just a single-point advantage, 16–15.

The minutes ticked away, each team unable to move the chains, until finally, with just over four minutes left, Parry McCluer got their offense going from their own thirty-four. Quarterback Neal Mohler passed to Eric Martin for nine yards and later to Steve McDaniel for nineteen more. Mohler's arm had led the Blues over Ralph Cummins's Clintwood squad in the 1979 state semifinals, and cheers from the home crowd rang out as they reached the Spartans thirty-six. Corner Greg Mance suffered a leg cramp on the tackle, but when he turned toward the sideline for a replacement, he was met by Steve's encouragement: "Get your ass back out there on that field!" Terrified, he immediately ran back in, determined to fight through the cramp and not disappoint his coach.

Two plays later, Mohler again looked for McDaniel, who broke a tackle and cut inside before being overtaken at the Giles twenty-two, a gain of fourteen with 1:38 left and the clock moving. Bobby Williams thought about a field goal but decided to stay with his offense. *There's no way we're going to stop them.* The Blues returned to the pass on the next play, but instead of McDaniel, Mohler looked to tight end Dirk Wilhelm on the deep route at the Giles ten-yard line. Seeing Todd Dennis cover McDaniel short, Greg Mance anticipated the throw to Wilhelm and stepped in front for the interception. From the Parry McCluer sideline, Bobby Williams could see him coming but was left helpless to alert his quarterback. The Giles sideline exploded in celebration. A supposedly untested backup, Greg Mance, had saved the day for the Spartans. Fittingly, four carries by Leon ran out the clock, and Giles was victorious. The junior tailback rushed thirty-seven times for 168 yards.

That was a tough ballgame, Steve thought.

Afterward, Coach Williams reassured his team, "I know we don't lose at home, but don't hang your heads—we haven't played a team this good in years. I wouldn't be surprised if Giles does something this year." The Spartans returned to the high school to dress, and as the Giles coaches waited outside the locker room, Williams brought Steve and his coaching staff ice-cold Coca-Colas. Steve stood amazed at the sportsmanship and class, especially after such a tight contest. He had such profound respect for the Parry McCluer mentor.

Despite the victory, Steve remained wary. He knew they would face numerous obstacles ahead, with James River next and Narrows on the horizon in just a few weeks. Still, as the Spartans loaded the Abbott bus to return to Pearisburg, the magnitude of their accomplishment began to sink in. The win was a definite confidence booster. Turd Martin, wide-eyed and grinning, screamed as he climbed aboard, "Woohoo! We won!"

The Bandana Express was back on track.

CHAPTER 11

EDGAR ALLAN MO

September 19, 1980
Giles vs. Narrows

STEVE DESCRIBED GILES and Narrows as "one hell of a rivalry," and on Friday night, when the two played, he knew it would be dog-eat-dog. Ragsdale Field was a madhouse two hours before kickoff. The Spartans dressed at Giles because of the close proximity, and when their bus arrived a little after six, Steve could not believe his eyes. He had never witnessed a scene in Giles County like the one playing out before him in Narrows. With the stadium well over capacity, the crowd was spilling out into the neighboring streets. Hot Rod Dennis was already blasting the siren on his green-and-gold wrecker so loud it could seemingly be heard all the way to Pembroke.

At the end of the first half, Giles and Narrows were deadlocked at 0–0, and the place was nearing bedlam. The top railing on the visitors' stands had already given way, sending fans flying off the back of the bleachers. A few well-trained thieves could have had their choice of plunder as the entire county was in attendance.

Five penalties and two turnovers had slowed the Spartans, along with inspired performances by Ricky Cook, Ben Richardson, and the rest of the Narrows defense. Steve had expected that Coach Patteson would ensure his team's readiness, and he certainly did. Heading to the locker room, Steve needed his troops to rise to the occasion and lift the Spartans out of the shadow of the Green Wave.

The week after the Parry McCluer triumph was not without its challenges for Giles. On Labor Day, Assistant Principal Charles Harris passed away suddenly at the age of forty-seven. It was a profound loss for the school and for Steve personally. Harris's youngest daughter, Rhonda, was also the cocaptain of the varsity cheerleaders, known as the "Bandanaettes." Still, the Spartans marched on, as Steve knew Charles would have wanted. That Friday, Giles overcame James River at home, 35–7, in a game that Steve, of course, felt was much closer than the score indicated. Steve Chafin returned an interception eighty-five yards late in the third quarter to put the Spartans up by two scores, sparking a second-half surge that finished off the Knights.

Because the Parry McCluer contest was played a week early, before most teams began their regular-season schedule, Giles was afforded an uncommon bye week to prepare for their duel with Narrows. It also aided the return of Don—Duck—Sparks. Entering the week, Duck questioned if he was at full strength, but Steve gave him the go-ahead. His legs were weak and wobbly coming off the practice field on Monday. Having missed nearly six weeks with a sprained right knee, he was still not in football shape, especially not for a Steve Ragsdale–run practice. Steve continued to tape his knee and secure it using a bulky brace, for he knew the importance of a return against Narrows, not just for Duck but for his family as well.

Many of Duck's relatives were from Narrows, including his father, Leonard. The oldest of four brothers, Leonard had been unable to play sports growing up but enjoyed watching his siblings excel, including his brother, Ronnie. A standout fullback for the Green Wave from 1963 to 1965, Ronnie Sparks was killed in Vietnam on April 6, 1968, and his jersey, no. 36, was retired shortly thereafter. Consequently, watching his son play against Narrows would be emotionally powerful for Leonard and the Sparks family. That meant a great deal to Duck, and he appreciated that Steve recognized the significance.

While the bye week gave Duck another week to heal, it gave Mo Ratcliffe an opportunity for added hijinks. With no game the next day, Mo and a few others decided to buy tickets to the Charlie Daniels Band concert in Roanoke on Thursday night. Yet, they had to wait until after practice to depart, which left them desperately short on time. As soon as Steve dismissed them, they piled in teammate Glenn Smith's dark-green metallic 1969 Dodge Coronet 440 and, with Mo riding shotgun, hurtled toward the Star City. Reaching speeds upward of one hundred miles per hour, they blared Molly Hatchet's "Flirtin' with Disaster" on the eight-track player. They passed cars on the shoulder, drove through medians, and blistered through the Interstate 81 rest stop at Ironto without letting off the gas. From the high school to the Roanoke Civic Center was a trip that should have taken well over an hour but reportedly clocked in at just twenty-seven minutes. It was a ride to remember, but they made it in time for the show.

A week later, Mo's mind was squarely on the Green Wave. It was all any of them could think about. The deep-seated animus surrounding the rivalry had caused the usual friction at the Celanese plant and the vocational school, and rumors were swirling again. There was talk of the desecration of bandanas at the Boom, a popular swimming hole and hangout in Narrows named for the sound of timber banging together as it floated down Wolf Creek in the days before the railroad. Other chatter included members of each squad making their way into enemy territory for mischievous purposes. Nonetheless, the hay was in the barn by Thursday, and all that remained was game day.

Like everyone involved, Mo could feel the anticipation in his gut, and his mind raced with plans and possibilities. He worked evenings after practice for a local janitorial business, J&L Cleaning Service & Supply, and that night, one of the locations tasked to him was the First National Exchange Bank. As he cleaned the office of bank president

Harold Chafin, he decided to write a poem about the Narrows matchup. He sat down and scrawled out the following opening lines:

> *Once upon a time, in the snake pit of Narz,*
> *from across the river came a long line of cars.*
> *The cars were red, the cars were white,*
> *the cars were full and ready to fight.*

In a nod to classic poet Edgar Allan Poe, he signed it Edgar Allan Mo and left it on Mr. Chafin's desk, whom he knew would be equally stirred come Friday morning. The contention between the two schools had almost reached its crescendo.

After two undefeated regular seasons and back-to-back New River District championships, Bill Patteson faced the colossal task of replacing sixteen starters, including Rusty Cook, now a running back at Virginia Tech. While citing the losses of Cook, Tony Robertson, Todd Oney, Terry Fleeman, and Junior Simpkins, Patteson was quick to acknowledge that 1980 was a new year. Marked by inexperience, Narrows had dropped their first three outings, hindered by their inability to score points. They had been shut out twice at home, 7–0 by Tazewell and 16–0 by George Wythe, and managed just a single tally in a 21–6 road loss to Alleghany. Like Giles, the Green Wave had started their season a week early. To complicate matters, Patteson had just learned that one of his top returners, Punkin Frazier, would require knee surgery and likely miss the entire season. Frazier had been a contributor as a sophomore and an all-district performer a year later, catching touchdown passes against Giles in both their 48–0 and 28–13 victories. He had moved from end to fullback for his senior year and was one of only three veterans, along with Ben Richardson and Ricky Cook.

Described by his coaches as a warrior, Ricky Cook was the unequivocal leader of the Green Wave. Coach Patteson loved his aggressive play at linebacker, but like Mo and Charlie, with whom he attended vocational school, it was his punchy attitude that inspired his teammates. His die-hard loyalty to the green and gold was fierce. Bob Foley of the *Bluefield Daily Telegraph* contended, "Cook goes just one step short of berserk on game nights." He was the vocal front man, and all noise filtered through him. Ricky and Charlie had a lot in common and, in matters unrelated, considered themselves friends. But they did not speak during rivalry week. Even with his team's 0–3 start, Cook refused to concede anything to the Spartans.

Wins and losses notwithstanding, many still considered Narrows the favorite. In truth, it was folly to think either team, regardless of record, to be a certain victor in this type of game. After all, the United States had just surprised the Soviet Union 4–3 in ice hockey at the Lake Placid Winter Olympics, teaching the entire country to believe in miracles. Nobody knew this better than Harry Ragsdale.

Harry could remember the Pearisburg upset of 1935 and the words of his first principal, William H. "Professor" Barrett. Aware they had already earned the Class B District Seven crown, Barrett told the *Pearisburg Virginian* in advance of the late-November clash, "It is like I have always said, you can scrap all the scores and expect a hard game between Pearisburg and Narrows." The old adage proved true, as the two-win Red Devils, coached by William L. "Shorty" Hargis, shocked the undefeated Green Wave in a snowstorm, 7–0, ending a thirteen-game winning streak for Narrows.

With this in mind, Harry did something early in the week he seldom did otherwise. He stopped one of Steve's players to interject a coaching point. Nothing could be taken for granted.

"Greg, I want to talk to you," Harry requested of wingback Greg Mance.

"Yes, sir," Mance replied as he jogged over.

"When you go through the hole on the reverse, you have to make sure you have your left foot planted and your toe turned toward the line of scrimmage. That way, you can cut back or accelerate forward. If you plant off your right foot, you're not going to be able to cut back."

Greg was taken aback by Harry's attention to detail. Techniques this precise had never occurred to him. He never thought of which foot to plant as he started upfield. He just ran. Mesmerized, Greg internalized what Harry had told him and hoped he would have a chance to utilize it at Narrows on Friday night.

The volatile rivalry had become a tinderbox, ready to ignite by week's end. As if the Spartans needed more provocation, Hot Rod Dennis had predicted a Narrows victory on WNRV. While not surprising, it piqued their interest when he confidently proclaimed, "Giles cannot beat Narrows!" On Friday morning, students in the mathematics wing ignored threats of expulsion and lined the driveway to the Giles County Vocational School, located adjacent to the Giles High School campus. By the time the Narz bus arrived, a multitude had gathered, cheering for the Spartans, shaking bandanas, and, no doubt, exchanging pleasantries with the opposition. The assembly swarmed the bus, forcing it to proceed slowly through the parting mass. This kept the school administration busy for several hours, but ultimately, no students were disciplined.

The pep rally was especially raucous that afternoon. The cheerleaders strolled the hallways, gathering students on their "spirit train" that led to the gymnasium. Detergent boxes were used as decorations, suggesting the Green Wave was all washed up, and bandanas were visible at every turn. The festivities were truly a sight to behold. A large sign on the gym wall declared, "Narz, the 8th wonder of the world . . . the only hole above ground," while Wild Neal Maggie performed a deafening rendition of his G-I-L-E-S chant to get the activities underway. Without a halt, the cheerleaders continued to rev up the crowd, and the sophomore class won the spirit stick, though it was hard for anyone to choose. But the roof nearly came off when Coach Ragsdale took the microphone.

Steve thrived in situations like this. After he thanked the students for their enthusiasm in greeting the Narrows vocational bus earlier that morning, he produced a green-and-gold flag and a piece of paper. The flag was one of many flying through Narrows. Steve informed them that he had discovered the flag taped to his front-porch railing, along with a note. Unfortunately, it was laced with so much profanity that he could only share a few excerpts. A vulgar attack on him and his players, the message spelled out how the Spartans would get beat on and off the field, and it was not for sensitive ears. As Steve fired up the student body, Mo smiled. Perhaps he and some of his cohorts knew where the Narrows flag and note came from, but they weren't telling. As far as they were concerned, it came from Ricky Cook. If Steve had any idea, he wasn't letting on either. In fact, he preferred it this way. The pep rally concluded with a flurry of excitement, and the stage was set.

Fans had been putting down blankets to save their seats since the early afternoon and began showing up at least three hours before the eight o'clock kickoff. Therefore, when the Spartans arrived, they had trouble getting their bus in and parked behind the visitors' stands. Ragsdale Field was bursting at the seams. The coaching staff emphasized focus and instructed their players to keep their helmets on as they walked to the locker room on the opposite side of the stadium. "They'll throw rocks at you at Narrows," Steve had told them. As the team deboarded the bus, they looked in awe at the mob of people on the Giles side. The atmosphere was phenomenal—a sea of red, white, and Columbia blue.

"Look at this, man," remarked Chris Woods as he turned to his buddy Greg Mance. "I never thought we'd have this many people down here this early."

"It's crazy, isn't it?" Greg replied. They could feel the electricity.

As soon as the ball left his hand, Greg Mance's first thought was, *He's going to kill me!* But his fumble on their opening drive was not the only misstep that had hampered the Spartans in the first half. Narrows had made adjustments to their 5–2 defense to take away Leon, aligning Ricky Cook and defensive tackle Ben Richardson on the long side of Giles's single-wing formation. Richardson and counterpart Dennis Wiley weighed in at 255 and 260 pounds, respectively, which gave the Green Wave a size advantage, something the Spartans had struggled with against Grundy. Likewise, Narrows had found some success running quick dives, primarily away from Charlie, but had been unable to sustain anything significant. The tension was so thick you could cut it with a knife, and a scoreless tie to start the third quarter only heightened the atmosphere.

Giles got the game's first big break almost immediately after intermission. On their second offensive play, Leon handed off to Greg Mance on the inside reverse. Steve instructed blocking back Timmy Martin, also back from injury, to feign a block on the defensive end, giving the illusion of a perimeter run and setting up the blocking inside. The adjustment worked beautifully as the junior wingback crisscrossed off-tackle. Recalling Harry's coaching point, he planted off his left foot, cut back, and found the middle wide open. The Giles crowd roared to their feet as Mance knifed through the heart of the Green Wave defense and blew past their safetyman Mike Burton for the game's first points, a fifty-six-yard touchdown jaunt. As he crossed the goal line, he glimpsed Hot Rod Dennis standing behind the end zone and yelled, "There's your prediction!" pointing right at him. To Greg, the look on Hot Rod's face was priceless. The extra point was off the mark, but the Spartans were out in front, 6–0, less than two minutes into the second half.

Narrows tried to mount a response on the following possession. On the drive's second play, Chuck Harless blasted through the line on a hard-charging run, pinballing off the Giles defenders and spinning his way to the Narrows thirty-nine for a gain of nine and a Green Wave first down. However, after two short runs, quarterback Mike Burton was pressured by the Spartan pass rush and hit by a pursuing Cecil Austin, jarring the ball loose. Narrows recovered, but facing a fourth-and-nineteen, Coach Patteson decided to punt the ball back to Giles.

Back on offense at their own thirty-four, Steve wasted no time going back to Greg Mance on the reverse play, and he dashed into the secondary once again. Narrows corner Chuck Harless was able to drag him down from behind at the Narrows thirty-seven, but not before a gain of twenty-nine. As the Giles fans cheered wildly, a skirmish broke out between Charlie and Ricky Cook back at the original line of scrimmage. Charlie had been moved to left end following the Parry McCluer game, and with him and Mo now side by side, their double-team got movement on the defensive tackle, Dennis Wiley. Even with Mance racing downfield, Charlie continued to block Wiley behind the play, arresting the attention of Cook. Charlie flashed an inflammatory grin, and Cook grabbed him by the face mask, drawing multiple flags. The Narrows captain was hit with an unsportsmanlike conduct penalty, and Giles was advanced fifteen more to the Green Wave twenty-two.

Patteson's defense stiffened, though, and minutes later, the Spartans were faced with a fourth-and-less-than-a-yard from just outside the Narrows twelve-yard line. Steve elected to go for it, and with the Green Wave packed inside, called 42 Buck. Taking the pitch from Timmy Martin, Leon cut inside the block of Don Sparks and, with one move, streaked into the end zone—touchdown! But there was a penalty flag on the field. Another false start against Giles, and now it was fourth-and-six. A thirty-four-yard field goal was outside the range of his rudimentary kicker, Rodney Freeman, who had already missed an extra point. Thus, Steve stayed with his decision to go for it and sent the play in with seven-man Turd Martin:

"42 Buck Pass." Leon took the pitch and looked to right end Chris Woods, who was open and heading toward the pylon, but the ball was underthrown and intercepted by Chuck Harless. Harless raced up the sideline with blockers out in front but was knocked out of bounds at the Narrows thirty-seven-yard line by Timmy Martin, saving a game-tying touchdown.

While a wasted opportunity for Giles, the Green Wave could not capitalize on the change in momentum. Narrows again went three-and-out, frustrated by nose guard Cecil Austin, who had wreaked havoc in the backfield all night, and punted the ball back to the visitors. The teams switched ends a few plays later, and Giles headed to the fourth quarter, clinging to a six-point advantage.

The Spartans then went to work eating clock and protecting their slim lead. In their most time-consuming drive of the game, the single wing moved seventy-four yards in fourteen plays, aided by two Narrows penalties. But the Green Wave defense managed to keep the Spartans out of the end zone yet again, and Steve was confronted with another fourth-down decision, this time with the ball resting on the Narrows eight-yard line. He opted for the field goal, which, at twenty-five yards, was just spitting distance from an extra point but clearly not a foregone conclusion. The Giles fans held their collective breath as straight-on kicker Rodney Freeman booted a high-arcing moon shot that, when it finally came down, hit the crossbar and bounced through the uprights—good! The Spartan supporters thundered, for the Bandana Express now led 9–0, and time was running out for the Green Wave.

With under a minute remaining, Narrows took to the air in a last-ditch effort at a comeback. Following a short completion by backup quarterback Rocky Blankenship, Steve put seven defenders back into pass coverage. On the next play, Blankenship dropped back and fired a pass into the flats, but defensive end Mo Ratcliffe stepped in front for the interception at the thirty-four-yard line. He sprinted down the home sideline, cut inside one defender at the ten, and rumbled into the end zone for the pick-six! The touchdown sent the visitors' side into absolute pandemonium, and Rodney Freeman's extra point was the icing on the cake. The final thirteen seconds were just a formality, and Giles was triumphant, 16–0. They had vanquished the Green Wave. Through the madness, the first person to shake Steve's hand in the middle of the field was Ricky Cook, signifying respect from the Narrows captain.

Afterward, several Spartans fans burst into the locker room just as Steve began his postgame remarks. His players were concerned at first, but when the entrants gave Steve an enormous hug, they quickly realized the significance of the moment. To their disbelief, he didn't even mind. The visitors were recent graduates and probably intoxicated, but representative of the rivalry's emotional weight. The burden had been lifted, and the members of the Giles community could hold their heads high. The celebration, in all its majesty, was in full swing. As the Spartans left through town, their fans were exuberant, some jumping up and down atop their cars. Even so, it didn't escape Steve's attention—there wasn't a single Narrows fan laughing at them this go-round.

When the buzzer went off, the town was dead in yarn,
and here came mean Mo with a head under each arm.
And so it's told for many miles,
1980 is the year for Giles.
—From the writings of Edgar Allan Mo

CHAPTER 12
DRIVE, DRIVE, DRIVE!

September 26, 1980
Giles vs. Blacksburg

THE GILES SPARTANS felt like celebrities after their victory over Narrows. At the Tastee Freez in Pearisburg, they no longer paid for food and drinks thanks to owner Odell Ratcliffe, Mo's first cousin once removed, and patrons supportive of Spartan Football. Storefront windows across town were decorated with bandanas and covered in messages of encouragement handwritten in soap, including at the Giles Shoe Center, a fixture in the community for nearly two decades. A football player pulled over for a traffic violation received a cautionary warning, a pat on the back, and well wishes of good luck in their next outing at Blacksburg. Where the Green Wave had adopted Queen's "We Are the Champions" as their late 1970s anthem of ascendance, the Spartans held all the bragging rights this year. Cruising Wenonah Avenue from the town pool to the dine-in Pizza Hut, they were on top of the world.

Monday's practice told a much different story. An uninformed bystander would have thought they had lost on Friday night, as Steve was determined to keep them grounded following the Grundy scrimmage. After a win was the ideal time to push his players, he believed, when the fruits of their labor were most evident. The spoils of victory were immense, but so was the required sacrifice. Practices seemed unending, water breaks were sparse, and players ate salt pills like candy. Like his father before him, Steve was a purist regarding the single wing. He was hyperfocused, blocked out all distractions, and would often be so immersed in what they were working on that he would lose track of time. The offense would drill a particular play over and over until Steve was pleased, knowing that the attention to detail would yield improvement in execution. In his players' minds, however, he was rarely satisfied.

One component of Steve's Monday practice routine was running Fungo Mountain. A hill adjacent to the practice field, Fungo Mountain was used for conditioning and building leg strength. It was named for a former player, but the hill was unmistakably Steve's, and he loved it. The Spartans were slated for five hills each week, but extras were added for each penalty and turnover, minus takeaways. Against the Green Wave, Giles had three turnovers and was penalized eight times, including five false starts. Even with three takeaways, thirteen hills would be decidedly cumbersome. While undefeated, Giles was still not performing up to their coach's expectations, and this week's matchup with Blacksburg would be another mental obstacle for the Spartans.

Steve didn't want his players to be nervous. *Nervousness implies that you're worried about your performance or you're worried about losing.*

Steve and the coaching staff had decided the entire team would spend some time on the blocking sled at the start of practice. The sled, a seven-man behemoth Steve inherited when he took over, was a builder of men, and while they dreaded it, the Spartan players knew it bettered their physicality, which set them apart. Their unique brand of shoulder blocking was quickly becoming part of the program's identity. Steve wanted it rough on the defender—as rough as they could make it. As they drove the sled relentlessly, Steve bellowed, "Drive, drive, drive!" from atop the steel structure. "My grandmother's damn ninety years old, and she could do better than that!" he reminded them. His players fantasized about running the sled off a cliff or into the New

River. Respect for Steve was not to be confused with how they felt in the heat of the moment—they hated him impulsively. Still, they pushed themselves onward, for they trusted the correlation between his methods and their success. Like incessant hammering, Steve repeatedly insisted they make the sled jump with each collision, and when they thought they could not continue, he again rained down from above, "DRIVE, DRIVE, DRIVE!"

Finally, after cycling through their lines countless times, the starting offensive line was back to the front. Coach Lowe was now perched above the players while Steve alternated between the sled and watching out in front, where he could observe the entire group. Coach Edwards, whom players thought resembled actor George Peppard from the television series *Banacek*, walked behind the players to keep anyone from lagging behind. When the first team hit the sled, it lurched forward, knocking Steve to the ground. Within seconds, it was on top of him, the legs of his offensive linemen still pumping like pistons. The assistant coaches noticed and blew their whistles, but not before the sled was halfway up his legs, crushing him underneath.

Steve hopped up, hoping to downplay the incident. "Hell's bells, boys! If y'all got that much energy, let's go do one-on-ones!" he exclaimed. But his players were stunned, unsure if they faced punishment or absolution. Deathly quiet, they awaited clarification. He adjusted his whistle and brushed the dirt off his legs, and as he did so, a grin of approval formed on his face. Steve rarely smiled on the football field, so when he did, it spoke volumes. "If y'all don't think that's funny, then y'all ain't alive," he said. When they realized Steve's comment was self-deprecating, they laughed, albeit nervously. They were awestruck that Steve was poking fun at himself. Just as important, he was pleased with how they hit the sled. That, by its very nature, was revitalizing. After all, Coach Ragsdale threw compliments around like manhole covers.

Afterward, Steve gave the team an extended break, not so much for them but for himself. Regardless, his misfortune had broken the tension, and the Spartans responded. It reminded them that football was still fun, and, for a brief moment, practice was almost bearable. Later, Steve dismissed them, adding, "If that's what it takes to get things going, I'm all for it—I hope y'all hit somebody in the game that hard!" Munching down a grasshopper, Mo decided to use the day's events as inspiration for his Thursday poem to Harold Chafin.

> *Our head coach is Ragsdale, he's as mean as a snake,*
> *when he bellers down our neck, a touchdown we will make.*
> *Now we don't have the bigheads, we are sure of our team,*
> *all that we want to do, is to fulfill our dream.*

Word of Giles's hard-line practices had reached Blacksburg, and head coach Dave Crist wondered how Steve kept his players coming back for more. Yet he couldn't ignore how hard they played. After battling to an even draw in 1979, Crist wasn't surprised by their 3–0 start.

Nonetheless, Giles was still the underdog. The Indians were ranked eleventh in the United Press International (UPI) Group AA state poll and unbeaten, with wins over Group AAA Salem, 6–0, and Radford, 34–7, plus a lone tie against Christiansburg, 27–27. Furthermore, Steve had never beaten Blacksburg as a football coach at Giles. The Blacksburg Middle School Braves, under Bob Holland and later Jim Shockley, had been the top eighth-grade program in the area during Steve's tenure from 1975 to 1977, winning twenty-seven straight. The current junior and senior classes had fallen to their Blacksburg counterparts, and the closest Steve had come was a 22–20 loss in 1977. With a 10–0 loss and a 6–6 tie at the varsity level, Steve was now 0–4–1. "If the Indians can stop the running attack, then Blacksburg should notch its second district win in as many weeks," pronounced the *Blacksburg Sun*.

The Indians had returned to the I-formation in 1980 after a two-year stint in the T, and this year, tailback Greg Keys was the leading rusher in the New River District, with 492 yards through three games. Leon was currently fourth with 310 yards. A week prior against Radford, Keys had registered 274 yards on twenty-seven carries, reaching pay dirt on three occasions. The speedster had also won the 220-yard dash in the previous spring's district track meet.

Harry could remember when he had likewise faced a celebrated running back, Shirley Crowder, William Byrd's prolific scorer of 1938. Narrows was 5–0 when they hosted the high-powered Terriers and head coach Paul E. "Nap" Ahalt, who would later serve as superintendent of Giles County Public Schools from 1953 to 1974. Crowder was lauded in *The Roanoke Times* as the leading scorer in the state, but Harry's boys, led by Junior "Toar" Skeens, kept him out of the end zone, and the Greenies dispatched the visitors from Vinton, 20–6.

Steve hoped the Giles defense could perform similarly against Keys and the Indians. While the single wing was front and center, the defensive unit had also found an identity. Championed by Mo and Charlie, they had begun referring to themselves irreverently as a collection of lowlifes and gradually adopted it as their mantle. The 1970s featured numerous NFL defensive units with catchy nicknames: Orange Crush, Purple People Eaters, and the Steel Curtain, to name a few. The 1972 Miami Dolphins had the No-Name Defense, and the 1980 Giles Spartans had the Lowlife Defense. They weren't sure how the name originated, but they embraced it. They were a gang of classic antiheroes, unrefined renegades ready to get after the city boys from Blacksburg.

"Here they are, doctors, lawyers, and professors' sons, and we ain't nothing but a bunch of corn-fed country boys," Steve reminded them immediately before the game. He could feel the enthusiasm building.

As Steve surveyed the visitors' locker room, Alvin "Turd" Martin caught his eye. Standing alone, Turd was smiling from ear to ear. Steve could tell by the expression on his face that he just wanted to get out there and play. He wasn't thinking about winning or losing or even making mistakes. Steve didn't want players to be nervous. He wanted energy—he wanted them to knock the tar out of somebody and have fun, and Turd exemplified this attitude.

"Can't anybody be *that* good," Blacksburg assistant Vaughn Phipps had stated ahead of the junior varsity contest with Giles in 1978, attempting to rebuff Leon King's much-talked-about prowess. However, Phipps withdrew his previous statement, Dave Crist recollected, after a brilliant display later that afternoon, noting, "By God, he is that good!" Leon intended to duplicate that jaw-dropping performance this year.

With the game underway, the Spartans began their first drive at their own twenty-nine-yard line following a Blacksburg punt, and the single wing went right to work.

After his 180-pound fullback, Greg King, converted a third-and-inches, muscling to the Giles forty, Steve called 42 Buck for Leon's first carry of the night. Greg again took the snap, bucked the line, and handed to Timmy Martin, who made the pitchout to Leon on the edge behind a pulling Don Sparks. Duck pinned the corner inside, allowing Leon to get to the sideline, and with a quick sidestep, he was by the safety at midfield. The pursuit attempted to cut him off, but Leon stopped on a dime and cut back inside, the two defenders unable to correct course. The Giles fans howled with adoration for their junior tailback as he zigzagged the defense and bolted down the sideline for the touchdown, an astonishing sixty-yard run on the buck lateral. The point-after was unsuccessful, but with 7:56 remaining in the opening quarter, the Spartans had jumped out to an early 6–0 lead.

Crist's troops responded, though, embarking on a fifteen-play, sixty-nine-yard march that ate more than five minutes off the clock. Greg Keys capped the drive with a three-yard scamper on an option play, and with the extra point, Blacksburg pushed ahead 7–6. Coming off the field, Charlie was determined these would be the Indians' only points.

In the second frame, another Blacksburg punt left the Spartans at their own sixteen, but the visitors again moved the length of the field, highlighted by a thirty-four-yard completion from Greg Mance to Charlie on the wingback reverse pass. The Spartan faithful, many in number, waved their bandanas and cheered their team with each first down. Later, a face mask penalty gave Giles a first-and-goal at the Indians nine-yard line before Leon scooted off-tackle from the three for his second score of the half. With his two-point conversion throw to Greg Mance, the Spartans reclaimed a 14–7 advantage just before intermission.

Despite Bill Brown's move to a seven-man line on defense, the Spartans widened their lead in the third quarter. Ripping off chunks of yardage on the ground, Leon and company moved from their own twenty-five into Blacksburg territory. Momentum was firmly on the side of Giles. Facing a pivotal third down at the Indians six-yard line, Steve went again to the reverse pass, which offered misdirection and utilized Greg Mance's versatility. Greg rolled left and found his blocking back, Timmy Martin, just over the outstretched arms of a defender for the six-yard scoring toss. Rodney Freeman, who had won the kicking duties for another week, tallied the extra point, and Giles led 21–7.

The Indians tried desperately to return fire as the game moved into the final stanza, but the night belonged to the Bandana Express. After holding the ball for nearly the entire quarter, Leon put the exclamation point on a convincing victory with his third touchdown, punching it in from seven yards out with less than a minute remaining. The extra-point attempt was blocked, but the outcome was already decided.

Giles dominated statistically with nearly four hundred yards of offense, and Leon finished with a staggering 282 yards, a school record, on thirty-five carries. When the *Roanoke Times & World-News* asked about Leon's heavy workload, Steve responded, "We executed better than we have all year by far. I don't worry about King carrying the ball too much. He's strong; he can run forever." The Lowlife Defense held the Indians to sixty-nine rushing yards, severely limiting district leader Greg Keys, and quarterback Lee Flowers was sacked multiple times in the second half, halting Blacksburg drives.

When the bus was ready to return to Pearisburg, Steve looked back at the scoreboard, still illuminated. The final score shone brightly, 27–7, and his heart was full. *I'll never forget this. Blacksburg might have everything . . . but there is one thing they don't have—they don't have Spartan Football!*

Mo was forced to miss the next game after suffering a concussion near the end of regulation, and the associated late hit did not sit well with Charlie, who had to be consoled afterward. Nonetheless, the win at Blacksburg was a turning point for the Spartans. Phillip "Fudd" Steele, a Newport boy, played in Mo's place at ten-man, and the Spartans rolled over the Radford Bobcats, 35–0, shutting them out for the second year in a row. Greg King paced the ground game, and Leon added three more touchdowns.

George Wythe came to town a week later, Mo returned, and the pageantry of homecoming week was patterned in paisley bandanas. Cheerleader Ronda Myers was named homecoming queen at halftime. Meanwhile, with the Spartans up just 6–0, Steve decided to employ the wing-T after the break. Without a genuine short-side series from the single wing, Steve had kept his wing-T formation, at which Timmy Martin slid under center to act as the quarterback, and Greg Mance aligned outside the left end. Using this adjustment almost exclusively, Giles drove eighty yards in eighteen plays to start the third quarter and pulled away from the Maroons, prevailing 27–0. The Lowlife Defense recorded their second shutout in a row and third in the last four games, and the Spartans improved to 6–0 on the season.

The win was not without cost, however. On the first of two fourth-quarter scoring drives for the Spartans, Leon launched himself across the goal line for the three-yard touchdown, and when he did, he came down directly on his left shoulder. When he woke up the next morning, he could not lift his left arm off his side. It was like it was strapped to his body, his arm's limited mobility and weakness accompanied by excruciating pain. As soon as Steve was notified, he got Leon scheduled to see Dr. Erma. Whatever the diagnosis, he knew he had a colossal problem just six days until their clash with undefeated Christiansburg to possibly decide the New River District championship.

CHAPTER 13

ANOTHER ONE BITES THE DUST

October 17, 1980
Giles vs. Christiansburg

LEON KING BELIEVED HE WAS INVINCIBLE. So when he tweaked his left shoulder late in the George Wythe contest, he never doubted he would be available the following week at Christiansburg. That is, until Saturday morning.

"Is it broke?" he asked.

"No, Leon, it's not broken. It's a sprain of the ligaments in the joint," Dr. Erma explained. He had an AC sprain, also known as a separated shoulder. After settling in Pearisburg in 1954, Dr. Erma worked on staff at Giles Memorial Hospital and ran a successful family practice. While she wasn't the official team doctor, she would evaluate injured players at Steve's request.

"Well, if it ain't broke, I'm playing!" Leon affirmed. "There ain't nothing wrong with me."

Dr. Erma left the door open for Friday night but suggested specialized padding combined with a shoulder harness to stabilize the AC joint. Full-time athletic trainers were yet to be widespread, so Steve was responsible for treating his own players. Facing a quick turnaround, he phoned Eddie Ferrell, the head football trainer at Virginia Tech, to see if he could design the added protection. Ferrell agreed but asked Steve to bring his tailback's shoulder pads so the support underneath could be custom fit.

At the start of the week, Steve cleared the trip with Principal Bill Puckett, but when Leon brought his shoulder pads to the coaches' office, Steve couldn't believe his eyes. He personally issued each helmet and pair of shoulder pads at the start of the year. While his assistants helped in many ways, Steve was careful to never delegate this responsibility. That way, he could ensure that each player was fitted correctly with the best equipment possible should there ever be a question. With that in mind, he was sure this was not the set he had issued Leon back in August. This pint-sized pair looked like something a little kid would wear.

I can't take him in that training room with those things! They'll laugh me off campus! I can hear them now: "You've put your best player in this little rinky-dink pair of pads?"

At some point, Leon had switched his shoulder pads for some he had found lying around the adjacent eighth-grade locker room. He didn't want any extra weight on his body that could hinder his ability to dodge and duck. If Steve had let him get by with it, he would have played without equipment, aside from his helmet. "Man, I can't take you over there with that pair of shoulder pads," Steve quipped, calling to mind his tailback's guts and gumption. Leon grinned and went to retrieve his original-issue pads.

After a productive visit to Virginia Tech, the two returned to Pearisburg. On the way back, Leon turned to his coach and asked, "Remember when Blacksburg won the state championship?"

He replied that he did.

"Well," said Leon, "wouldn't it be nice if we won it this year?"

Steve just smiled.

"This is not a good program," Christiansburg head coach Phil

Robbins was told during his interview in 1977. "But if you have any hope of winning, it's with the eighth- and ninth-grade classes. If you can get those two groups together in a few years, you'll have a chance." Indeed, the Blue Demons had endured their fair share of adversity. After twenty-six straight losses, the program nearly folded in 1939. A new coach, former Notre Dame monogram winner Francis J. "Boodie" Albert, revived the sport a year later but left after one season, returning to his alma mater, Covington, where he coached for thirty-three years. After World War II, difficulties remained, and aside from isolated seasons under Sumner D. "Tex" Tilson, James E. "Buddy" Earp, and Omar Ross, Christiansburg toiled in mediocrity. Following the same trend, Harry held a 19–5–2 career mark against the Blue Demons.

After interviewing at three schools, Robbins took the job at Christiansburg. Even though there had only been one winning season since 1963, and they were coming off a 2–8 finish, the Emory & Henry graduate embraced the challenge. After the first day of practice, he told his wife, "There's more athletic talent out there than I had in the entire six years I was at John Battle, but they are horrible." Still, he continued to stress the phrase, "I believe," and with just three run plays and two passes from his I-formation, Christiansburg edged George Wythe 14–7 to start the year, their first win in a district opener in twelve seasons. His players had bought in, and so had the community.

Robbins was now in his fourth year at the helm of the Blue Demons. They had continually improved in his first three seasons, from 3–7 and 4–6 to 6–4 in 1979. Entering this season, Christiansburg had been picked to win the New River District by the *Roanoke Times & World-News* and the *Blacksburg Sun*, and at 5–0–1, they were off to their best start in almost a quarter century. The foretold potential of the now-upperclassmen had resulted in a roster of twenty seniors and nineteen juniors loaded with talent.

The Blue Demons' offense averaged thirty-eight points per game and was paced by another highly advertised running back, junior

Mark Franklin. Steve told the *Virginian Leader* of the six-foot, 208-pound fullback, "He's the leading scorer in the district, a real horse, and by far the best we've faced all year." Franklin also ranked atop the district leaderboard in rushing. "He's bigger than most of our linemen, and he's faster than our backs," Steve continued in the *Roanoke Times & World-News*. "And it's not like he's the only guy we have to worry about . . . They've got two or three other weapons they can use just as effectively."

Joining Franklin in the Christiansburg backfield was tailback C.K. Allen. Praised by Coach Robbins for his tenacity, the senior had accumulated close to eight hundred yards and was third in the district's rushing and scoring races, giving the navy and gold a potent one-two punch. The trigger man was senior quarterback Dewey Lusk, who had led the league in passing a year earlier and completed nearly 60 percent of his throws, the majority to Stevie Allen, an All-Region IV selection at wide receiver in 1979.

On Tuesday that week, sportswriter Dave Scarangella penned a story for the *Roanoke Times & World-News* titled "Giles' Single Wing Double Trouble" and featured a picture of the backfield trio of Leon, Greg King, and Greg Mance. Each had been the leading ground gainer in at least one contest. Scarangella returned to the newsroom and told the other reporters, "You guys think you've seen the single wing, but you've never seen the single wing like *this*."

All the acclaim and notoriety concerned the Giles head coach, for Steve could recall the result following Scarangella's feature article, "Giles Resurgence," a year prior. On top of that, the Spartans had made their first-ever appearance in the UPI Group AA Top 10, ranked at number six that week, and a win against Christiansburg would match the record for most wins by any Giles football team in a single season. Everyone in the community was on cloud nine, but Steve needed his players firmly on the ground. He needed a message to refocus his troops ahead of the biggest game of the regular season. By happenstance, he was gifted just that.

Midweek, Steve was approached by former assistant Jack Williams, now the program's videographer, who revealed that, after running an errand in Christiansburg, he had driven by the Blue Demons' practice field and saw them practicing in shorts. *I've never believed in going on a football field in a pair of shorts.* This was an ideal angle, and Steve couldn't wait to use it as a rallying cry. It struck at the core of everything he valued as a football coach and was just what he needed to rouse his squad. *You don't play in shorts on Friday night! If you're practicing in shorts, you're just learning to play high.*

Since his time at the eighth-grade level, Steve had prided himself as an in-your-face, dyed-in-the-wool disciplinarian who insisted on physical practices every day of the week. *After that first week in August, we're not putting on a pair of shorts the rest of the year! We're going out in pants and shoulder pads—and we're going to use them, too!* Conversely, the Spartan players believed they won because of how they practiced.

"They've got no more respect for us—hell, they're over there practicing in shorts," he announced. "Here we are, busting our tail ends. Boys, they've got a good football team, but they can't be hard-nosed like we are!" Steve could tell by the look in their eyes that he had stirred their emotions, and for the remainder of the week, he repeated the fundamental notion that they were the better team because they practiced harder. After all, the only time the Spartans left the locker room in shorts was when they went home.

———

The bass intro alone was enough to fire the enthusiasm of even the most indifferent of Giles fans. Queen's song "Another One Bites the Dust" had become the Spartans' soundtrack for the 1980 season. It was a favorite at pep rallies and after games, and this week, it was the number one song in America on the Billboard Hot 100 chart. It was also the title of Mo's weekly poem to Harold Chafin. "You go on in there and write that poem, and I'll do the cleaning," suggested teammate Barry Harrell, who worked with him at J&L Cleaning Service & Supply for the same $3.10 an hour. "You're going to jinx us if you don't!" To ward off superstition, Mo got right to work, closing with the following verse:

> *Now a reminder to all our Spartan fans,*
> *who are always yelling and clapping their hands.*
> *Keep wearing red and keep on grinning,*
> *come to our ball games, and we'll keep on winning.*

For away games outside of Narrows, Steve preferred to reach their destination early to give his players a chance to walk the field. It allowed them to stretch their legs, familiarize themselves with the playing surface, and visualize success, all while drinking a Nutrament shake administered by the coaching staff. It was typically an uneventful routine. However, when the Spartans walked the field on Friday night, the Blue Demon mascot appeared on the sideline and did the unthinkable. He put a bandana on the end of its pitchfork and lit it on fire in front of the entire Giles team. Mo and Charlie were beside themselves, for they likened this to the burning of an American flag, a sensitive issue for many. Patriotism had returned to the national forefront in recent months as fifty-two American hostages still remained in Tehran, Iran, following the takeover of the US embassy by militants 349 days prior. "Coach, let me go get him!" Mo implored, and within seconds, it reverberated throughout the group.

Big mistake, Steve thought.

Harry could remember a time his team had also been taunted. It was 1961, and the Green Wave had returned to Dublin, where they had last lost 39–14 to the Dukes two years earlier. Before the season, a new electronic scoreboard was installed at Soldiers Field, and Pulaski

County's newspaper, the *Southwest Times*, called it "the most modern in the New River I-B District." As Harry's boys prepared to take the field, the scoreboard lit up with the 1959 final score, a message of mockery that did not go unnoticed. Narrows whipped the Dukes 34–0 for their twenty-second win in a row.

The Blue Demons played their home games at Christiansburg Middle School, which, by most standards, was inadequate to host a game of this magnitude. School officials acknowledged that parking was scarce, seating was limited, and restroom facilities were lacking. Nonetheless, a crowd comparable to the one at Narrows four weeks earlier awaited pregame. By Tuesday, Coach Robbins had convinced everyone in town that they wouldn't get a seat if they didn't get there at least two hours in advance. The stakes were high, as the winner would control their own destiny in the battle for the district title. It was also the first time either school had been in this situation, and attendance reflected it.

The police had to part the multitude so the teams could enter the stadium for warm-ups, and the Spartans received a hostile reception from the Christiansburg faithful. People were already standing on the roof of the school building and climbing up the outdoor basketball goals to see. Because of low seating capacity, fans were five deep around the fence, which was in close proximity to the field. Steve was in awe at the noise level. *I can't hear anything.*

Instead of sending out small groups periodically, the Spartans went out as a cohesive unit. They took the field in single file and dispersed into their lines to do stretches and calisthenics. Steve admired the meticulous coordination of precision drill teams and wanted the exercises to be exact, with everyone in lockstep and sounding off in unison. He always ran the warm-up himself and, up until then, used verbal commands for direction. Yet, for the first time, his players couldn't hear him, even with his booming voice, and he had to start using a whistle instead.

The question of how Leon's injured shoulder would hold up against the Blue Demons' experienced defense loomed as the Spartans began their first possession following a Christiansburg punt. On the second play from scrimmage, Leon carried the ball off-tackle, where he was hit simultaneously by a host of Blue Demons and nearly fainted from the pain. As he lay on the turf, the opposing players shouted, "Yeah, we got him!" Hearing this, Leon resolved there was no alternative but to continue. He got up and returned to the huddle, his shoulder now numb. Two plays later, the Spartans punted the ball back to Christiansburg, who would have excellent field position near midfield.

To start their second drive, Dewey Lusk gave to Mark Franklin, who plowed straight ahead for six yards. After the play, defensive tackle Turd Martin came up favoring his shoulder and told his teammates, "Don't hit him in his thighs!" He thought Franklin's tree-trunk legs resembled those of Houston Oilers running back and league MVP Earl Campbell, who had just rushed for 178 yards against Kansas City the previous Sunday.

Behind Franklin, Lusk, and C.K. Allen, Robbins mixed elements of the option with traditional I-formation staples, and the Blue Demons moved into Giles territory. A pivotal completion from Lusk to David Linkous moved the chains on fourth-and-four from the Spartans thirty, and five plays later, Lusk hit tight end Paul Bibb on a seam pass from the six-yard line for the touchdown. The scoring strike was the culmination of a twelve-play, forty-eight-yard drive, and with the extra point, the Blue Demons grabbed an early 7–0 lead with 3:22 left in the opening quarter.

Across the field, Mo told himself, "All right, they scored. It's out of the way. Let's play." He knew his teammates would feed off his demeanor. Following a short return, the Spartans set up at their own thirty-one. On first down, Leon handed to Greg Mance on 23 Reverse, and Greg broke several tackles en route to a twelve-yard gain.

Mo and Charlie opened the hole with a crushing double-team on the defensive tackle and returned to the huddle reinvigorated. "They ain't shit! They're soft!" they screamed.

"Let's get after their ass!" their teammates responded.

After Greg Mance added six more, Leon exploded up the gut on "48," an inside trap made to look like its off-tackle counterpart, 44, and danced his way to the Christiansburg thirty-seven, a fourteen-yard gallop. The single wing moved into high gear, and the first quarter ended with Giles knocking on the door at the Blue Demons fourteen-yard line. The Giles fans were also back in the game, passionately waving their bandanas.

Three plays into the second period, Greg King capped the sixty-nine-yard march with a one-yard plunge. The extra point was off the mark, and with 11:02 left before the half, Giles trailed 7–6. Leon accounted for forty-six yards on the eleven-play drive, but the pain permeating the left side of his body was starting to take its toll. Nonetheless, momentum was now on the side of the Bandana Express.

Christiansburg couldn't get anything going on their next possession, and the Spartans got the ball right back at their own thirty-eight. Leon continued to play inspired. After his second down run netted seven yards and gave Giles a fresh set of downs, he took the pitch on 42 Buck to the edge and picked up fourteen, whirling forward for five after the initial contact. Christiansburg's local newspaper, the *News Messenger*, described Leon as "a speedy, spinning runner who had more moves than a tournament chess player."

After the play, Christiansburg tailback C.K. Allen, who also played defensive end, was shaken up. Seeing him leave the field emboldened the Spartans as it solidified everything Steve had told them during the week. "Yeah, looky there," he pointed out to the players on the sideline, "he's been practicing in shorts while we've been practicing in pads!" The reminder aimed not to disparage Allen but to feed the belief that they were the more physical team. For those in the huddle, it further highlighted Leon's gutsy performance. He was nearly in tears, his left arm seemingly adhered to the side of his body, but he never said a word and wasn't coming out. It motivated his teammates—it was more determination than they'd ever seen.

Leon carried the ball five more times on the drive, a grand seventeen-play, sixty-two-yard advance that included three fourth-down conversions and spanned almost eight minutes. Greg King barreled over again from one yard out, giving the Spartans a 12–7 edge. Steve chose to go for two, but Leon was upended shy of the goal line by Mark Franklin, a linebacker on defense, and the score held. The Giles sideline winced as the collision knocked Leon for a complete flip, but he again got back up, much to the chagrin of the competition.

Christiansburg attempted to respond with only 2:06 remaining until intermission, and following a forty-yard completion from Dewey Lusk to wideout Stevie Allen, the Blue Demons were in position. However, with seventeen seconds remaining, C.K. Allen was stopped short on fourth down, and the Lowlife Defense had held. The Spartans would also receive the second-half kickoff as they headed to the locker room up 12–7.

After the break, the single wing was on the move again. On third-and-three from the Blue Demons forty-one, Leon cut inside on "47," a fake reverse, and scurried up the middle for ten behind the blocking of right end Chris Woods. Play 47 was run to perfection by Harry's 1962 tailback, Jerry Huffman, and a favorite of Steve's in these situations. Later, Leon connected on a pass over the middle to Greg Mance, who shook off a defender at the fifteen and sprinted to the end zone for the thirty-two-yard touchdown. A two-point toss from Leon to Chris Woods and Giles had taken a commanding 20–7 lead less than five minutes into the third quarter.

Coach Robbins knew his team needed a spark, so on the ensuing kickoff, he called a designed reverse. Stevie Allen handed to Mark Rorrer, who picked up a wall of blockers and raced untouched across midfield before finally being wrestled down at the thirty-four. The return of fifty-one yards energized the home side and gave the Blue

Demons renewed spirit. Even so, Christiansburg failed to leverage the field position, as Lusk was sacked multiple times, and the drive ended in a turnover.

As the game moved to the fourth quarter, the Blue Demons took over once more, seeking to draw closer. On third-and-twelve, Dewey Lusk heaved to Stevie Allen, who made an acrobatic, falling-away catch near midfield. Christiansburg next faced a fourth-and-five and again turned to Allen, this time on a split-end reverse for six yards and the first down. Clearly, the Blue Demons were not going down without a fight, as Lusk ran the option and pitched to C.K. Allen, who bolted into the secondary on the next play for a gain of twenty. Minutes later, Mark Franklin powered over from the three, and with the extra point, Christiansburg was within a score, down 20–14 with 6:41 left to play.

Looking to capitalize, the Blue Demons attempted an onside kick, and the gamble seemed to pay off when they recovered, sending the Christiansburg stands into hysteria. But it was not to be, as the officials ruled the kick was touched just inches shy of the necessary ten yards, and Giles took over.

The Spartans remained composed, needing to melt the clock to protect their lead, and Steve kept the ball in Leon's hands. On fourth-and-one, he called 42 Buck, and with blocks by Mance and Don Sparks, Leon accelerated around the corner for a gain of nine and the first down. He refused to be denied, and no matter how many times he got knocked down, he continued to get back up. His fortitude defied his teammates' logic as they helped him back to the huddle.

In the end, the twelve-play drive would decide the outcome, as Leon punched it in from one yard out with fifty-two seconds remaining. As he dove across the goal line for the decisive touchdown, he collapsed, his effort unparalleled. His brother tallied the two-point conversion, and Giles extended their lead to fourteen. The Blue Demons added a score in the game's final seconds, but it was inconsequential, as the Spartans remained unbeaten, 28–20.

After a challenge from Steve during the week, Greg King played his best game of the year at linebacker, combining with Charlie for twenty-four tackles and limiting Mark Franklin to just seventy-two yards. Leon, on the other hand, had a herculean night, rushing twenty-eight times for 142 yards, overtaking Franklin for the district's top spot.

Between a throbbing shoulder and utter exhaustion, he struggled to remain conscious afterward. In an abundance of caution, Steve called for an ambulance and asked Don Lowe to ride with him to the hospital. At 150 pounds, Leon had always possessed the will of a warrior, a readiness to fight, but on the way to Pearisburg, Coach Lowe saw something different, something more. He saw the heart of a champion. A boy who had become a man. After a battery of tests, he was released. When he walked into the lobby, it was full of people, all there to check on him, Giles's favorite son. It was a heartwarming show of support from the community. Leon had been on the verge of tears all night, but for the first time, it wasn't because of the pain.

CHAPTER 14

OH SH*T!

November 6, 1980

AFTER SLUGGING IT OUT with Christiansburg, Steve decided it wise to rest Leon against non-district foe Roanoke Catholic the following Friday night, despite his tailback's objections. No matter, Greg Mance played tailback, and the offense continued to roll. Mance rushed twenty-three times for 156 yards and scored three touchdowns as the Spartans overwhelmed the Celtics 34–6. Their eighth win marked the most in school history.

The subsequent week's game against Carroll County was moved to Thursday night to avoid Halloween. Leon returned to action with 158 yards on twenty-one carries, and Giles cruised over the winless Cavaliers, 38–7, in a fog-shortened contest, clinching their first-ever New River District championship.

While it was a time of celebration, Steve also warned them against engaging in tomfoolery on Halloween, and with their personalities, it was for good reason. He frequently counseled them against risky behaviors that could derail the team's success. "I don't care how many times you see that commercial on TV about how much pure Rocky Mountain spring water is in Coors beer—it's a damn lie!" he had told them earlier in the year. "Drink more water, less beer, boys. All right?"

Nonetheless, with no game the following night, only a handful of football players were in school on Friday.

Still, heading into the first week of November, the Spartans were 9–0, ranked third in the state, and preparing to travel down Interstate 77 to Galax on the final night of the regular season. On Tuesday, Ronald Reagan was elected the fortieth president of the United States, which kept the government classes busy, and every evening Walter Cronkite apprised the nation of the number of days the American captives had been held hostage in Iran, now over a year. Otherwise, it had been a routine week in Giles. That is, until the day before the game.

A typical Thursday practice consisted of team offense until Steve was satisfied and then a review session, where he discussed possible scenarios for the following night's game. Players were also given a test on the scouting report, which was given to them weekly on purple-inked mimeographed pages. They were responsible for knowing the name, number, and weight of the opposing players. When the Spartans came out for practice this Thursday afternoon, however, Mo and Charlie, two team captains, were nowhere to be found. They were complete no-shows.

Steve was furious. They'd scantly missed a practice in five years, and their attendance this season had been impeccable. With just one win in the district, Galax was not expected to pose a significant challenge, but that was completely irrelevant. Not surprisingly, Steve was strict about attending practice. When he took over, that was one of his primary expectations. "You're going to practice! If you ain't going to practice, you ain't going to be on our football team! There ain't going to be none of this 'I'm this, I'm that'—hey, you're practicing!" he had warned his first group in 1978.

The day's practice continued as scheduled, but in the meantime, the assistant coaches discovered that Mo had gone to the town pool for a fistfight, and Charlie had gone to back him up. Mo was dating a girl, they learned, whose ex-boyfriend had become bothersome, and even though he had already graduated, Mo was ready to confront him.

While he had no qualms about a bare-knuckle brawl, Mo thought the guy might bring reinforcements and had enlisted Charlie to accompany him. The assistants immediately reported their findings to Steve.

"They didn't show up—to hell with them! They're off the team," declared Steve in the coaches' office after practice. He wanted to have an undefeated season, he knew the team and the community did as well, but he couldn't excuse the fact that two of his captains had inexplicably skipped practice. Don Lowe agreed this was justified based on the standards they had set forth the past three seasons. He and Steve usually had strong opinions but were not always in agreement. At the same time, Vic Edwards was often the mediator and voice of reason, ensuring they came to sensible conclusions.

Vic spoke up. "You know, technically, the day's not over. They haven't missed it, Coach. They missed the time. They're tardy. But they ain't missed it." He contended an adequate punishment would be a makeup practice later that night.

Slowly, Steve began to come around. Finally, he said, "You mean to tell me you two are willing to come out here tonight? Because we're all going to be here, and we're going to work their hind ends off. Y'all are willing to do that?" They agreed, and the decision was made.

Steve called each of their fathers, whom he knew relatively well. They were both loyal fans, but more importantly, he knew they would support his judgment. "Hey, Charlie didn't show up to practice today," Steve disclosed. John Mullins came to practice regularly but could not attend that Thursday. "Now, if he's going to continue to be on our football team, he's going to have to show up and make this practice up tonight! If he doesn't, that's it. He's gone."

"He'll be there," John assured him. Mo's father responded similarly.

Charlie still wasn't home. After he and Mo arrived at the pool and the opposition hadn't shown up on time, he put a dip of Copenhagen in and opted to go hunting. It was bow season for whitetail deer, and Charlie knew his father wouldn't be at practice. When he returned to the house at sunset, though, John Mullins was waiting.

"How'd practice go?" his father asked.

"Good," Charlie replied.

"That's good, because Coach Ragsdale called and wants you at the school at eight o'clock." Charlie had not only skipped practice, but he had lied to his dad.

"He's done what, John? Little Charlie just went hunting." His mother, Karen, was blissfully unaware of the ramifications.

Mo had yet to learn of these developments. He had returned to his house with some other friends, and before his father could speak with him, the phone rang. It was Charlie.

"Man, we're in trouble." His voice was shaking. "Coach Ragsdale called my dad and said I better be at the high school at eight o'clock. If you want to be on the team, you better be there too."

"Oh shit!" Mo said to himself. When his buddies saw the look on his face, they asked him what was happening. "Y'all ain't going to believe this, but I've got to go to the school. If I ain't there at eight o'clock, I'm kicked off the team!"

Mo knew Coach Ragsdale wasn't bluffing. He played no favorites. Without hesitation, Mo jumped in his car and drove straight to the school. Harold Chafin would have no poem waiting for him on Friday morning, needless to say. When he arrived, all the coaches' vehicles were already there. "Oh shit!" he reiterated.

Mo parked and went in. The locker room was open, and the coaches were all in the coaches' office. Charlie was sitting on a bench in the locker room with a solemn look on his face. Mo sat beside him, but no words were exchanged between the two.

Steve told Vic Edwards, "I'm going to bring them out here on the field, and when we come through that gate at the concession stand, I want you to hit that light switch in the press box."

He then entered the locker room and addressed his two captains. "Boys, if it was left up to me, I'm telling you, you'd be off the team today." He was livid. By now, Mo and Charlie were both on the verge of tears. "However . . . the other coaches have asked me to give you an opportunity to make the practice up and continue to wear the colors. Whether you'll ever play again, I don't know." Mo and Charlie thought they would come in another time, but that's not what Steve had in mind.

"So, here's the deal. You get your uniform on, we're going out on that field, and we're going to have a practice. Take it or leave it. It's up to you. You practice, and you're back on the team. No practice, that's it."

Both agreed but were petrified.

"I'm telling you—get your damn shoulder pads on! *Now!*" Steve crowed, the inflection in his voice rising sharply.

Mo and Charlie looked at each other and then hurriedly got dressed. Neither knew what to expect. It was pitch dark, after all. Once ready, Steve promptly led them toward the stadium, along with Coach Lowe and eighth-grade coach Rusty Kelley. Coach Edwards was already up in the press box.

"How in the hell are we going to practice in the damn dark out here?" Mo asked himself as they walked around the corner of the building on the way to the field. Likewise, Charlie wondered how extensive it could be based on the circumstances. Turning on the stadium lights unscheduled was highly unlikely in any situation, much less for only two players. The energy crisis of the previous few years, marked by double-digit inflation, had made stadium lighting more regulated. To offset rising utility costs, some schools had even considered daytime games.

Steve stopped and unlocked the gate. When they stepped through, the stadium lights suddenly clicked on, and their eyes became as big as baseballs, agape and stunned. Mo looked at Charlie, an unforgettable look of frozen horror etched on his face. "Oh shit!" Mo reprised once more. Charlie felt like he couldn't breathe.

"OK, boys, we're going to start practice," Steve announced. He told them to line up as if the entire team was there. As they began their exercises, one acted as the leader, calling out the initial count, "one, two," and the other responded, "three, four," just as the team would have had they been present.

When they reached ten, they switched roles and moved to the next exercise. This pattern continued until they went through all their stretches and calisthenics. Once finished, Steve sent them up to the practice field to retrieve blocking dummies from the equipment shed. "You better not get the light ones either!" he added. They returned from the blackness dragging eighty-pound cylinders.

From there, Mo worked on his pulls, except after he went through the hole, he had to run thirty yards and hit the blocking dummy. After each turn, he immediately ran back to do it again. Charlie, on the other hand, was working on his pass patterns. "I want you to do a ten-yard square out," Steve instructed, but when Charlie ran the route, Steve took the ball and threw it as far as he could straight down the field. Charlie then ran a fly route, and Steve threw the ball out of bounds. This continued through several pass routes.

As minutes turned into hours, they rehearsed all their assignments for offense, defense, and special teams. With the entire team, there was rest time between repetitions, but since there were only two players that night, it was a continuous activity from start to finish. Not to mention, Steve was in their ear the whole time.

The stadium lights had begun to attract curious spectators. Everyone knew electricity was too expensive for them to be on arbitrarily. After what felt like forever, practice concluded with countless one-on-ones at the goal line. "Come on, boys, the game's on the line!" the coaches barked. Over and over, the two hit each other with all the effort they could muster.

Finally, Steve called them both in. He told them to remove their helmets and take a knee. "Boys, what kind of practice do you think we had this afternoon?" he asked. When he didn't get a response, he went on. "It was the worst practice we've had all year, being that two of our captains laid out on us."

It had never dawned on them that practices were not individual workouts or a means to an end. In their adolescent minds, they weren't concerned with the overall impact of a single day's practice. What they were doing was important to them, and they were due a missed practice. But now they realized they were only thinking of themselves, not the team. As captains of the 9–0 Giles Spartans, the Bandana Express, Mo and Charlie were respected fan favorites and heroes to many, including countless elementary school students who wrote to them weekly. They were bold, fearless, and self-assured. Nevertheless, Steve had just taken the wind completely out of their sails. They had not grasped the influence and obligations of being a leader until now.

"Boys, I'm disappointed in you. You are our captains. We have a tradition—if you miss practice, regardless of what you miss practice for, you run five conditioning laps. But you boys are special . . . You get to run ten!"

Mo and Charlie ran their ten laps and returned their dummies to the equipment shed. They had lost track of time. It had to be eleven o'clock. By now, probably twenty people were watching the two-man practice, including their fathers. Steve told them they had to apologize to the team the next day but noted, "I still don't know whether I'm going to play you or not."

As the boys exited the field, neither the players nor the fans spoke. They hung their gear in silence and headed home. It was the most demanding practice either had ever had in their playing careers at Giles High School. On the way home, Charlie reflected. He felt God had grounded him through Coach Ragsdale and vowed to be a yes-sir, no-sir young man going forward. The practice had indeed changed his life.

Harry could remember numerous players who had acknowledged his lifelong influence, but none more than Kenneth French. Captain of the 1941 Narrows eleven, French dropped out of school in the eighth grade, but Harry convinced him to return. He found him a job and taught him to excel on the gridiron, where, as a lineman, he earned a scholarship to the University of Georgia. When he left on the train to Athens, Harry was there with money for the trip. While the 1942 Bulldogs went to the Rose Bowl, French went to war, serving under General George S. Patton. He wrote to Harry monthly and, later, returned to his old coach for advice. Now the athletic director at William Fleming in Roanoke, French told everyone he owed it all to Harry Ragsdale.

The next morning, Steve passed a group of football players in the hallway before school, all clustered around Mo and Charlie. As he walked by, he heard one of them say, "You won't believe what he did—he turned the damn lights on!" He grinned and knew the experience would have a lasting impact. Word circulated around town that it cost upward of five hundred dollars to turn the lights on for two players. If so, it was worth every penny to Steve. Leadership forged in the crucible of a cold November night carried no price tag. Mo and Charlie's dogged persistence was essential to the program's ethos, and Steve was proud to be their coach.

Before getting on the bus to Galax, the two apologized as instructed. They did not start the game, but they did play. Leon carried sixteen times for 103 yards, Greg King scored three touchdowns, and the Spartans walloped Galax 51–14. The triumph gave them, like Bo Derek, the "perfect 10."

Giles had anticipated a playoff opener against Gate City, but a series of upsets that night left the Southwest District runner-up undecided. With Gate City, Virginia High, and Grundy all tied for second place, a meeting would be held Saturday morning in Abingdon to determine who would travel to Pearisburg for the first-round contest.

Elsewhere across the state, Mike Grammo kicked a thirty-one-yard field goal with seven seconds remaining to lift Park View (Sterling) over rival Broad Run 11–10. With the victory, the Patriots secured the Northwestern District championship and a spot in the Region II playoffs.

CHAPTER 15

INTERSTATE 77

November 14, 1980
Region IV Semifinals
Giles vs. Grundy

BY THE FINAL WEEK'S contest at Galax, Don Sparks had rebounded from his early-season knee injury and was playing superbly. While he struggled initially, he showed marked improvement with each outing, and the *Bluefield Daily Telegraph* praised him as "one of the district's premier linemen." Even so, Steve had continued to tape Duck's knee before every practice, and each Monday, the conversation between the two invariably turned to the previous week's game.

"How do you think you played on Friday night, Don?" Steve would ask as his eight-man stood on the training table, having his knee sprayed with Tuf-Skin. Duck's favorite player in all of sports was Mickey Mantle, who wore no. 7, so when the red jerseys debuted in 1979, he chose no. 77.

"I didn't play very well, Coach. I could've done better," he always replied.

Steve never told him any different, but thought to himself, *God, son, you're killing them out there.*

While not physically imposing, Duck was agile, with nimble feet and outstanding body control, and like several others on the offensive line, had played in the backfield in youth league. Aided by the ability to block below the waist, he dropped defenders in the open field on plays like 42 Buck. *It's like he's cutting them down with a sickle.* In fact, the Galax coaches had referred to him as "Interstate 77" because when he pulled, the hole was "two lanes wide and went straight through town." Duck took it personally, his role of blocking for Leon, and genuinely felt he could improve. Not because he lacked confidence but because he was always chasing perfection. That's what Steve had instilled in them with the teachings of Lombardi. While unable to play in the scrimmage against Grundy, Duck was ready for the rematch with the Golden Wave on Friday night.

As the New River District champion, the Spartans were slated to host the Southwest District runner-up in the Region IV semifinals. However, with a three-way tie heading into the weekend, it was not clear who Giles would face until a meeting on Saturday gave Grundy the nod, the Golden Wave edging Virginia High on points by the slimmest of margins, 0.023. Abingdon, the Southwest District champion, would host Narrows, who, after opening 0–4, had rattled off six wins in a row to overtake Christiansburg as the New River District runner-up.

Following their preseason meeting with the Spartans, Grundy started 2–2 before also winning six straight, including a 14–7 triumph over Abingdon, the Falcons' only loss of the season. The 8–2 finish was the first winning season for the Golden Wave since 1966. In many ways, their rise over the previous three years had paralleled Giles's success, but while 1980 had turned out to be "The Year of the Wave," Grundy had also endured a horrific tragedy.

Less than a month prior, on October 19, two students were killed, and a third was seriously injured in a homecoming-weekend car accident. Among the deceased was beloved senior captain Mark Van Meter, while teammate Mike Bailey, who had played opposite Van Meter for three years at guard, was hospitalized with life-threatening injuries. The wreck devastated the school and the community. "I walked into the funeral home . . . and that's the saddest I've ever been in my life," head coach Larry Bradley told several newspapers. Van Meter was buried in his football jersey, and the Golden Wave dedicated the rest of their season to his memory.

Back in August, Giles was manhandled by Grundy, but the Spartans were a different team now, in large part because of that odyssey over Big A Mountain. "We learned a lot from that scrimmage and found the kids who wanted to play," Steve explained to the *Bristol Herald Courier*. "Our offensive and defensive lines have shown a lot of improvement."

The Spartan players knew it would be a benchmark for their progress over the last three months, and they were intent that they would not be physically beaten like they were in the scrimmage. Reminiscent of Christiansburg, their mindset stemmed from how they practiced, and Steve was sure to remind them. Still, Giles would have to find a way to negate the Golden Wave's size advantage. "They're a real physical football team, nothing fancy, no razzle-dazzle, they just run over top of you," Steve continued in the *Virginian Leader*.

Tailback Junior Coleman, Grundy's "Mr. Football," had rushed for 1,550 yards, going over a hundred yards in all ten games, and scored 126 points, tops in the Southwest District. "I believe that he is the best high school running back that I've seen for his style," said Larry Bradley. Coleman was nursing an injury after suffering a hip pointer in the Golden Wave's final regular-season game against Patrick Henry (Glade Spring), but Grundy was battle hardened from their district schedule, and Steve was worried their offensive style would keep the Giles offense on the sideline. *We have to keep them from controlling the football on us with their size and strength. You have to have the ball to score.*

Leon had finished the season with 1,250 yards rushing, and his brother Greg had scored 84 points, ordering them just behind Christiansburg's C.K. Allen and Mark Franklin, respectively, in the final NRD rankings for each statistical category. Collectively, the backfield stable of Leon, Greg, and Greg Mance had combined for 218 of the Spartans' 307 total points. Not to mention, each had also thrown for multiple touchdowns, a hallmark of the triple-threat ace since the days of Pop Warner. Despite a smaller lineup, Steve hoped the single wing's deception would showcase the Spartans' edge in speed and agility.

To illustrate this, Steve had begun periodically showing them film of Harry's teams. He wanted them to see the misdirection in his father's offense and, in one instance, showed them Narrows's 1961 season finale against Blacksburg. Steve spotlighted the long-side defensive end attempting to defend 42 Buck, which Harry called "Buck 32," just as Princeton had. "Watch this—nobody touches this defensive end!" Steve pointed out. Intentionally unblocked, the defensive end came across and then froze, looking inside and out, trying to find the football, all while standing flat-footed. He was lost, and the ball was gone. Steve also seized the opportunity to highlight the effort and toughness of defensive lineman James Rombow, who played much of the second half with a fractured leg. Needless to say, he wasn't the first of Harry's players to battle through broken bones.

Furthermore, in recent weeks, Steve had field-tested what he called "36 Buck." Previously, his buck-lateral series did not have a complementary play in the six-hole, but he felt it was needed for a more complete game plan and thought it would be particularly effective against the many variations of the 6–2 defense they encountered. They tried it in practice, and it worked like a charm.

The single wing is our tradition, Steve thought.

As interest surrounding the game increased, so did the press coverage. "It's a beautiful offense, but it can be stopped," declared Tony Lotito in the *Bluefield Daily Telegraph*, the headline "The Ancient Single Wing Presents Problems Galore" accompanied by a crudely drawn diagram. The seventy-one-year-old Lotito, a member of the Emory & Henry College Sports Hall of Fame, had been the head coach at Bluefield College in 1941, the final year before the program was abandoned, and later at Beaver High School. He was also a contemporary of Harry Ragsdale. "When I defensed it, I usually used a six-man line, and I think this is the thing Grundy will probably use," Lotito predicted.

Harry could remember facing Tony Lotito when both coaches were early in their careers. It was late October 1932 when the Green Wave traveled to Pocahontas, a coal-mining town outside Bluefield in Tazewell County, and Lotito was in his second season at the helm of his alma mater. It was Narrows's first year playing competition outside Giles County, and although they had topped Christiansburg the previous week, they were soundly defeated by Lotito's eleven, 20–0, with several Green Wave players badly injured. While the only loss of the season for Harry, it was a necessary learning experience for the young twenty-five-year-old.

A six-man line was precisely the scheme Coach Bradley and his staff had prepared for the Spartans. David Henry Stiltner, an all-district linebacker in 1979, anchored a mammoth Grundy defense that had surrendered just sixty-four points all season and posted four shutouts. The Golden Wave also had seventeen pass interceptions, but Bradley knew preparing for Giles was primarily about stopping the run. "It'll be a lesson in old-timey football . . . That buck lateral is the darndest thing you've ever seen," he admitted to Bob Foley of the *Bluefield Daily Telegraph*. "They certainly deserve their number two ranking in the state of Virginia." 1979 state runner-up Jefferson Forest had closed the regular season in the top spot.

It was the first-ever playoff game for both schools and with that came the fanfare surrounding preparations. Bradley's club received a boost midweek when they found out Mike Bailey, who was not expected to be released from the hospital until December, would be on the sidelines in Pearisburg. Meanwhile, officials at Giles learned Spartan Stadium would require modifications to meet the VHSL's minimum standards to host the event, including additional seating to reach a seating capacity of six thousand and a fence around the field for crowd control. This was a significant concern heading into the week, but they were determined to meet the requirements. After nineteen years, they weren't about to let the game be moved.

Twenty-five hundred temporary bleacher seats were procured from Virginia Tech and installed atop the hill behind what had now become the home stands, increasing the total seating to seventy-five hundred. Steve had decided after the 1979 season to move the Giles sideline across the field, opposite the press box. The seating accommodations were better on that side, and with a coach in the press box, he believed it would be beneficial to have a set of eyes on both sides of the field. The regular bleachers just went to the top of the hill, so when the temporary ones were added above them, it created a two-tier appearance. When Steve saw the effect, he thought, *That is so awesome looking.*

At the same time, the high school and booster club worked to have a fence constructed around the field. Eventually, athletic director Gary Clark contracted Sears, which had a retail location between Pearisburg and Narrows, to install a four-foot chain-link fence, and the $5,800 barrier was completed the day before the game.

With help from the Virginia Tech grounds crew and former assistants Jack Williams and David Chapman, the school's art teacher, the coaches also painted the field with increased flair to complement the stadium improvements. They styled the east end zone with "Giles," the west end zone with "Spartans," and the center of the field with a Spartan-head logo. On the bank under the scoreboard, they added "Bandana Bunch," another in a series of nickname variations that included Bandana Gang, Bandana Boys, and Bandana Bandits. Overall, it was a tremendous effort in just one week, and Steve resolved that adorning the field for playoff games would become a tradition moving forward. Nevertheless, he attempted to shield his players from the numerous distractions and keep them focused solely on the game.

Friday was proclaimed "Bandana Day" by longtime Pearisburg mayor Clarence J. Taylor, who had served in the role since 1946. The team symbol was everywhere, from shirts, hats, ties, and flags to rearview mirrors and car aerials. The Tastee Freez was bustling with talk of the Spartans' first playoff game, and an increased number of spectators had begun attending practice to have a nervous look-see. The energy that accompanied nearly two decades of anticipation was palpable.

Before the game, as the team relaxed in the hallway of the agriculture building, each player sat in the same spot they had all year. They dared not change their routine. Mo was humming the chorus to one of his favorite tunes, Nazareth's "Hair of the Dog." He had told Charlie during the week, "If Junior Coleman comes around our end, we're going to get his ass good!" The combination of excitement and expectation often caused Charlie to vomit in pregame. To compensate, he ate the salt pills of the reserve players, even more so now that the underclassmen from junior varsity had moved up, providing the starters with fresh practice fodder. While Leon sometimes left school on game days with similar bouts of sickness, these moments were spent contemplating the task ahead. Steve knew exactly how to push Leon's buttons in a situation like this, just as he did for each of them. "Now, Leon, they've got a running back, Junior Coleman . . . They're real high on him. You do what you got to do," he whispered, and that was all the motivation Leon needed.

After receiving the opening kickoff, Grundy began at their own thirty-two, and the Lowlife Defense set up in a tight 6–2 scheme designed to combat the Golden Wave's power running game. Steve moved strong safety Todd Dennis to the defensive line beside Cecil Austin, and their quickness immediately gave the Grundy offensive line problems, forcing a three-and-out on the first series. A booming fifty-four-yard punt by David Henry Stiltner rolled dead at the Giles ten-yard line, and the Spartans went on offense.

The single wing was also greeted by a six-man line, only with overshifted spacing, similar to the alignment Parry McCluer had employed in week one. After a first down and gain of three, Leon handed off on the inside reverse, but Grundy defensive lineman Brad Mullins penetrated into the backfield and made the tackle on Greg Mance for a three-yard loss. Mullins had been coached to follow the pull of the nine-man, Barry Farmer. On third-and-ten, Leon just missed a wide-open Mance down the middle of the field on "40 Pass," the closest thing Giles had to a drop-back pass, and the Spartans would have to kick the ball back to Grundy. Following a Steve Chafin punt, the Golden Wave would start their second possession at their own forty-yard line.

Like the rest of his coaching staff, Steve paced the sideline in red polyester pants, a red jacket, and a high-crowned team cap, and he glared as the power-I seemed to gain traction first, with Bradley's troops advancing across midfield and into Giles territory. Yet, when quarterback Curtis Elswick broke into the secondary and gained what appeared to be another first down, free safety Mark "Diesel" Chapman jarred the ball loose and recovered the fumble at the thirty-yard line. Diesel was another Spartan player unknown to the visitors, as he cemented his starting role after the preseason scrimmage.

To open the next series, Grundy's Brad Mullins continued to wreak havoc, making two more tackles for loss, and the Spartans quickly faced a third-and-seventeen from their own twenty-three. Steve returned to 40 Pass, only this time Leon completed the throw to Mance, who made a move and lunged ahead for the first down at the Giles forty-one. With the pickup of eighteen, Larry Bradley could feel the pace quicken in Giles's favor. Two plays later, Leon grabbed momentum by the horns with a spectacular seventeen-yard run on the buck lateral, weaving across midfield and eluding tacklers down to the forty, and the Giles fans were on their feet.

Greg King then bulled his way forward on three straight carries, two on 36 Buck, clobbering Golden Wave defenders for ten and another first down. Steve knew these punishing inside runs would only make the buck lateral more effective, and after a gain of seven on the next play, he again called 42 Buck. Leon took the pitch and followed Don Sparks, whose cut block seemingly pulled the rug out from under the corner, and in two shakes of a lamb's tail, he slashed through the secondary and into the end zone for the twenty-three-yard touchdown. It was pandemonium in the home stands as the Spartans had drawn first blood, the partisan crowd decidedly more rambunctious in the playoff atmosphere.

Grundy jumped offside on the extra-point try, so Steve elected to go for two, and Leon tossed to Greg Mance for the successful conversion. Larry Bradley realized his defense had missed an opportunity on third-and-seventeen. Nonetheless, Leon's scoring jaunt concluded a ten-play, seventy-yard drive, and with forty-four seconds remaining in the first quarter, Giles led 8–0.

Following a Bobby Munsey kickoff, Grundy started their next drive at their own thirty-yard line. A Pembroke boy, Munsey began kicking extra points full-time against Radford but had yet to kick off until this week. Harry had recently told Steve that his weakest area was his kickoff team, so he decided to move the sophomore into the starting role in hopes of improving their defensive field position.

As the first quarter came to a close, it again looked like the Golden Wave might be on the move. Junior Coleman and Chris Whited, who had just returned to action after being injured for most of the season, moved the ball to midfield on carries of seven and thirteen yards, respectively. Regardless, the drive fizzled soon after, and the subsequent punt sailed into the end zone for a touchback.

After Greg King started the next drive with a well-organized wedge play, Steve wasted no time revisiting 42 Buck. Don Sparks buried the corner into the Grundy sideline as Leon took the pitch and accelerated for thirteen yards before being pushed out of bounds. Just feet away, Larry Bradley likened Sparks to a bulldozer. Another first down moved the ball to the Giles forty-five before Greg Mance completed the reverse pass to Timmy Martin for seventeen more, and the single wing was at full throttle once again. Within minutes, Steve came back to the wedge on fourth-and-one, and Greg King steamrolled his way for six yards to move the chains again.

Finally, on the eleventh play of the drive, having noted the Golden Wave's overzealous pursuit earlier in the game, Steve called 47, the fake reverse with the tailback keeping inside. From the twenty-three, Leon faked to Greg Mance and shot up the middle. An oblivious Golden Wave defender celebrated after tackling Mance, only to turn and see Leon crossing the goal line. Grundy again jumped offside on the PAT, and once more, Giles capitalized. Mance passed to Martin for the two-point conversion, and with 6:11 left in the half, the Spartans had stretched their lead to 16–0.

Down but not out, the next possession proved the best thus far for the Golden Wave. On the drive's first play, Junior Coleman took a toss sweep and, following several nice blocks, found running room to the outside and up the sideline. As he broke into the open field, a slight stumble allowed Mark Chapman to catch Coleman from behind at the Giles forty-three, saving the touchdown. Still, the thirty-five-yard gallop gave Grundy new life. Conversely, it renewed the challenge for the Lowlife Defense. While Coleman had eclipsed the century mark in all ten games, they had not allowed a hundred-yard rusher.

Larry Bradley continued to feed Coleman, who, despite being hobbled by injury, repeatedly blasted the interior of the Spartans' defense on isolation plays. The Golden Wave appeared to be gaining confidence as Coleman powered them to two more first downs in reaching the Giles twenty-two, and Steve began to worry if they could make a stop. The defense stiffened, and the visitors were confronted with a fourth-and-one just outside the twelve-yard line, but again, Coleman willed his way for the necessary yardage. With a first down and goal-to-go from the nine, the Grundy fans urged on their team, hoping to pull within a score before halftime.

On the eleventh play of the drive, when it seemed Coleman

would carry the ball once more, Coach Bradley elected for a play-action pass. Bill Wooldridge, who was splitting time with Curtis Elswick at quarterback, faked to Coleman and hurled a throw to the end zone intended for Ricky Blankenship. Everyone in the stadium watched intently as Mark Chapman dove in front of Blankenship for the interception. Steve breathed a sigh of relief. It was a touchback for the Spartans, and the Grundy drive was halted.

The 16–0 score would hold until intermission. At the break, the Giles faithful listened attentively for an update from the Abingdon–Narrows game, and when a 14–7 halftime lead for the Falcons was announced, they celebrated in response. Even in the playoffs, there was no love lost between the bitter rivals.

Grundy came out in a 5–3 defense to start the third quarter, but the Spartans picked up right where they had left off. On their second play, Chris Woods and Greg Mance executed a textbook double-team, Don Sparks flattened the linebacker, and Leon exploded off-tackle for ten. The Giles single wing looked like a well-oiled machine to open the second half.

As the Spartans advanced toward midfield, Leon threw a strike over the middle to Greg Mance, who broke a tackle and sprinted to the Grundy thirty-three for a gain of twenty. From there, Giles continued to churn out yardage and grind the clock. The entire backfield got in on the act, and with under six minutes left in the quarter, the Spartans found themselves four yards away from another score. Sharpened by hundreds of repetitions in practice, Steve confidently called 44 for the fourth time on the drive, and his offensive line cleared the way for Leon to go over the top for the touchdown. Leon's third tally was the culmination of a thirteen-play, seventy-two-yard march, and with Bobby Munsey's extra point, Giles now led 23–0.

The Spartans would complete the scoring on the first play of the fourth quarter when Leon ripped off a forty-one-yard run on the buck lateral, again following Don Sparks, who mauled the cornerback. His fourth touchdown electrified the home crowd, and red bandanas waved vehemently from the hillside to the concession stand, dubbed the Bandana Bar. Greg King added the final two points after Grundy jumped offside for the third time. In addition to his four scores, Leon rushed for 173 yards on twenty-two carries. *He does things with the football you just can't teach.*

Grundy, on the other hand, was limited to two first downs in the second half and never threatened again. Charlie had fourteen tackles, but the standout on defense was Mark Chapman, who concluded his spectacular performance with his second interception of the night in the waning minutes. It was the fourth shutout of the year for the Lowlife Defense, and they still had not allowed a hundred-yard rusher on the season.

Not only had Giles defeated the Golden Wave, but they had done so in dominating fashion, 31–0. Afterward, Larry Bradley quickly acknowledged Giles's stark improvement. "Tonight, they were one of the best teams I've ever seen," he asserted to Doug Doughty of the *Roanoke Times & World-News*. Speaking of Duck Sparks, he said, "That number seventy-seven was just tremendous, but that's the way their whole team was tonight."

In the coaches' office, assistant Rusty Kelley made a startling discovery while totaling the stats. "Coach Ragsdale, we didn't have any penalties. I don't think we made any mistakes," he said. Steve smiled. *We were like clockwork.* While pleased, he knew the road to the Region IV championship still ran through Abingdon, 27–7 winners over Narrows.

CHAPTER 16
THE BANDANA EXPRESSWAY

November 21, 1980
Region IV Championship
Giles vs. Abingdon

AS THE FULL moon rose on the third Friday night of November 1980, a record eighty-three million Americans, 76 percent of the entire television audience, were set to watch the prime-time drama *Dallas* to find out "Who Shot J.R.?" The question had become a national obsession, gripping the country for months, but for thousands in Giles, even the fate of villain J.R. Ewing wasn't enough to keep them from making the two-hour trip to Abingdon for the Region IV championship.

The Spartans were traveling down Interstate 81 when the driver of the Abbott bus they had chartered began hearing chatter on the CB radio from passing tractor trailers. One of the truckers asked, "What's going on there with all them bandanas? Where you going?"

"I've got the Bandana Express! We're heading to Abingdon," the bus driver radioed back.

"You must have a hundred cars behind you," the trucker interjected. "I've never seen so many, and they got bandanas hanging all over the place—out the window, off the antennae, everywhere!"

The convoy exemplified the community's devotion, which Steve reflected on often. *Football is important.* Fans had lined the street in front of the Giles County Courthouse to send them off earlier that afternoon, even renaming the stretch of road between there and Abingdon "The Bandana Expressway."

For the 10–1 Abingdon Falcons, it was their second straight appearance in the regional title tilt, having defeated Narrows 21–0 at Ragsdale Field a year earlier before falling at Jefferson Forest, 10–7, in the state semifinals. This season, a good nucleus of talent returned, especially at the skill positions, but for first-year head coach Curtis Burkett, returning to the playoffs was not without its obstacles.

After four seasons at the helm, Region IV Coach of the Year Bob Buchanan resigned following the 1979 season, and offensive coordinator Berkley Clear was tapped to succeed him. However, Clear quit a month later over a dispute with the school system, and the team was left without a head coach. After careful consideration, Burkett, who had served as defensive coordinator under Buchanan, decided to take the job, citing the solid foundation already established. Even with a new coaching staff, Burkett's leadership solidified the respect of his players almost immediately. Eleven games later, the Emory & Henry alum was the Southwest District's Coach of the Year, and his team was looking to ride home-field advantage all the way to a state championship.

Their home field was, after all, the perfect championship setting. New in 1978, Falcon Stadium replaced Latture Field, a historic venue on Main Street, and featured large-capacity concrete grandstands. The Washington County facility was one of the finest in Southwest Virginia, and by the time Giles walked the playing surface in pregame, both sides were already packed to the gills.

In anticipation of subfreezing temperatures that evening, Steve had told his team about the fabled "Ice Bowl," the 1967 NFL championship, when Vince Lombardi led the Green Bay Packers over the Dallas Cowboys 21–17. He explained that while the game-time temperature in Green Bay was negative thirteen degrees Fahrenheit, the Packers never lost sight of their objective, even at the expense of linebacker Ray Nitschke's frostbitten toes. Steve often shared tidbits of

Packer lore as they related to moments throughout the season.

The Spartan players knew Abingdon was an exceptional team. *They're the best team we've faced all year.* When Steve switched on the projector that Monday, they saw an Abingdon team that was strong at every position.

Operating out of a pro set, their split-back veer featured running back Sterling Ellison, who was selected as the district's Offensive Back of the Year alongside Junior Coleman after finishing the regular season with 1,033 yards at 7.65 yards per carry, both school records. With good wheels and inherent big-play ability, his coach described him as a "once in a lifetime" talent who, as a competitor, was "just like his name."

Directing Burkett's option attack was junior signal caller Greg Eades. Untested to start the year, Eades had rushed for over three hundred yards and thrown eleven touchdown passes, ten to returning All-Group AA wide receiver Trudell Hiller.

A gifted multisport athlete, Hiller had hauled in sixteen catches for 511 yards and an eye-popping 31.9 yards per reception, another school record. Moreover, Hiller's twenty-two touchdown grabs for his career placed him at eighth in all-time VHSL history. The fleet-footed senior wideout also clocked in at 4.5 in the forty-yard dash and was being recruited by multiple schools to play at the next level. Where Grundy had trouble matching up with the Spartans' speed, Abingdon would not.

They're capable of scoring on almost any play. The Falcons' option game especially worried Steve, as one of his starting defensive ends, Chuck Stone, had missed three days of school with the flu. Normally, Steve would have expected attendance at practice regardless of the circumstances, but with stakes this high, he couldn't risk exposing the rest of the team. Stone returned on Thursday but had still lost ten pounds by the end of the week.

On defense, the Falcons ran what Curtis Burkett termed a "40 scheme", also known as a split-four or split-six, that had allowed only forty-three points in the regular season, including four shutouts. Gone were all-staters Steve Knight, now at the University of Tennessee, and Mike Briscoe, but the front four still featured seniors Joe Pope and Wade Lopez, as solid a defensive pair as any in Region IV.

At five foot eight, 210 pounds, Joe Pope was a fireplug with a lower body two axe handles wide. An all-region selection as a junior, he was recently named the top defensive lineman in the Southwest District for the second consecutive season. What he lacked in size, he made up for in technique and determination, and his quickness and low center of gravity made him a nightmare for opposing blockers. Defensive end Wade Lopez had an uncanny ability to diagnose opposing offenses, giving Burkett a coach on the field. Despite recovering from a broken wrist, he had fifteen tackles and three sacks in his previous two games, and Steve anticipated he would be camped out on the long side of their single-wing formation.

His conjecture was correct, as Coach Burkett was naturally concerned about the Spartans' formidable buck-lateral series and the hard-running King brothers. Still, after film study and conversations with other coaches in the region, he felt the dagger was Greg Mance on the reverse and decided to align Joe Pope over center Randy Martin in opposition. Burkett was also keenly aware of Giles's ability to throw the ball.

As expected, many of Giles's rushing statistics were already school records. Leon currently had 1,422 yards on the season. The development of an accomplished aerial assault, on the other hand, was atypical in the single-wing repertoire. Leon had quietly completed seventeen passes for 327 yards and four scores, while Greg Mance and right end Chris Woods had eight catches apiece. The pair had combined for sixty-five receiving yards against Grundy. Several opposing coaches, including Larry Bradley, had acknowledged the validity of their passing game, and Curtis Burkett was no different. "Giles doesn't throw much, but their tailback can put it up. When they throw, they usually go for the home run," he advised the *Bristol Herald Courier*.

Harry could remember when he, too, had an unprecedented passing combination. In 1939, the Pulaski Orioles stood in the way of a perfect regular season when they came to Narrows in late November. In front of the largest crowd of the year, halfback Ted Johnson passed to left end Bill Morris, one of four brothers who played for Harry, for a remarkable four touchdowns, and the Green Wave prevailed 35–6. The *Bluefield Daily Telegraph* claimed the feat was a national record, though it was never substantiated. After serving in World War II, Ted Johnson started at blocking back for Virginia Tech in the 1947 Sun Bowl, their first-ever bowl appearance.

Since the Spartans had three captains, Steve rotated two to go to midfield each week for the coin toss. On this occasion, he sent Charlie and Mo, with Charlie designated as the speaking captain, but only after giving him instructions for each scenario. "If we win the toss, we want to receive," Steve explained. "If they win and take the ball," he continued, "we want to kick that way," and he pointed south toward the scoreboard.

"Ok," Charlie affirmed.

Nevertheless, when the duo got to midfield, things quickly went awry. An excitable player, Charlie was always restless before kickoff, so when the referee turned to him and said, "You've won the toss," he blurted out precisely what Coach Ragsdale had advised.

"I want to receive *and* kick that way!" he exclaimed, pointing intently toward the scoreboard.

"What are you talking about?" the official asked.

Charlie reiterated, "I want to kick that way!"

"Are you sure that's what you want to do?"

Becoming increasingly agitated, Charlie doubled down. "The coach told me, *kick that way!*"

The referee said, "OK," slapped Charlie on the shoulder pad, and indicated that Giles had won the toss and elected to kick off. "Kicking that way!" the official echoed, pointing toward the south end zone just as Charlie had explicitly indicated.

Steve started yelling, "Whoa, whoa!" and came out for an explanation.

"Your man said you wanted to kick that way!" the head of the split officiating crew clarified.

In an unfavorable development, Abingdon would receive to start the game and still have the choice to do so again at the outset of the second half. Steve already wanted to avoid giving dangerous return men Trudell Hiller and Sterling Ellison undue opportunities, and now they would have to kick off to open both halves. He was beside himself.

Steve instructed kicker Bobby Munsey to squib the opening kickoff, but that meant good field position for the Falcons at their own thirty-five. On the first play from scrimmage, Greg Eades bobbled the snap but quickly recovered and scurried up the middle unnoticed. In a flash, the wiry quarterback slipped past Mark Chapman and was off to the races in front of the home crowd. Corners Steve Chafin and Greg Mance gave chase, finally dragging him down at the Giles sixteen, but it was a run of forty-nine yards to begin the game for Abingdon. Clearly, this was not the start Steve had wanted.

Dive plays to running backs Sterling Ellison and Danny Foster netted eleven more, and the Falcons had a first-and-goal at the five-yard line. Burkett returned to Foster on the next play, but there was a fumble on the exchange between him and Eades, and the ball was loose. Barry Farmer pounced on it for the Spartans, and in an instant, Abingdon's scoring opportunity was lost. Recovering his second fumble in as many weeks, Barry had taken his lumps as a sophomore but was finally seeing the fruits of his labor as a senior.

The frozen turf crunched under the players' feet as the Giles single wing took over at the six-yard line. Greg King tried the middle on his first carry but was stuffed for no gain, brought down hard by a host of Falcons, including senior captain Daniel Roe, an all-district linebacker. The aggressive Abingdon defense played with confidence, but Steve took notice of their convergence on the fullback.

As the teams unpiled following the play, defensive end Wade Lopez came face-to-face with Mo Ratcliffe. "You're scared," Lopez blustered.

Mo sneered and countered sharply, "I ain't been scared of nothing in my entire life."

By their second play, Steve was ready to call 42 Buck. Leon took the pitch from Timmy Martin and sprinted to the edge unabated. Following a block by Don Sparks, he darted past a diving Lopez and made a move to the outside before being slung out of bounds at the twenty-five-yard line by safety Trudell Hiller. It was a gain of nineteen, and the Spartans had breathing room.

Next was the offense's bread and butter, 44, and Leon thundered off-tackle and into the secondary. Hiller was forced to make the tackle again, and the Giles sideline erupted. Seventeen yards and another first down for the Spartans at their own forty-two. Two plays later, Leon converted a third-and-five, and they were into Falcons territory.

Steve continued to call Leon's number, but after three straight carries, Giles faced a fourth-and-two at the Abingdon forty-yard line. Steve came back to 44, and Leon ripped off an explosive eighteen-yard run, downfield blocking by Mo and Charlie allowing him to rumble all the way to the Falcons twenty-two for the first down.

On third-and-eight, Turd Martin brought the play in from the sideline: 23 Reverse. As the offense came to the line, Charlie took his mouthpiece out and got the attention of the Abingdon defender inside of him. "Hey! We're running a reverse this time, and the ball is coming right through here! Me and him are going to take your ass down the line and dump it on the ground!" Mo looked at him, shocked, as Charlie rarely spoke to the opposition. He thought of inquiring, but Charlie had already put his mouthpiece back in and was ready to go. Mo couldn't help but grin.

Sure enough, Mo and Charlie's double-team got a great push, but

Greg Mance was still tripped up by Joe Pope short of the line to gain, forcing another fourth-down situation, the second of the drive for the Spartans. In this situation, Steve opted for the tighter 46, and Leon followed Mo for six yards and the first down, nearly breaking away for the score. The Giles fans shouted encouragement, for it was first-and-goal at the Falcons ten.

After a three-yard plunge by Greg King, Steve again called the buck lateral. Greg Mance and Don Sparks sealed the edge, and Leon scampered into the end zone untouched, raising the ball in celebration as he crossed the goal line—touchdown, Giles! It was a masterful sixteen-play, ninety-four-yard drive. Bobby Munsey kicked the extra point, and the Spartans were up 7–0 with 4:19 remaining in the first quarter.

The Falcons' next possession also crossed midfield but abruptly stalled. Burkett opted to punt and play field position from the Giles forty-three, but the kick was short and took a Spartan bounce, rolling dead at the twenty-nine.

On first down, Greg King ground out five on 36 Buck, but Abingdon shifted to a 7–1 defensive scheme and was able to force a three-and-out. It was then that the Spartans made an uncharacteristic mistake. Set to kick the ball away, long snapper Dean Marshall snapped the ball over punter Steve Chafin's head. In a heady move, Chafin retreated into his own end zone and took a safety rather than risk setting up an easy touchdown. With thirty-eight seconds remaining in the opening stanza, the home squad was on the board, trailing 7–2.

After the free kick, the Falcons advanced to the Giles forty-three following an eight-yard run by Danny Foster on the last play of the first quarter. Yet, after the teams changed directions, Greg Eades pitched to Sterling Ellison, who lost control and fumbled the ball forward, where it was recovered at the Giles forty by a pursuing Chuck Stone, despite being weakened by the flu. It was the second turnover for the Falcons.

From there, the Bandana Express drove right down the field. Leon hit Chris Woods for fifteen yards, and Greg Mance busted loose on the inside reverse for sixteen more, reaching the Abingdon twenty-nine in just two plays. After a pass-interference penalty, a fifteen-yard run by Leon out of the Spartans' short-side wing-T set gave Giles a first-and-goal at the Falcons two. The junior tailback capped the seven-play, sixty-yard drive minutes later, diving over for his second touchdown from one yard out. Steve elected to go for two, and Leon passed to Chris Woods, who made a diving catch in the back corner of the end zone for the conversion. With 9:20 left before halftime, the Spartans now led 15–2.

On the next series, Abingdon responded with an impressive drive of their own. Starting at their own thirty, the Falcons moved seventy yards in fifteen plays, but not without controversy. On fourth-and-seven from the Giles twenty-five, Greg Eades launched a long throw to split end Trudell Hiller that Mark Chapman appeared to knock away just short of the goal line, but a pass-interference penalty moved the chains for the Falcons.

Steve usually paid little attention to the officials, but this night was different. Abingdon went back to the air on third-and-twelve when Eades hurled a pass to the back corner of the end zone, again looking for Hiller, who was well covered by two Giles defenders, Chapman and Greg Mance. Mance went up in front of Hiller and came down with the interception, but another flag indicated pass interference. Steve was irate at the call. *Damn, something's got to give here!*

The Falcons needed three plays to score from the seven, with Danny Foster running behind guard Don Henderson, whose family owned a local chain of grocery stores, for the one-yard touchdown. Richard Hughes' extra-point attempt missed wide, but Abingdon had narrowed the Spartans' lead to 15–8 with 3:49 left in the half.

After an exchange of punts, Giles got the ball back at their own thirty-three with less than a minute remaining. Steve noticed that Joe Pope had become highly aggressive over center Randy Martin, attempting to slap the ball away and penetrate into the backfield. So on second-and-five, he went to one of his favorite play calls, 47. Greg Mance faked the reverse, Timmy Martin trapped Pope, and

Leon bolted into Abingdon territory, eluding multiple defenders to the forty-seven.

Still, time continued to tick away, and two plays later, Leon's pass to the end zone sailed incomplete with just one second remaining, time enough for one final play. From the Abingdon thirty-eight, Steve's choices were limited, but he settled on 40 Pass in hopes that Greg Mance could shake free down the middle. Plumes of steam exhaled from each of their face masks as the Spartans broke the huddle and readied for the snap. Even with the Falcons' secondary aligned deep, Leon was able to find Mance at the ten-yard line, but he was dragged down short of the goal line by corner Robert Mitchell with time expired.

But there was yet another penalty flag on the field.

The entire stadium waited anxiously for the signal. It was a personal foul on Abingdon. After several minutes of deliberation, the officials ruled Giles would receive an untimed down before the half. It was Curtis Burkett's turn to question the call, but likewise to no avail.

From the four-yard line, Leon calmly tossed to Greg Mance for the touchdown. The two-point conversion failed, but in an astounding turn of events, instead of taking a seven-point edge to the locker room, the Spartans now led by two scores, 21–8.

Even so, a miraculous sixty-seven-yard drive in less than a minute couldn't save Charlie at halftime. "Hell, we can't even get the damn coin toss correct! What in the hell were you thinking, Mullins? Kick off? I guess we're going to have to go back out there and kick off to them again," shouted Steve.

On their first drive of the second half, Abingdon marched seventy yards in eleven plays to answer the Spartans' score before intermission. Shifty runs by Sterling Ellison, a penalty on Giles, and a twenty-four-yard diving catch by flanker Korky Skeens moved the ball into the red zone, and the Abingdon crowd was alive once more. Trudell Hiller picked up fifteen on a well-designed reverse, giving the Falcons a first-and-goal at the four, and three plays later, Ellison followed all-district tackle Craig Cuskey on a quick hitter for the one-yard touchdown.

The extra point was off the mark for a second time, but it was back to a seven-point game with 7:04 left in the third quarter.

Neither team could mount a meaningful drive for the remainder of the period. The Spartans moved to the Abingdon thirty-five on their next possession but eventually turned the ball over on downs, while the Falcons crossed midfield but punted back to Giles a few minutes later. The stalemate continued on during the following series as Coach Burkett mixed the defensive calls, moving between six and seven-man lines. On third down, the Spartans attempted to run 44, but defensive end Wade Lopez hit Leon right as he turned up into the hole, knocking him for a complete aerial flip. *We're not going after them like we did in the first half*, Steve noted. The Abingdon players celebrated, and the third quarter ended with Giles clinging to a 21–14 advantage.

The bitter cold was bearing down on both teams. With excellent field position to start the fourth, Greg Eades narrowly missed an open Korky Skeens streaking down the sideline. Then, on third-and-ten from the Spartans forty-three, Eades looked for split end Trudell Hiller on a deep post. The throw was too high for Hiller but not for safety Mark Chapman, who made an acrobatic interception at the twenty-seven-yard line. The Lowlife Defense had come up with another turnover, and the Giles diehards waved their bandanas feverishly.

The teams traded punts while the clock ticked under six minutes remaining in the game. Pinned deep in their own end, Leon picked up five and a first down as the Spartans fought to protect their lead. Burkett's defense rallied, however, and with 3:42 to go, Giles faced a third-and-ten from their own twenty-two. The Falcons desperately needed a stop to give their offense time to mount a game-tying drive. Steve went to a variation of 40 Pass, with Greg Mance running a drag route across the formation, but the completion from Leon was well short of the sticks. Steve Chafin's punt rolled dead at the Abingdon forty-three, and the Falcons would get the ball back with 2:41 left to play.

After Sterling Ellison gained barely a yard on first down, Eades went back to Trudell Hiller, but the throw was high and nearly intercepted again by Mark Chapman. Now under two minutes to go, Danny Foster tried to get outside but could only muster three on third-and-nine, and it was apparent Abingdon might be down to their final play. To make matters worse, a false start made it fourth-and-eleven at their own forty-two.

With their backs against the wall, Eades took a five-step drop and ventured one last time to complete the deep ball to Hiller, despite being double-covered by Chapman and corner Steve Chafin. He heaved the pass as far as he could downfield, and all three leaped to make the grab. Somehow, Hiller came down with the ball—a spectacular catch for the Falcons at the Giles twenty. The thirty-eight-yard reception ignited the home side, and the Falcons were back in business with 1:37 left in regulation.

By now, Coach Burkett had decided they were going for two and the win if they scored. They were well prepared and had already practiced the play they would run should this situation arise. Steve, on the contrary, could sense the swing in momentum. *This looks bad.*

Aiming to capitalize, Burkett returned to the option. Moving right, Eades faked to Foster and pitched to Ellison, only this time, the defensive end, an ailing Chuck Stone, tipped the ball with his left hand, deflecting the pitch. The ball was batted backward, some ten yards behind the line of scrimmage, and players from both teams raced to make the recovery. After what seemed like an eternity, Turd Martin, hustling from his backside defensive-tackle position, dove on the fumble and refused to relinquish it. The Spartans and their fans rejoiced, for they had thwarted Abingdon's comeback.

It was the fourth turnover for the Falcons, and barring disaster, Giles could run out the clock for the 21–14 victory. "I didn't feel safe until the horn blew," Steve told several newspapers afterward. "It sure wasn't easy. Lordy, I'll tell you that much," he added. *We played too cautious in the second half.* Abingdon was the first team to shut them out after intermission. Nonetheless, the Spartans were Region

IV champions and would host Region III winner Jefferson Forest in the Group AA semifinals.

"Hey, Coach, I'm like the guy from Green Bay," Mo yelled in the locker room later. "My toes are frostbitten, just like his." Steve laughed amid a chorus of cheers. At the same time, Bob Teitlebaum of the *Roanoke Times & World-News* asked to interview Alvin Martin, and his teammates shouted, "That's Turd! That's Turd!" The atmosphere was sublime.

Leon rushed for 151 yards on thirty-two carries while completing five passes for an additional seventy-three yards. Charlie led the Spartans defensively with thirteen tackles. The Lowlife Defense held Sterling Ellison to eighty-four yards on the ground and had still not allowed a hundred-yard rusher on the season.

On the way back to Pearisburg, Steve wanted to reward his team with a steak dinner, so they stopped at a restaurant just off Interstate 81 in Chilhowie. With an eye to next week, he directed the still-recovering Chuck Stone, "Nobody eats off your plate." The assistant coaches remarked how Steve loved the salad bar, making three trips before eating his steak. The boys usually only got a small cheeseburger and fries after an away game, so they were on top of the world. On this night, what could have resembled shoe leather was the best steak they had ever eaten. It was a time of fellowship and camaraderie, but their journey was by no means over, and if they thought it was cold at Abingdon, nothing could prepare them for what they would experience one week later.

CHAPTER 17
THE GAMBLER

November 29, 1980
Group AA Semifinals
Giles vs. Jefferson Forest

WEATHER CONDITIONS ARE ONE INGREDIENT that makes playoff football on any level special, and the team that deals with the bad weather better has a definite advantage, Steve reminded himself. Snow was blowing sideways in gusts near forty miles per hour, and with temperatures already in the low twenties, the windchill was close to zero degrees Fahrenheit. The Jefferson Forest players had taped over the earholes in their helmets to muffle the sound of the whistling squalls as they rushed past. To their bespectacled head coach, Glen Styles, the surreal setting and its cacophony made him think of static white noise on a television set.

With Giles holding fast to a razor-thin lead and the Cavaliers set to receive the second-half kickoff, Steve strategically elected to kick into the stiff wind to start the third quarter. He knew the decision may cost the Spartans field position, but after witnessing the powerful leg of all-state kicker Mickey Stinnett, there was no way he was going to afford the visitors the wind at their back in the game's final period. With that in mind, what came next made perfect sense.

"I didn't come here to play conservative football," Steve told his team as they huddled around him. "We're going to start the second half with an onside kick."

While the weather forecast for Saturday afternoon was freezing cold, a hot new tune was burning up the local radio airwaves by midweek. Cheerleaders Pam Dunn, Babette Farmer, and Rene Lucas, with help from the staff at WNRV, had recorded their own version of the NFL Atlanta Falcons' team song, "Falcon Fever," by Steve Carlisle, and it was an immediate sensation. Calls flooded the radio station every hour requesting "Spartan Fever," with listeners reliving all twelve of their victories within the song's lyrics, from Parry McCluer to Abingdon.

Steve, on the other hand, was intently focused on preparation. Practices were always mentally and physically grueling, but even more so in the elements. A plummet in the mercury was not enough to bring them off the practice field—only the threat of lightning would do that. In the cold, Steve cinched his red-hooded sweatshirt tightly around his face and continued. The players could only take solace in the fact that it was over when darkness fell, at least until this particular week when the stadium lights suddenly clicked on instead. "All right, boys, down to the game field!" ordered Steve, and they practiced for another hour under the lights.

Perhaps it was the eighty yards in penalties against Abingdon, but Steve was extra cantankerous this week. He felt his team was too tentative in the second half against the Falcons, playing not to lose instead of playing to win, and was insistent that would not happen against Jefferson Forest, the 12–0 champions of the Seminole District and Region III. *We're going to throw caution to the wind.*

Located in Bedford County, Jefferson Forest High School opened in 1972, and Glen Styles had been the school's head football coach since the beginning. An Emory & Henry graduate, Styles held a career record of 78–73–4, including a previous head-coaching stop at Rustburg from 1966 to 1971, with a 24–2 mark over the past two seasons.

Like Abingdon, the Cavaliers utilized a pro set, but while Styles called his offense the "twin veer," a term popularized by Arkansas head coach Lou Holtz, Jefferson Forest ran a much different style of option attack than the Falcons. In fact, Steve likened them to Christiansburg.

All-state running back Monzell Jefferson had graduated, but the Cavaliers still featured a heavy dose of inside running from this year's Seminole District Back of the Year, Toby Thompson. At just under six feet tall and 215 pounds, Thompson had forearms like Popeye and stalwart calves. With his fullback-type frame, the senior had bludgeoned opposing defenses with quick-hitting downhill runs to the tune of 1,159 yards and twenty touchdowns. Styles's offense also boasted the district's top offensive lineman in six-foot-five tight end Kenny Fuqua. A towering physical presence, Fuqua averaged nearly eighteen yards per catch, making him an attractive college prospect.

Still, after watching film and reviewing their wins over Martinsville, 21–0, and Alleghany, 24–7, in the first two rounds of the playoffs, Steve considered their defense and kicking game to be the strength of their team. Even with the departure of previous defensive coordinator John Schleupner and players like Jeff Calloway, an all-region defensive lineman, the Cavaliers had succeeded in holding their twelve opponents to a stingy eighty-one points, including five shutouts. Led by senior linebacker David Allen, also a state-champion wrestler, this year's group had tallied fifty-six takeaways as well, including a staggering thirty-four interceptions. As a product of Brookville High School, Styles was familiar with the single wing, having grown up watching Vince Bradford run it so well at nearby EC Glass. By contrast, his players had never seen it, and preparing for it in a lone week of practice was daunting. While their base defense was a 4–4 scheme, Steve expected multiple looks from new assistant Don Woods.

Jefferson Forest's special teams featured Mickey Stinnett, one of the state's few soccer-style placekickers, who was a returning All-Group

AA selection and had booted thirteen field goals over the past two seasons. In fact, it was Stinnett's twenty-seven-yard field goal late in the 1979 semifinals that propelled the Cavaliers past Abingdon, 10–7, in the newly opened Sabre Stadium, aptly named by Styles.

This year, it was Region IV's turn to host the semifinals. The VHSL had also decided to return the state finals to the home team's local field on a rotating basis after a one-year stint at a neutral site. Thus, instead of the title tilt being at the University of Virginia in Charlottesville, where the Spartans had watched Jefferson Forest play Southampton a year earlier, the winner of Saturday's contest would host the state championship in one week's time.

The Cavaliers had been in the top three of the UPI Group AA state poll for most of the year and had finished in the number one spot. Four-time champion Southampton had missed the playoffs for the first time since 1971, meaning a new contender would represent the eastern part of Virginia in the state finals. In the matchup between Region I and II, Tabb was slated to travel to Sterling to face Park View. While Region II was the designated host location, the Patriots' home venue, Bill Allen Field, did not meet the VHSL's facility requirements to host a playoff game, so the game was moved to Herndon High School in neighboring Reston.

While still readying his team for Jefferson Forest, Steve received a phone call from an unexpected source offering to scout the Park View–Tabb game for the Spartans—the source was Blacksburg head coach Dave Crist. Accompanied by his wife, Faye, and sons, Brian, Steven, and Michael, Crist was going home to Luray to visit his parents for Thanksgiving and offered to travel the remaining hour and a half to Fairfax County. Remembering the help he had received from other district coaches in 1977, he felt it was the right thing to do. Grateful for his generosity, Steve accepted his offer.

With their game on Saturday, Steve decided a ten o'clock curfew was needed for Friday night. The other coaches divvied up the roster while he gave instructions: "Boys, you're going to have to be in bed early. One of the coaches is going to call you, and we don't want your mother or father answering, saying, 'He's in bed,' or whatever. If you don't answer, you're not gonna play." He made it abundantly clear—they had to speak with the coach themselves.

Whether they were cruising Wenonah Avenue, shooting pinball at Peel's, or warming their girlfriend in their letterman's jacket, they had to be mindful to get home by ten. Of course, some cut it closer than others. Up to his typical weekend antics, Mo beelined home to take the call, then unbeknownst to the coaching staff, slyly slipped back out to continue the night's adventures.

By the next morning, the concern had shifted to the inclement weather. *It's windy as the devil,* Steve observed. It was intermittently blowing snow, and the top of Angel's Rest was glazed with ice. *And cold as blazes.* The Saturday after Thanksgiving was rifle season for whitetail deer, so hunters emerged from the woods, added bandana red to their already copious layers of camouflage, and made their way to the stadium.

The gates opened three hours before the 1:30 p.m. kickoff, and even with the almost-unbearable windchill, the crowd was massive, albeit slightly below the ten thousand expected earlier in the week. Those who persevered came equipped with everything from ski masks to heavy blankets, determined to witness history.

It was the first Saturday game the community had ever experienced. The field was freshly painted, just as it was against Grundy, and WNRV was scheduled to air live coverage, with Jeff Nichols and Harold Chafin providing commentary. Aided by the daylight, the Giles supporters rose to their feet at first sight of their team heading toward the stadium. It was a warm reception for the Spartans, a multitude of waving bandanas and clanging cowbells accompanying the shouts of approval.

On the contrary, Jefferson Forest did not find the environment quite so welcoming. Glen Styles thought the American flag, rigid from the wind, resembled a sheet of plywood. In fact, he questioned whether the game should have been played at all, given the horrid conditions. The Cavaliers had traveled from Central Virginia, where it was about twenty degrees warmer that morning than in the mountains of Giles.

Harry could remember when he had also faced a Bedford County club in the state semifinals. Narrows traveled to the county seat in December 1939 to take on the Bedford Otters for the Class C Western Half-State Championship. Coach Simon M. "Cy" Painter's troops took an early lead, but the Green Wave stymied the Otters' formidable passing attack and stormed back for a 25–6 victory. Allen McClaugherty and Ted Johnson shined through the rain and muddy red clay, reminiscent of Harry's childhood home in Lunenburg County. The following week, eastern champion Warrenton refused to play Narrows, and the Green Wave claimed their second consecutive state crown, closing the decade on a twenty-one-game winning streak.

Pregame warm-ups in Pearisburg were anything but. Greg Mance's teeth were chattering. Mo wore long johns under his uniform. The Spartan players had studied their scouting reports and were well aware of the physical stature of Jefferson Forest players like Thompson and Fuqua. Even though the visiting team typically wore white, the top-ranked Cavaliers were dressed in solid black, with only the slightest hint of red and white, a psychological tactic orchestrated by Styles. With the wind at his back, Mickey Stinnett was kicking field goals from near midfield, and his extra points were sailing way over the outer fence and onto the adjacent baseball field. Steve and his assistants were in awe of his leg strength.

After Giles won the toss and elected to receive, Stinnett boomed the ball through the end zone for a touchback. To emphasize his head-on approach, Steve called a pass play on the first play from scrimmage into the teeth of the wind. While it was incomplete, he felt it would let the Cavaliers know his squad would not be playing it safe. After all, Leon had thrown for 447 yards on the season to go with his 1,573 yards rushing.

Leon gained six on second down, but Kenny Fuqua and David Allen combined to stop Greg Mance at the twenty-seven-yard line a play later, resulting in an opening three-and-out. The Cavaliers were indeed showing a variety of defensive alignments. Steve Chafin's punt rolled dead at the Jefferson Forest thirty-seven, and Coach Styles's offense, under the direction of quarterback David Hughes, took the field for the first time.

Toby Thompson muscled his way for four yards on the drive's first play, then carried off the left side again behind all-district linemen Tommy Nichols and Edward Sanderson. Charlie met him in the hole, but Thompson spun out of the tackle and nearly broke into the open field. He was tripped up by a diving Barry Farmer, but only after a gain of seven and a fresh set of downs at the Cavaliers forty-eight-yard line.

The Lowlife Defense was also shifting between fronts, using their base 5–2, or Spartan Five, and the tight 6–2 they had used successfully against Grundy. From the latter, Todd Dennis got penetration on first down, allowing Charlie to subdue Thompson for a one-yard loss. "Pin your ears back and GO!" Steve had told his defensive unit earlier in the week.

It was evident Styles was looking to establish his stud running back early when Thompson returned to the same dive play for the fourth straight time, this time for four. In the final regular-season game against William Campbell, Thompson had willed his team to an undefeated season despite a badly pulled hamstring, carrying five consecutive times on the game-winning drive of a 13–12 triumph. Incidentally, Thompson's father, John, was also Jefferson Forest's principal and instrumental in the program's success.

Opposite halfback Sherwood Spinner gained but a yard on third-and-seven, and it appeared the Spartans had likewise forced a punt. Yet, when the Cavaliers broke the huddle, they lined up for a field goal. Mickey Stinnett's playoff long was thirty-five yards, a Group AA regional playoff record, but from the Giles forty-eight-yard line, this would be an unbelievable sixty-five-yard attempt, two yards longer than Tom Dempsey's NFL record. Everyone in the stadium believed it to be a fake, but when the ball was snapped, Stinnett blasted it right down the pipe. The kick, which seemed improbable, landed just five yards short, a testament to Stinnett's ability combined with gale-force winds at his back. Steve was amazed. *Boy, did that kid kick that ball . . . He almost made it.*

Nonetheless, the Spartans took over at their own twenty. On first down, Leon followed Mo on 46 for thirteen yards, energizing the Giles aggregation and prompting Steve to call it again, earning five more. Don Sparks trapped the defender aligned over right end Chris Woods, driving him out of the hole and into the backfield, and he was quickly replaced with Toby Thompson. Styles attempted to two-platoon, but in big games or crucial situations, players like Thompson and Fuqua were used on both sides of the ball.

After Leon moved the chains with a seven-yard sweep out of the short-side wing-T set, Greg King wedged the center of the line for two to the Giles forty-seven. It was then that Steve called 42 Buck for the first time.

As highlighted in Harry's film several weeks prior, the defender positioned over the right end was deliberately left unblocked on the buck lateral. Schematically, he had to be conscious of being trapped on six-hole plays, even more so with the addition of 36 Buck. Steve had seen it many times over. The opposing player would come across and freeze, looking inside and out, trying to find the football, and in a blink, be left trailing Leon to the perimeter.

In this instance, bruiser Toby Thompson's reaction was much the same. Greg King bucked the line and handed to Timmy Martin, who lateraled wide to Leon on the pitchout. Thompson gave chase, but as soon as he turned to face his own goal line, Mo hit him squarely in the chest, streaking like a blur from the secondary. Steve had taught those playing ten-man, whose regular assignment was to block the safety downfield, to peel back toward the line of scrimmage if they could not get to him, and he had executed it flawlessly.

"Man, I just knocked the dog shit out of somebody!" Mo told his teammates when he came back to the huddle, and they watched as Thompson was attended to on the field for several minutes.

The play itself netted just nine yards, but its impact was far greater. For the Spartans, it demonstrated that Jefferson Forest was not invincible. With an imposing snow-covered mountaintop in the background and their top running back being helped to the sideline, the harsh wind became even colder for the highly touted Cavaliers.

Jefferson Forest had a seasoned playoff team, though, and their defense mustered a stop when the Spartans turned the ball over on downs at the visitors' forty-one. With Toby Thompson out of the lineup, the Cavaliers struggled to move the ball but still managed to get on the board first when, after the teams exchanged punts, Coach Styles employed what he called a "gadget" play.

On second-and-ten from midfield, quarterback David Hughes faked the dive and ran the option, but the pitch was caught instead by flanker Mike Lindsay going the opposite direction on a reverse. Lindsay, the team's backup quarterback, pulled up to throw and launched the ball deep to receiver Steve Stadtherr, who had snuck behind the coverage amid the uncertainty. Stadtherr made the catch inside the fifteen-yard line, evaded the Giles secondary, and lunged headlong across the goal line for the fifty-yard touchdown. On the final play of the first quarter, Jefferson Forest had grabbed an early advantage and, with a perfect Mickey Stinnett extra point, led 7–0.

Oddly enough, the Spartans appeared to be settled by the score. After all, it wasn't their first time falling behind to start. They had faced early deficits against Parry McCluer and Christiansburg, among others. The subsequent kickoff rolled out of bounds, giving Giles the ball at the forty-yard line, and the Bandana Express once again roared to life. Leon motored down the sideline on 42 Buck for twelve, and two plays later, his brother added a matching dozen on "38 Buck," a straight-ahead fullback run from the buck-lateral series. Greg King looked like a runaway freight train as he barreled up the middle, rousing the Spartan fans.

Steve returned to the buck lateral on the next play, and Leon again bolted for a long gainer. Don Sparks led the way for sixteen yards before Leon was knocked out of bounds at the Jefferson Forest eighteen by safetyman David Huffman. For Huffman, Duck seemed much larger than his five-foot-ten, two-hundred-pound frame as he pulled to the perimeter.

Next up was Greg Mance, who, for the first time, made considerable yardage on 23 Reverse, winding his way to the nine-yard line. After the play, Mance noticed his bandana, which had been tucked in his belt, was missing.

"Where's my bandana?" he asked as he returned to the huddle. "Have y'all seen my bandana?" Searching the field, he finally located it—a player in the Jefferson Forest secondary had it in his waistband. It must have fallen off when he got tackled, he realized. "That guy took my bandana!"

"Who took your bandana?" his teammates asked.

Mance pointed him out.

"Oh, I see it. I'll get it back," Mo announced. But before any other words were exchanged, blocking back Timmy Martin called the next play, 36 Buck, and the huddle broke, sending them to the line of scrimmage.

When the ball was snapped, Greg King charged forward, shrugged off a defender, and plowed his way into the end zone standing up. The rugged nine-yard scoring run concluded a six-play, sixty-yard march, and after spotting the visitors a 7–0 edge, Giles was within a point of the Cavaliers.

Steve stayed with his aggressive game plan, choosing to go for two, and Leon went in untouched around right end as the home-siders boomed. The Spartans had answered, inching ahead 8–7 with 10:30 left in the half. In the aftermath, Mo approached the opposing player with Greg Mance's bandana and firmly stated, "That's not yours!" as he jerked it out of his belt. When he met Mance coming off the field, he had the red cloth in his mouth. "There's your bandana, Greg," he said with a smile.

That tally would remain until halftime. Both offenses saw success but could not string together another scoring possession. With the teams headed inside and the snow blowing harder now, Steve understood the start of the third quarter would be critical in determining who would advance to the state championship.

As the football tumbled end over end across the midfield stripe, time seemed frozen, like everything else that afternoon. Bobby Munsey had perfectly executed a surprise onside kick, the Spartans' first of the season. The bandana bunch loved their coach's daring strategy, and it reflected in their eyes as players from both squads converged from all directions.

Cecil Austin got a hand on it first but could not grasp the loose pigskin before a scrum ensued at the Jefferson Forest forty-six-yard line. The officials dug through the mass of players until, suddenly, Bobby Munsey emerged from the pile and raised the ball above his head—he had recovered his own kick! Simultaneously, the referee signaled in favor of Giles, and the hillside assembly went wild!

For many, Kenny Rogers was synonymous with "The Gambler," a 1978 hit song that also inspired a television movie. However, on this day, the moniker belonged to the Spartans' twenty-nine-year-old head coach. Bob Foley of the *Bluefield Daily Telegraph* was already crafting his possible headline: "Coach Steve Ragsdale: Call Him The Gambler." Conversely, Steve didn't consider it a gamble at all. Any kickoff into the unyielding wind would have resulted in a similar starting position for the Cavaliers, he believed.

Following the recovery, Giles was riding a wave of momentum. Leon, who topped one hundred yards on his first touch of the second half, carried six more times, while Greg King rumbled for a crowd-pleasing thirteen-yard romp, again on 38 Buck. On fourth-and-two from the Jefferson Forest eighteen, Leon once more showcased his tenacious spirit, reaching the first-down marker with a determined second effort on 44, the off-tackle smash. Minutes later, he finished the nine-play scoring drive with a spinning seven-yard touchdown on its tighter companion, 46. The two-point conversion failed, but the Spartans were now in front 14–7 with 7:47 showing.

Things didn't get any better for the Cavaliers on their next possession. On first down, Glen Styles revisited the option reverse pass they had scored on earlier in the game, but Mike Lindsay was sacked by defensive end Chuck Stone for a loss of nine. On the next play, quarterback David Hughes threw to Kenny Fuqua on a screen pass, but Mo and Todd Dennis sniffed it out for a five-yard loss. *If we can neutralize them in the third quarter, we'll get the wind in the fourth*, Steve thought. With an incompletion on third-and-twenty-four, the Spartans would get the ball right back, but it would be a long haul as Mickey Stinnett uncorked a sixty-six-yard punt that rolled dead at the Giles fourteen.

The Spartans caught a break on the next series when Jefferson Forest appeared to recover a Greg King fumble, but the play was ruled dead, much to the chagrin of Styles and the out-of-town contingent. Any potential shot in the arm faded immediately when Greg Mance broke three tackles en route to a twenty-eight-yard gain on the wingback reverse. After converting another fourth-and-short, Steve called 47, and Leon faked the same reverse, zipped inside, and jetted forty-three yards for an electrifying score. Styles's concern deepened, knowing the Cavaliers only had 2:51 remaining with the wind. Leon tacked on the conversion run, and the advantage stretched to fifteen, 22–7.

Less than a minute later, the wheels started to come off for Jefferson Forest. Heading left, they attempted to run the option, but an errant pitch from David Hughes to Sherwood Spinner was fumbled, and Greg King recovered at the Cavaliers forty-one. *Our defense has played one heck of a game.*

On the second play after the turnover, Leon took the buck lateral but instead passed to Chris Woods along the sideline for nineteen yards, and the single wing was cooking once again. Three more totes for the junior tailback, and the third quarter ended with the Spartans knocking on the door at the Jefferson Forest ten-yard line.

Four plays into the final stanza, Leon added his third touchdown, triumphantly leaping over from one yard out. Steve employed the reverse pass on the two-point try, and Greg Mance flipped to Timmy Martin for the successful conversion. Following the thrilling three-touchdown explosion, the Bandana Express had an emphatic 30–7 lead with 10:24 left to play, and the revelrous Giles County crowd could sense the Spartans were closing in on their first-ever appearance in the state finals.

But the once-favored Cavaliers didn't quit. On the ensuing kickoff, Mike Lindsay took the return toward his bench, pulled up, and threw a lateral pass across the field to Kenny Fuqua, who promptly sprinted eighty-nine yards down the Giles sideline for the touchdown. On WNRV, Harold Chafin apprised his listeners, "That was one of those razzle-dazzle plays!" A Toby Thompson two-pointer made it 30–15, and Jefferson Forest was back within two scores with 10:06 to go.

Barely two minutes elapsed before the Spartans had to punt, thanks to a revived defense led by Fuqua, David Allen, and defensive lineman Jessie Johnson, and David Hughes called for the fair catch at his own twenty-nine. Three plays later, the Cavaliers were across midfield, and Steve began to worry. *That kickoff did for them what the onside kick did for us.* Hughes then completed passes to Steve Stadtherr and Toby Thompson, and with 5:30 remaining, Glen Styles's club was in scoring position at the Giles twenty-yard line. Working against the clock, Styles returned to the air on the next play, but Hughes's pass was off the mark and intercepted by none other than Mo Ratcliffe! His teammates were beside themselves with exhilaration as the entire Spartan fan base celebrated the timely takeaway.

While Jefferson Forest did get a one-yard touchdown run from Toby Thompson in the game's final minutes, it was too little, too late for the Cavaliers, as a failed conversion pass left the game out of reach, and Giles was victorious, 30–21. Even with his late score, the Lowlife Defense held Thompson to forty-five yards rushing and his team to a paltry seventy-two. Charlie delivered a superb performance with twelve tackles, and Mo contributed ten more.

The offensive output for the Spartans was quite the opposite. Leon carried a Group AA state playoff record thirty-four times for 232 yards as the single wing rolled up 406 yards of total offense. "I'm used to carrying the ball a lot," Leon told the Lynchburg newspaper, the *News & Daily Advance*, in the locker room afterward. "Coach likes to keep me busy," he explained.

When asked about his team's bold mindset, Steve answered plainly, "Like I said at halftime, we didn't come out here to play it safe." Bob Foley would encapsulate it fittingly in his postgame write-up: "Well, of such are state championships made—and riverboat gamblers born."

By now, Harry had made his way inside and, after hearing his son's remarks, provided a father's point of view. "You've got more nerve than I do," he declared, and they shared a reassuring laugh.

However, all eyes quickly turned to the following week's matchup, for news had reached Giles that their opponent would be Park View, 14–13 winners over Tabb. Steve knew what this meant to the community. He had once compared playing football to climbing a mountain, and after thirteen games, his team, the Bandana Express, had reached the pinnacle—the state championship game.

CHAPTER 18

HULLABALOO

December 1–5, 1980

"**YOU MAY NOT BE ABLE TO PLAY,**" the emergency room doctor told center Randy Martin. At four in the morning, the day after the Jefferson Forest game, the usually reserved senior had awoken in severe pain to find his right calf swollen to the size of a cantaloupe. A hospital visit revealed a blood clot and the dim prospect of playing in the state championship game.

"I'm going to play," the Pembroke boy responded definitively. Randy hailed from a remote area of the county known as "Big Stony," located in the vicinity of Stony Creek, but played youth football for the Pembroke Trojans.

Steve met him at the front entrance to the school when he arrived on Monday morning. Seeing Randy on crutches, he knew he had a serious problem. While Dean Marshall was a capable substitute, the one player his offense could least afford to lose, besides Leon, was the center.

After the 1979 season, Steve was tasked with replacing two-year starting center Billy Williams. The single-wing center had to be hardworking, reliable, and conscientious. *He can't be a darn helter-skelter kind of kid.* Narrows' centers Richard Charlton (1936) and Jim Johnson (1940) had even been captains for his father, showcasing their dependable nature.

The center's chief responsibility was to make precise spiral snaps, what traditionalists called passes, to various locations based on the play, and they had to be tough and unwavering. Because his head was down, some teams tried to beat the daylights out of him. With blocking secondary, it was also where Steve could play a kid who may not be able to start anywhere else. He saw Randy as an ideal candidate, a hard-nosed country kid who had been a backup for Benny Hendricks, and he informed him of the move.

While surprised, Randy had quietly embraced the challenge of learning a new position in his final season. He worked tirelessly, both with Steve and at home. Harry frequently sat in his lawn chair and watched Randy snap, especially during two-a-days. One afternoon, the distinguished mentor asked, "Do you see that stripe down your helmet?"

"Yes, sir," Randy acknowledged.

"If I'm a defensive lineman, and you turn your head to look at where you're snapping the ball, I'm going to know where it's going," he advised. Harry had always taught a two-handed snap, which was customary at the time, but he and Steve had developed a one-handed adaptation two years earlier, which Randy now utilized. "If you turn the ball a little bit and point it, I'll know where it's going. When you come up to the line, everything's got to be exactly the same . . . every single time," Harry concluded. The teacher's lesson made complete sense to his pupil.

As the season progressed, Randy became an essential cog in the Spartans' offensive attack. His pinpoint snaps provided for smooth execution, and he defined dependability. The weekend before the Radford contest, he lacerated his thigh with a chainsaw cutting firewood, requiring stitches, but he never missed a practice and played the entire game. The *Bluefield Daily Telegraph* recognized him with a feature article before the Abingdon game, in which Bob Foley labeled him "Dandy Randy." Now, with his availability for Saturday's championship in question, his worried coach faced the possibility of a problematic personnel change.

Nonetheless, Steve had a practice to prepare for that afternoon. On Sunday, he had gone to Dave Crist's home to collect the two 16mm reels they had received in the exchange with Park View, along with the scouting report Crist had prepared from the Patriots' semifinal win over Tabb. Accompanied by the steady sound of the projector, he and the coaches tirelessly watched film, strategically analyzing every aspect of their opponent, an 11–2 Northern Virginia squad with a plethora of talent and a flair for winning close games.

Situated in Sterling, a suburb of Washington, DC, in Loudoun County, Park View High School opened its doors in 1976 to alleviate overcrowding at nearby Broad Run. From the beginning, Principal Richard Bonieskie had high expectations for the school and its sports programs. On the gridiron, the Patriots won just twice in their inaugural campaign but, under the guidance of head coach Ed Scott, were 32–21 overall and had not had a losing season since. Like Giles, their success was relatively newfound. They captured their first district title in 1978 but had never advanced past the first round of the playoffs until this year.

Park View's primary offensive weapon during the regular season had been running back Allen Pinkett. Averaging over eight yards per carry, the five-foot-nine, 170-pound junior had rushed for 1,485 yards and scored one hundred points in his first ten games, exceeding even Leon's totals. His other statistics were also impressive: a six-foot-four high jump, ten seconds in the hundred-yard dash, 4.5 in the forty, and a three-hundred-pound bench press. He was sure to garner interest from multiple high-profile colleges in his upcoming senior year. "He's one of the best backs we'll face on any level," said Osbourn head coach Tim Sarver following Pinkett's 148-yard performance in week four, a 7–6 victory for the Patriots. The tale of the tape should have set up a duel between two talented running backs, but that wasn't the picture the Giles coaching staff got when they reviewed Park View's previous three games. Rather, Steve hardly mentioned Allen Pinkett when he went through the mimeographed scouting report with his team on Monday afternoon.

The film of the Patriots' first-round playoff opponent, James Monroe, was of poor quality and barely visible. Pinkett rushed for seventy-three yards on fifteen attempts, but it was a defensive struggle, and the play of the game came on an acrobatic thirty-five-yard run late in the fourth quarter by senior tailback Todd Turner. Pinkett had predominantly played fullback in Scott's two-tight-end, multiple I-formation, with occasional rotations at tailback. Park View later scored, Mike Grammo booted the decisive extra point, and the Patriots won 7–6. Pinkett, however, had gone largely overlooked.

The second film, the region finals against Harrisonburg, was better but still somewhat misleading. Park View handled the Blue Streaks 29–19, avenging a playoff loss from two years prior, and Pinkett ran for 136 yards, but most of that came on a single fifty-one-yard touchdown gallop early in the first quarter. Instead, halfback Dave Bell caught the eye of the Giles coaching staff. The senior utility player gained 110 yards on just nine carries, mostly on an Ed Scott favorite, a counter with Bell aligned as a wingback. The cunning misdirection play had also been highly effective in wins over Osbourn and Broad Run earlier in the season, and Steve made note that his defense needed to be ready for it. Bell also had two receptions for twenty-four yards and a touchdown from quarterback John Nettles, who completed six passes for sixty-one yards.

We've got to stop their passing attack.

Against Tabb, muddy field conditions and a cold wind contributed to nine combined fumbles. Pinkett, slowed by a sore shoulder, had two of his own and his lowest rushing output of the year, just thirty-eight yards on seventeen carries. Even so, Coach Scott urged his club to put Park View "on the map," and they did just that thanks to the strong right arm of Nettles. The six-foot-two signal caller threw touchdown passes to tight end Chip Buckman and later Dave Bell, leading Park View to a 14–13 triumph over the Tigers and first-year head coach Charlie Hovis. It was the fourth one-point victory of the season for the Northwestern District and Region II champions and the second of the playoffs. Even with early-season losses to Group AAA Stonewall Jackson (Manassas) and county foe Loudoun Valley, they had now won seven in a row.

Upon examination, Allen Pinkett had averaged just eighty-two yards per game on the ground in the postseason. Thus, the Giles coaching staff saw him as a solid part of a five-man backfield rotation, which also included Rocky Coppola and Terrance Lardy, but most of the Spartans' defensive focus was on the versatile Dave Bell and the passing of John Nettles. After all, the Lowlife Defense had not allowed a hundred-yard rusher all season.

Still, Steve could sense the Patriots' big-play potential. "They had Harrisonburg down 14–0 after the first four minutes. That's something that bothers me because you can't afford to get behind early," he told Dave Scarangella, who would be providing coverage for the *Roanoke Times & World-News*. Furthermore, Todd Turner, the hero of the James Monroe game, had been sidelined with a lower-back injury sustained against Harrisonburg and, unbeknownst to Steve, ruled out for the state championship game. Unfortunately for Giles, this would press Pinkett into an increased workload at tailback, and he would be at full strength for Saturday.

That same weekend, Park View obtained the Grundy and Abingdon films in trade and sent a young assistant named Pat Elliott to scout the Spartans against Jefferson Forest. It was Elliott's first year on the staff, but he was not altogether unfamiliar with the single wing. Before relocating to Virginia, Elliott had worked under Charlie Linn at Pattonville High School in St. Louis, Missouri. Linn had played tailback for legendary single-wing grid boss Norris Patterson at William Jewell College and utilized similar blocking at Pattonville. Despite difficulty following the ball, Elliott recognized the fundamental schemes and feverishly took notes to relay to Ed Scott. Of equal importance, though, Elliott observed the community support and told of an enthusiastic following accented by the red bandana.

While the Park View players had never encountered the offense, Scott had previously faced one other single-wing team in his career. From 1969 to 1975, the William & Mary graduate served as head coach at Clifton Forge High School, and in 1970 and 1971, the Mountaineers defeated Pocahontas County, West Virginia. During his tenure atop the Alleghany County program, he amassed a record of 39–30–1, giving him a career mark of 71–51–1 heading into the clash with Giles.

Defensively, Scott was a staunch believer in the 4–4 defense and planned to stay with his base defense against the Spartans. "We have to make some adjustments, but I really won't change anything," he divulged to the *Bluefield Daily Telegraph*. Scott believed his players should focus on what they could control, the execution of their respective assignments, rather than the workings of their opponent. Preparing for the Giles single wing and its stable of backs, who had collectively rushed for over three thousand yards, was no exception. They had faced skilled ball carriers before, including James Monroe's Charles McDaniel and, most recently, Wayne Kirby from Tabb.

The leading tackler for the red, white, and blue-clad Patriots was inside linebacker Scott Lageman. The 190-pound junior, who also played offensive line, had eighty-five stops during the regular season and would be planted firmly on the long side of the Spartans' unbalanced line. Complementing his alignment opposite the strength were defensive linemen Tom Locascio and Frank Hughlett. After an impressive senior season, Locascio was regarded, along with Ben Richardson of Narrows, as one of the top defensive tackles in the state and a candidate for All-Group AA honors. With eighty-four tackles and three sacks, he had also been named to the All-Suburban First Team by the *Washington Star*. Hughlett, also a senior, registered sixty-eight tackles and three sacks and was an all-district selection at defensive end. While the heaviest of the trio, Locascio, weighed just two hundred pounds, they were long and rangy, with all three standing over six feet tall.

Unlike many games where Giles faced a size disadvantage, the matchup with Park View was much more favorable, as neither side boasted exceptional bulk, particularly up front. In his usual fashion, though, Steve downplayed any perceived benefit for the Spartans. "It scares me that they are not very big," he explained to the *Loudoun Times-Mirror*. "It's been my experience that when you get real big kids in high school, they're usually too slow . . . At 180, 190, they've got something there they can move around." Moreover, while the Patriots weren't mountainous, they were strong, thanks to an ahead-of-its-time weight-lifting program championed by Scott.

On Friday morning, Park View had a spirited pep rally and final send-off as the team headed for a waiting charter bus amid NBC television cameras. In addition to local dignitaries and politicians in attendance, Washington Redskins assistant Kirk Mee congratulated the Patriots on behalf of head coach Jack Pardee and the entire organization, adding, "After you win the game Saturday . . . come back and help us beat San Diego on Sunday."

Following a six-hour bus ride from Sterling Park, Park View practiced at Blacksburg High School that afternoon and prepared to stay in Christiansburg overnight. Coach Scott reminded his team of the expected crowd and hostile environment they would likely encounter, punctuated by a fandom that identified itself through high school football and the Bandana Express. He reiterated that, while different from what they were accustomed to experiencing in Northern Virginia, they were to remain intent and focused on their individual responsibilities, not external factors. Still, even Scott would be wowed by what awaited them the next morning.

The thing that concerns me is that the boys will get caught up in all the hullabaloo going on around here and not play the way they should.

As the week moved along in Giles, Steve was tugging at a familiar emotional thread. Even though the Spartans had finished undefeated and ahead of Park View in the final state poll, he still painted his team as the underdog. This week, the storyline was the ultimate tale of the country versus the city—"little ol' Giles" against metropolitan Washington, DC.

Meanwhile, center Randy Martin was earnestly attempting a return to the lineup. After several days of doctor-recommended whirlpool treatment, he was able to stand unassisted and snap without contact. Although playing seemed far-fetched, Randy persevered, and his mobility improved with each day. By Friday, he was ready to discuss it with Coach Ragsdale.

"How does it feel?" Steve asked.

"It feels fine," Randy replied categorically. There was no way he was answering anything to the contrary. Steve suggested they stay afterward and work out on the game field so he could make his definitive evaluation.

With the Spartans' final practice complete and the sun nearly set behind Angel's Rest, Steve and Randy snapped alone under the stadium lights. In the distance, Steve could hear the honking of horns as about two hundred vehicles had assembled in town for an impromptu bandana parade and pep rally. *It's like a madhouse up here. Everyone's gone crazy.*

After watching his center's performance, Steve decided to give him the go-ahead to try to play. How long the senior could hold up remained to be seen. In the meantime, the calm before the storm was unmistakable, and Steve took it all in. With a breath of crisp December air, he admired the extra bleachers and fencing, added just weeks prior, as well as the playing surface, freshly painted in all its playoff splendor. Spartan Football had made great strides in three seasons, but Steve knew they weren't to the finish line yet. Then, as he turned to leave, he noticed something that appeared to be suspended in the night sky. It was a large red "1" glowing proudly above Pearisburg.

In 1949, Roanoke debuted a hundred-foot electric star atop Mill

Mountain, billing it as the largest of its kind anywhere. Fourteen years later, Pearisburg erected a forty-five-foot homage to the iconic landmark as part of its holiday lights display, placing it partially up Pearis Mountain. While initially intended to be temporary, the white star remained a tradition and was illuminated annually at the town's Christmas parade. This year, a triumphant red "1" was constructed in the center to celebrate the accomplishments of the Spartans.

While the lighting of the star wasn't scheduled until Monday, the numeral alone had been lit early at the behest of Mayor Clarence Taylor. Steve was blown away. With Christmas less than three weeks away, the Giles faithful were hoping for an early gift on Saturday, pointing out that "Noel" spelled backward was . . . Leon.

CHAPTER 19
TIGHT AS A BANJO STRING

December 6, 1980
Group AA Championship
Giles vs. Park View

THE SUN ROSE on a sparkling morning in Giles. The radiant blue skies and mild temperatures, expected to be in the sixties by kickoff, were a sharp contrast from the previous week's semifinals against Jefferson Forest. To provide his players some measure of normalcy, Steve continued their Friday-night curfew and held a team breakfast, but ignoring the day's spectacle remained difficult.

After breakfast, he allowed them some downtime before they began their pregame routine. Some returned home, while others retreated to the mountains, but for many, it meant listening to their favorite music. Leon's song of choice was "Love's Theme" by The Love Unlimited Orchestra, a chart-topping hit on the Billboard Hot 100 in 1974, and he visualized running all over the Park View defense as he listened. For Mo, it was usually something by Pink Floyd, but for his final game as a Spartan, he blared Styx's "Come Sail Away" as loud as he could play it.

"Let's ride around the community," Steve suggested, and the coaching staff loaded into Don Lowe's car to look at all the decorations around town. As they drove down Wenonah Avenue toward Main

Street, there were signs in every yard, messages on every storefront, and bandanas tied to everything imaginable. They savored the moment.

Conversely, when Park View left Christiansburg en route to Spartan Stadium, their coaches and players had no idea the scene that lay ahead. As the team's charter bus crossed Brush Mountain and reached the Giles County line, it was met by hundreds, if not thousands, of Spartan loyalists lining both sides of US Route 460. Nearly fifteen miles from Pearisburg, the multitude was shaking red bandanas and holding signs welcoming them to "Bandana Country." Everyone, including Ed Scott, could feel the electricity in the air.

This only continued the closer they got to the high school. A sign hung on the side of Hilltop Grocery in Newport that read: "We're district champions, got the region too. Look out state, we're after you!" A few minutes later, a massive banner was spotted at Fairchild Incorporated, a manufacturing plant in Pembroke, before another at Pembroke Elementary School that listed the names of fifteen Spartans who "got their start in football here." Nevertheless, even with the distractions, the Patriots appeared calm and composed upon arrival.

Fans were already in line when the gates opened at 10:30 a.m., and an hour before kickoff, vehicles lined both sides of US Route 460 as thousands streamed steadily across the road toward the stadium. From the police and fire departments to the school faculty and staff, everyone in the community had a role. Even Principal Bill Puckett was helping park cars.

Jeff Nichols and Harold Chafin were on the air, as they were again providing coverage for WNRV. Dave Scarangella, who had witnessed the rags-to-riches evolution of the program firsthand, was on his way to the Giles press box, which, like its counterpart at Narrows, was built by students at the county vocational school. Once he arrived, Scarangella learned his usual spot was taken by another radio station, WAGE from Leesburg, and its commentators, John Sieber and Paul Draisey. Thus, he chose to roam the Park View sideline as he took notes for his reporting. In all, at least eight different publications planned coverage, including newspaper giant *The Washington Post*. Pacing opposite Scarangella was WDBJ Channel 7 sports reporter Roy Stanley, accompanied by a cameraman to capture highlights for the evening broadcast.

In the hallway of the school's agriculture building, the Spartans readied themselves. Many had shed excess clothing in response to the warm weather. One of them, Randy Martin, was preparing to play full speed for the first time in a week. At the same time, Charlie had consumed nearly ten salt pills and was on the verge of vomiting from restless energy. In light of the Abingdon incident, he was surprised when Steve appointed him captain for the coin toss, along with Greg King.

As the clock ticked toward the 1:30 p.m. start time, the Patriots took the field first for warm-ups and were greeted by an already incredible crowd. The seating capacity, which had been increased to seventy-five hundred, was filled to the brim. Approximately three hundred Park View supporters, mainly parents and the marching band, had made the trip, but the spectators were decidedly partisan. There were more red bandanas than Allen Pinkett had ever seen, and he admired how the Giles community had rallied around its football program. Pageantry aside, though, he was ready to put on a show.

The stadium erupted as the Spartans emerged for the first time. Dressed in red jerseys and led by their three captains, they took the field as a single unit and filed off into their lines for stretches and calisthenics. The stands were chock-full of homemade decorations, including cardboard cutouts, bandana flags, and an oversized "Bandana Express" banner crafted on rolled-out freezer paper. Among them, Don Sparks spotted a white plastic duck, typically used as a lawn or garden ornament, with "77" painted on the side and a red bandana around its neck.

Despite the ovation and the mad clattering of cowbells, the Patriots, donning helmets identical to their NFL namesake, kept their heads down. As an extension of Ed Scott's coaching philosophy, they were not allowed to look across the field at their opponent during pregame. Scott viewed preparation as independent of their opponent, including during warm-ups, and his players had bought into that mindset.

"[Ed Scott] is a very personable young man who has done a remarkable job at Park View," stated Harold Chafin on WNRV. A consummate gentleman off the field, the slim, well-mannered thirty-seven-year-old brought intensity and passion to his football team. His players noted how, when he became especially animated, a particular vein protruded from his forehead, visible because of his balding head. Scott often told them he wanted to see the "fire" in their eyes and was masterful at recognizing when they were not ready to play. This, however, was not one of those occasions.

Chafin reviewed the starting lineups as both clubs exited the field for last-minute instructions from their respective head coach. When they returned, the overflow crowd had covered the hillside, leaving standing room only along the fence and under the scoreboard at the east end of the stadium. Some overzealous onlookers had even climbed the towers to which the stadium lights were mounted, hoping to gain a better vantage point of the action. Flying overhead in his Piper Super Cub, Bluefield photographer Melvin Grubb captured an aerial shot that was sure to grace the cover of the *Bluefield Daily Telegraph* the following day.

It was a spectacular scene. Many of Steve's peers were there, from Dave Crist, Norm Lineburg, and Phil Robbins to Larry Bradley and Glen Styles. With more than ten thousand in attendance, it was the biggest turnout ever for a sporting event in Giles County and an unprecedented audience for both teams. While unnerving for some, Allen Pinkett was primed to perform on the grand stage. After all, he planned to play in front of even larger crowds someday.

After naming the Spartans' defensive starters, public address announcer Clarence "Mullie" Mulheren introduced Giles High School freshman David Coulson, who gave a moving invocation before the national anthem. Each team's designated captains, Tom Locascio and

Dave Bell for Park View and Charlie Mullins and Greg King for the Spartans, then met at midfield for the coin toss.

Using the brim of his high-crowned Giles cap to shield his eyes from the bright sunshine, Steve observed in his distinctive red polyester pants and jacket, though some of his assistants had opted for their short-sleeved white polos because of the surprisingly warm weather. To the delight of the locals, the Spartans won the toss and elected to receive.

All-district kicker Mike Grammo teed up the opening kickoff for the Patriots, as play-by-play man Jeff Nichols informed his radio listeners, "All we need is a whistle from the referee, and we'll be underway with this 1980 Group AA state championship football game." The ensuing kick sailed through the end zone, and Giles would begin their first possession from the twenty-yard line.

Just as he had many times during the season, Steve planned to start his attack off-tackle, and when the Spartans broke the huddle, Park View was indeed in their base 4–4 defense. On the command of Timmy Martin, Leon carried off the right side on 44 but was brought down hard by Tom Locascio after only two yards, the defensive tackle shedding a down block in impressive fashion.

Steve followed this up with 46 on second down, but Leon managed just three more as multiple Patriots were in on the tackle. With third-and-five upcoming, the stands were already buzzing with anticipation. Leon handed to Greg Mance on the wingback reverse, and running behind Mo and Charlie's double-team, he weaved his way to the thirty-yard line and a Giles first down. Seeing this, Ed Scott quickly called a time-out to address his defense less than two minutes into the game.

Even so, the Spartans had another first down three plays later and seemed to be on the move at their own forty-three. But the Park View defense stiffened. The Patriots were now stemming their defensive line on the short side of the single wing, shifting just before the snap, and when Steve returned to 23 Reverse on the next play, defensive tackle

Terry Tretick sliced into the backfield and dropped Greg Mance for a three-yard loss. It was apparent that Randy Martin's limited mobility hindered him from making the necessary block on Tretick.

Leon dropped back to pass on second-and-long, but Tretick again got penetration, hitting him just as he threw, and the ball fell to the turf incomplete. Facing third-and-thirteen, Giles employed their short-side wing-T set, and Timmy Martin pitched to Leon sweeping left. The quick pitch had been effective in recent weeks, but this attempt yielded just four yards, and the Spartans would have to kick the ball away. Following a thirty-five-yard Steve Chafin punt and an eight-yard return, the Patriots would start their first drive at their own twenty-nine.

After a two-yard pickup by Dave Bell, Pinkett got his first carry of the game. With a flanker set wide left, he darted right for five yards on an off-tackle play designated as "4 Wham." Steve was concerned because he recognized their defensive scheme could be vulnerable against two tight ends. The structure forced the defense to balance, and the backside defensive tackle, Barry Farmer, was positioned inside his offensive equivalent, Scott Lageman, creating an advantageous blocking angle for Park View. Unfortunately for Giles, Ed Scott realized this as well.

On the following play, the Patriots ran 4 Wham again, and Pinkett burst through the line like he was shot out of a cannon. Wearing a neck roll and white no. 24 jersey, he was in the secondary faster than anyone the Spartans had ever seen. He zoomed across midfield before being dragged down by free safety Mark Chapman at the Giles thirty-nine, a gain of twenty-five yards in the blink of an eye.

Not only was Barry Farmer displaced by alignment, but extra strain was put on defensive end Chuck Stone and linebacker Greg King, who were also on that side of the defense. Ed Scott called 4 Wham for a third straight time, and Pinkett exploded off right tackle, accelerated into the open field, and went nearly untouched for the thirty-nine-yard Park View touchdown. Far cornerback Steve Chafin discovered he couldn't catch him, even with a downfield pursuit angle. In just four plays, the Patriots had moved seventy-one yards, and the hometown fans sat in stunned silence.

We can't play until we get behind a touchdown, Steve had facetiously told himself after the come-from-behind win against Jefferson Forest. They had even trailed against last-place Carroll County before roaring back to win convincingly, 38–7. Now, he only hoped his boys would hold true to form.

Mike Grammo came on for the extra-point try, but it was off the mark, sailing wide right. It was just the fourth miss all season for Grammo, including two that were blocked, and Ed Scott hoped it would not become a factor as the game continued. Nonetheless, the Spartans looked rattled as Park View took a 6–0 lead with 6:19 left in the first quarter.

Following a return to the thirty-four-yard line, the Spartans began their next drive. On the first play, Steve again called the wing-T quick pitch, but as Leon swept left, he was hit by corner Ken Sieber and a pursuing Terry Tretick and fumbled. Outside linebacker Rocky Coppola was the first to have a shot at it, then safety Joe Boone, who tried to pick it up, but the ball careened forward and was recovered at the Giles thirty-nine by Tretick. While an all-district selection at offensive guard, it was Tretick's defensive play that was having an impact thus far, and Ed Scott excitedly leaped into the air as the officials signaled in the direction of Park View.

We're as tight as a banjo string.

With the sudden turn of events, Scott saw an opportunity to go for the home run. Quarterback John Nettles faked left to Pinkett before reversing field and launching a long throw downfield to tight end Joe Boone, streaking down the sideline. Boone laid out for the catch, but it was just out of reach and incomplete. On second-and-ten, Nettles handed off to Pinkett on a draw, and he slipped through the line for eleven and a first down at the twenty-eight-yard line.

Nettles took off over center on the next play on what appeared to be a quarterback sneak and would have scored if not for a touchdown-saving tackle at the sixteen by corner Greg Mance. The twelve-yard scamper was not a haphazard short-yardage scheme but rather a designed one-step draw that Scott had used successfully throughout the season, including a forty-yard scoring romp by Nettles in the Patriots' week-eight victory over Handley.

After back-to-back runs of more than ten yards, Steve made a defensive adjustment, switching the Spartans to their 6–2 alignment. The change proved effective, as Pinkett and Dave Bell were stopped at the line of scrimmage on consecutive plays, bringing up a third-and-ten at the Giles sixteen. "The Spartans need desperately to halt this drive," acknowledged Harold Chafin. "They can't afford to let Park View score here."

Foreseeing a passing situation, Steve moved back to the Spartan Five, and when John Nettles attempted play-action, he was unable to locate an open receiver and wrestled down by defensive linemen Cecil Austin and Turd Martin for a nine-yard loss. With the sack, the Patriots were out of field-goal range. Ed Scott settled for another draw on fourth down, and while Pinkett got eleven yards back, he was well short of the line to gain, and the Spartans took over on downs.

Any sense of accomplishment was short-lived, however. Aiming once more to establish the off-tackle area, Leon headed right but was hit for a one-yard loss by Tom Locascio. Then, on second-and-eleven, the usually sure-handed tailback dropped the snap, and Locascio recovered at the eleven-yard line. The Giles sideline looked on in disbelief. A week removed from live repetitions, perhaps the timing was off with Randy Martin, but regardless, it was Leon's second fumble in as many possessions, and the Park View players celebrated.

It's like we're sleepwalking.

Four plays later, Pinkett powered over from one yard out for his second touchdown, and the small delegation of supporters from Northern Virginia cheered mightily. Having missed the first extra point, Ed Scott decided to go for two following the score. Nettles faked right to Pinkett and then looked left to tight end Joe Boone. Moving toward the back of the end zone, Boone flashed open, but the pass was thrown short, allowing Steve Chafin to recover and deflect the ball away. Yet, with fourteen seconds remaining in the opening quarter, the Patriots had widened their advantage to 12–0.

"Our boys, the Spartans, appear to be a little flat," Harold Chafin described on the local airwaves. Steve, on the other hand, saw more than that. Not only were they awestruck by Allen Pinkett, but they were timid and unsure of themselves. The squad that had boldly overtaken Jefferson Forest was nowhere to be found.

As the kickoff-return team took the field, Greg Mance looked back at the scoreboard in consternation and noticed Leon pacing back and forth. "Man, we're giving this damn game away," he shouted toward Mance. "We're giving it away!" In truth, Leon had already fumbled more times than he had in any outing all season. Not to mention, the entire team had only two turnovers in the previous three playoff games combined. His subsequent return to the twenty-seven-yard line closed the first period of play and not a moment too soon for Giles.

Leon gained four to start the second quarter, but Greg King was immediately stonewalled by Locascio, and the Spartans were up against a third-and-five at their own thirty-two. Steve's thoughts remained bleak. *We can't get anything going.* Trying to jumpstart his offense, Steve called the reverse pass. Taking the handoff from Leon, Mance rolled left and looked for Charlie on the deep route, but the ball was overthrown and intercepted near midfield by corner Dave Bell, who returned it to the Spartans forty-four-yard line before being pushed out of bounds. *Hell's bells.*

As Charlie made his way up the sideline in front of the Giles bench, Steve fiercely instructed his senior captain, "You go in there and tell them they're embarrassing themselves!" he screamed. Charlie could feel his coach's frustration collecting on his face mask.

Allen Pinkett zipped up the middle for seven yards on first down and, with that, topped the century mark, notching 105 yards on the afternoon. In his first ten carries, he had achieved what no other running back had all season against the Lowlife Defense. He showed no signs of slowing down either, as on the next play, he added six, dragging multiple Spartan defenders to the thirty-one-yard line on a quick dive from Nettles.

Pinkett is running all over us.

Giles swapped back to their 6–2 look and, after runs by Bell and Nettles, had Park View in a third-and-three situation. But the Patriots continued their onslaught when Rocky Coppola, spelling Pinkett at tailback, took the toss sweep, broke outside, and got loose down the sideline for seventeen yards before finally being collared by Mark Chapman at the seven. Slow to get up, Chapman was clearly favoring his leg, which would further complicate matters for Steve and the coaching staff.

Pinkett was back in the game on first-and-goal, and Ed Scott returned to 4 Wham, only from a power-I set instead. Before the Giles defense even knew what happened, Pinkett rocketed off-tackle and scored standing up. "Nobody even touched him! Again, a huge hole off the right side, and now things are getting rather serious," voiced Jeff Nichols.

By God, we're getting humiliated.

The touchdown, Pinkett's third, capped a six-play, forty-four-yard drive for the visitors. In a bid to make up for lost points, Scott called the same play on the two-point conversion, but Pinkett was upended short of the goal line. Still, another failed attempt seemed inconsequential because, with 8:07 left in the first half, Park View was up handily, 18–zip. The Spartans had rallied from behind before, but three scores seemed insurmountable. Watching from the stands, Harry was worried plenty.

Steve had long believed teams playing for a state championship were in a totally different category than the rest of the competition, and as he sent his kickoff-return unit into formation for the fourth time, he felt ashamed.

We ought not to even be here. This is out of our league.

Little did he know, their circumstances were about to get even worse. On the resulting kickoff, Mike Grammo attempted a squib kick, but the low line drive inadvertently ricocheted off front lineman Jeff Williams, a freshman skill player who had moved up from junior varsity and been inserted on special teams, and the Patriots' Terrance Lardy recovered at the Giles forty-three. The unthinkable sequence added insult to injury for Steve. *It's 18–0, and it looks like it's going to be 60–0.* Completely shell-shocked, the Lowlife Defense trotted back onto the field to try to stop the bleeding.

CHAPTER 20

RESURGENCE

IT WAS A NIGHTMARE SCENARIO for the Spartans: three turnovers, down 18–0, and Park View had just been gifted an accidental onside kick. *We can't afford to get behind by four touchdowns. That will be the game. It'll be over.*

On first down following the recovery, Allen Pinkett resumed his ground assault, gaining five on a toss sweep. However, a play later, he was submarined by Turd Martin for a one-yard loss, and the Patriots faced a third-and-six from the Giles thirty-nine. Quarterback John Nettles then went to the air. Rolling right, he found tight end Chip Buckman, but the pass fell incomplete along the home sideline, barely off the hands of his intended receiver. As Park View retreated into kick formation, Steve realized his defense had the stop they needed. *Somehow.*

With a three-score advantage and just over six minutes until halftime, Ed Scott had elected to punt in hopes of pinning the Spartans deep in their own territory. Precisely as he intended, Scott Lageman's kick bounced inside the ten-yard line and rolled dead at the five. From the stands watched Lageman's thirteen-year-old brother, Jeff, an up-and-coming football player who also dreamed of leading the Patriots to a state title. "When you're hot, you're hot, and right now, Park View is definitely hot," proclaimed Jeff Nichols.

Steve called 42 Buck to start their next drive, but as soon as Leon caught the pitch from Timmy Martin, he was swarmed under by defensive end Frank Hughlett and barely got out of the end zone, narrowly avoiding a safety at the one-yard line. Steve took note of Hughlett's aggressive play, but the Spartans now had their back against the wall. *We have to get going, or we're going to get buried.*

As they returned to the huddle, Mo peered around the stadium, which was eerily quiet. Behind him, the H-frame goalposts loomed, the vibrant ribbons that spiraled around them like festive barber poles, a sober reminder of the fans' previous enthusiasm. Familiar faces no longer reflected the joyous optimism of pregame but rather a sudden avalanche of bewilderment and dismay. Leon held his emotions in check, but Mo knew he had to be torn up inside. Leon had inspired his teammates countless times with his resilience. It was why they would never surrender. But they hadn't faced a deficit this steep since 1978, Steve's first year at the helm, and Mo understood he needed to speak up.

His eyes met a contingent of Narrows green on the Park View side. It was fitting, as his path, in many ways, began as a sophomore against the Green Wave. Four seniors—Barry Farmer, Greg King, Timmy Martin, and Mo—played that night, and Steve's words afterward remained with them. His numerous lessons, Mo realized, were more than fleeting inspiration but wisdom for the coming climb, an ascent to this very moment. "Come on, boys. Let's keep our heads up," he asserted, spurring them on. They were more than teammates. They were brothers. They were family. The bandana represented unity and hope, but at this juncture, it meant even more—it signified the resurgence of the Giles Spartans!

Leon handed off on the wingback reverse, and Greg Mance found a crease, hopping over a defender and lunging forward to the seven-yard line. The crafty cutback, aided by excellent execution from center Randy Martin, gave the offense room to operate with third-and-eight upcoming.

Steve liked to utilize the passing game with his team backed up in their own end, as he felt most defenses expected them to be conservative and simply run the ball. With that in mind, Leon dropped back to pass in the shadow of his own goal line. He looked over the middle, double-clutched, and rifled a throw to Chris Woods over the twenty to the twenty-six-yard line before he was brought down. This version of 40 Pass proved to be an expert chess move by Steve. "We let them out of a hole," Ed Scott lamented on the Park View sideline. He could immediately sense a shift, like the stirring of a sleeping giant, and he knew his team had missed an opportunity to put the Spartans away.

As the offense moved up the field, Steve relayed the next play from the sideline. He often stood with his hand on the messenger's shoulder as he contemplated, and sometimes, just as they departed for the huddle, he would pull them back to give special instructions. On this occasion, the call was 42 Buck, and drawing seven-man Rodney Freeman toward him, he added, "Tell Greg to block number sixty." Mance was surprised by the adjustment to block Frank Hughlett, as that was not his regular assignment, but the directive had come straight from Coach Ragsdale.

On the snap, the backfield executed the buck-lateral sequence, and Timmy Martin pitched the ball to Leon. Mance blocked down on Hughlett, and when he did so, the outside linebacker, Rocky Coppola, squeezed hard off the edge, thinking the off-tackle play was coming. As Don Sparks pulled wide, he and Leon cleared Coppola, allowing them to reach the perimeter with a full head of steam. Duck then rolled the corner, Ken Sieber, and Leon dashed into the secondary, reviving the home crowd. Safety Joe Boone closed, but Leon made a lightning-quick cut to the inside, leaving Boone grabbing at air as he fell to the ground. A deafening roar followed as Leon snaked back across the grain and into the open field, so loud that Jeff Nichols's call of "He may go all the way!" was barely audible on the radio.

As he crossed midfield, Harold Chafin couldn't contain himself and frantically hollered, "Go, Leon, GO!"

Nichols continued in dramatic fashion: "Thirty-five, thirty, twenty-five, twenty." The Patriots gave chase, but Leon bulleted toward pay dirt. "Fifteen, ten." Dave Bell dove at his feet, but Leon skirted just out of reach. "Five, TOUCHDOWN! And there are no flags!" A seventy-four-yard sprint to glory and a new Group AA state playoff record.

"These Spartans may be down, but they're not out!" declared Chafin emphatically. Ed Scott regretted not having Allen Pinkett on the field defensively, for his speed might have saved the touchdown. Instead, the Bandana Express had seized all the momentum in a single play. Bobby Munsey booted the extra point, and with 4:12 left in the first half, Park View's lead had been trimmed to 18–7.

Midway through the 1979 season, Dave Scarangella had written an article about how the Giles resurgence surprised their coach. At the time, Steve found the word choice ironic, but as he stood in amazement at his fearless little tailback with the heart of a lion, it was finally coming to fruition. He had watched Leon confound opponents since youth league and was reminded how much he revered his competitive drive. Across the field, Scarangella was equally astonished as he scribbled on his extra-long legal pad.

After Munsey's kickoff rolled into the end zone for a touchback, the Lowlife Defense returned to the field looking to get their offense another possession before intermission. Initially, it looked like the Patriots would continue to run roughshod as Pinkett dodged multiple tacklers on his way to eleven yards and another first down on the drive's opening play. But when Ed Scott called his favorite counter with Dave Bell aligned as a wingback, a play the Spartans had explicitly worked on defending, Charlie drilled Bell in the backfield for a one-yard loss. Two plays later, Giles held on third down and, following a time-out and a thirty-yard Scott Lageman punt, got the ball back at their own thirty-six with just over two minutes on the clock.

Steve wasted no time coming back to the buck-lateral series. Leon stayed outside with the pitchout for ten before his brother Greg worked the inside for eight, and the Spartans were across midfield to the Park View forty-six-yard line. Randy Martin operated with sustained precision, showing no evidence of his injury. With the clock running, Greg Mance faked the wingback reverse on the next play, Timmy Martin trapped a penetrating Terry Tretick, and Leon shot up the middle on 47 for ten more. While the running game was moving in bunches, Steve realized he would have to put the ball in the air with the half winding down.

Despite the earlier interception, Steve called the reverse pass from the Patriots thirty-six. Mance took the handoff and, moving left, saw Charlie open deep, but pressure off the edge by Dave Bell, who had been moved to outside linebacker, caused him to retreat back to his right. He peeked at Leon on the throwback but had to take off and could not get out of bounds, forcing Steve to call a time-out with fifty-two seconds to go.

With one time-out remaining, he gave his offense two plays in the huddle. Leon gained three on second-and-eight, and after hustling to the line, Mance attempted once more to get the ball to Charlie on the reverse pass, but while he was open momentarily, the throw was knocked away at the last instant by a diving Allen Pinkett, now in at cornerback.

Staring down fourth-and-five from the Park View thirty-one, Steve reached into his back pocket for the buck-lateral pass. Following the run action, Leon came to a halt, looked deep, and chucked a long throw down the sideline. The ball was slightly underthrown, but Chris Woods came back for it, went up among two defenders, Ken Sieber and Joe Boone, and somehow made a sensational grab at the nine-yard line. It was a completion of twenty-two yards, giving the Spartans a first-and-goal, but the clock was still running at seventeen seconds and counting.

Careful of time management, Steve wanted to run one more play before using his last time-out, and 42 Buck had been Giles's best thus far. Leon took the pitch and bolted to the flank. There was brief running room, but the Park View defense closed fast, and he was corralled at the five-yard line by Sieber, Boone, and a pursuing Tom

Locascio. Steve urgently called his third and final time-out with five seconds remaining.

Believing this would likely be the last play before the half, Steve called blocking back Timmy Martin over to get the call and any points of emphasis. A seasoned signal caller, Martin occasionally joked between plays that he hoped Coach Ragsdale would call "14 Buck," a designed run for the blocking back, and his calm demeanor in the huddle was an anchor for the rest of the offense.

"This'll probably be it for the quarter," predicted Jeff Nichols as the Spartans headed to the line and readied in the single-wing formation. Leon took the snap and, moving right, extended the ball to Greg Mance on the reverse, escorted by pullers Barry Farmer and Turd Martin. But the performance was a ruse—Leon had hidden the ball on his hip and pulled up to pass. Standing on the ten-yard line, he looked right. Chris Woods stayed in to block for maximum misdirection, so Leon peeked at Charlie, dragging across from left end, but he was covered. He looked back left. Mance had carried his reverse fake wide, and Timmy Martin had continued up the seam. Leon hesitated, then hurled a throw to Martin in the middle of the end zone. The entire stadium watched in suspense as the ball fluttered and fell short, nearly intercepted by linebacker Don Presley. The Patriots' defense threw up their hands in celebration, assuming they had made the necessary stop. However, as they turned to the scoreboard, they could not believe their eyes—there was still one second on the clock!

Ed Scott was floored. To the Park View coaches, the play seemed to last an eternity. It was inconceivable to them that there could be any time remaining. "There's no way you can run a play like that in five seconds! I don't understand how any time could be left on the clock," pleaded the dumbfounded Scott. His protest fell on deaf ears, though, and one second remained.

Giles would have one more opportunity from the five-yard line. With a second life, Steve sent the play in with Rodney Freeman: 42 Buck Pass. "Well, we'll see what they try now," said Jeff Nichols just before the snap. After smooth King-to-Martin-to-King ballhandling, Leon rolled right, looking to the end zone. Chris Woods made for the back of the end zone, and Greg Mance blocked for two seconds before releasing on a delayed route into the flats, which put him just inside the goal line.

At the last moment, Leon tossed to Mance. Ken Sieber, who had two interceptions in the semifinal contest against Tabb, was in tight coverage, but Leon delivered a strike at the pylon. Mance leaped, was hit in midair by Sieber, and came down right at the boundary, falling out of bounds. With time expired, Ed Scott peered down the sideline, awaiting the ruling.

"Did he catch it?" exclaimed Jeff Nichols. "*He did!*" The line judge was in position and immediately ruled it a touchdown. "They're saying Park View knocked him out while he was in the air. It is a touchdown, and that's a big, big play," concluded Nichols after some deliberation. In the final two minutes and twelve seconds, the Spartans had marched sixty-four yards in ten plays, but not without controversy. Bobby Munsey added the extra point, and the score was 18–14.

Giles was within striking distance and reinvigorated, but even with the late score, Steve still needed to address the fundamental first-half issue. Until the final five minutes of the second quarter, his team had played like they were afraid to lose. *They just seemed plain scared.* They had let the big-game atmosphere consume them.

Leaving the field, Steve immediately thought of Harry. In his mind, he traveled back to when he first heard the story of his father's halftime speech during the Green Wave's year-end clash with Blacksburg in 1961. Like Steve, Harry had an undefeated squad, but the Indians, captained by Jim Breland, a 1966 consensus All-American at center for Georgia Tech, held an early advantage and headed to the locker room up by a touchdown. Harry's former players still talked about the events that followed nearly two decades later. Steve was just ten years old, but he could still recall how motivated they were after halftime, coming back to win and carrying their coach off the field in triumph.

Steve glanced to where Harry was watching from the stands with his mother, Sarah. His father, who had no doubt chewed his fingernails down to the quick during their turbulent first half, was the greatest mentor he had ever known, a man of immeasurable influence, and he had again provided the necessary insight. Drawing inspiration from Harry's fabled Blacksburg address, Steve decided it was time to send his boys a message of the same tone and tenor. *I need to get them fired up.* As they entered a classroom in the school's agriculture building, he understood exactly what he had to do. *I have to shock these kids.*

CHAPTER 21
SEESAW

I WANT TO SHAKE THEM UP and get them mad so they forget about winning and losing and just go play football. Steve had always encouraged his boys to play with the brakes off, with reckless abandon, and that's how he would approach this halftime speech.

The team had already been sequestered in the agriculture shop classroom for several minutes. The room was filled with rows of tables instead of desks, and the players were seated in chairs behind them, with some standing in the back and around the periphery. They looked pleased with themselves following Leon's five-yard touchdown pass to Greg Mance on the final play of the first half. That is, until Steve came storming in and slammed the door.

On one of the tables up front, the managers had arranged drinks and snacks, including cups of water and Coca-Cola, along with Hershey's chocolate bars for a quick energy boost. Seated nearby was Mark Chapman, who was receiving treatment for his leg, injured tackling Rocky Coppola earlier in the game. Without warning, Steve smacked all the cups off the table, sending liquids flying across the room. Charlie and Turd Martin were sitting at the table where the drinks were located and bore the brunt of the splash. The blowup instantly stirred Charlie's emotions. Already willing to lay his life on the line for Spartan Football, this further intensified his conviction. Turd, on the other hand, generally had a more devil-may-care attitude, but the fit of rage got even him keyed up.

Steve then grabbed a wooden tabletop podium off the teacher's desk and forcefully threw it, sending it crashing loudly onto the floor and into numerous pieces. Its only remaining use would be for kindling. For some of the younger Spartans, the destruction of the podium was the pinnacle in a fog of surreal events. They heard nothing else. For the rest, the rampage inevitably carried on.

Steve was kicking and throwing objects around the room in a frenzy when he suddenly stopped and exploded. "Where's Cecil Austin!" Cecil was likewise seated at the front of the room, and Steve got right in his face and asked, "How many tackles have you made, son?"

"One," replied Cecil plainly.

As expected, Steve's response was apoplectic. His face was red, his eyes were bulged and bloodshot, and white froth had already collected in the corners of his mouth. Some players watched while others looked down, hoping to avoid eye contact with their coach during his blistering tirade. Greg Mance prayed. He had thrown an interception and was terrified he would be next for a verbal undressing.

After that, Steve took aim at someone toward the back of the room, but rather than maneuvering around the tables, he started walking straight through them and then dramatically climbed across. Players scattered as the furniture began to move. To them, the line between motivation and madness had blurred. Finally, he reached his target, Chuck Stone, and the scene continued.

Next was Greg King. "What in the hell are you doing out there letting them run all over top of you?" admonished Steve, merely inches away from him. It was evident he was seeking out members of the defense, particularly on the side that Pinkett had run the off-tackle play so effectively in the first half. Usually calm and jovial, Greg could feel the indignation rising inside him.

As Steve proceeded around the room, he was like a mad dog, sparing none in his path. Spit was flying everywhere as he thundered ferociously for what felt like ten minutes. His language was not for the faint of heart. They had experienced Steve's wrath before, some since the eighth grade, but nothing like this. The usual ass-chewings he doled out paled in comparison, and they were gobsmacked. They had never seen anyone that angry.

When Steve deemed his message adequately delivered, he reviewed their halftime adjustments. He was so animated as he drew on the board that the chalk kept breaking, aggravating him further. He explained that Charlie and Greg King would periodically be asked to switch sides in the second half, giving the Patriots a different look on defense. As with most of their personnel, the two inside linebackers played the right and left, respectively, and did not flip based on the offensive formation.

Occasionally, the session was interrupted by a stray thought that reignited his fury. "All right, ALL RIGHT," he interjected to begin, the volume and pitch of his voice rising sharply. Other times, a coaching point triggered an outburst. "Farmer? *Where's Farmer!*" Eventually, though, he returned and detailed a blocking variation for 42 Buck based on their success at the end of the half. Greg Mance would still block down on defensive end Frank Hughlett, but Chris Woods would now make a short pull and hook the outside linebacker, who would have to squeeze in expectation of the power play, 44. This version was a callback to how Princeton blocked the buck lateral, as depicted in Caldwell's *Modern Single Wing Football*.

Once completed, Steve addressed his team one final time before returning to the field. "Boys, you all don't have to be scared anymore about Park View. You don't need to be scared of losing this football game. You have pretty much taken care of that," he reiterated. By now, they were well aware of how they had played for most of the first two quarters.

"We're not supposed to win this game. We're not even supposed to be here. We've had a great season, and we sure don't have any reason to hang our heads," Steve acknowledged. He was steadily recasting his team as the long shot, the outsider with nothing to lose. At the same time, he called to mind his grandmother's only postgame question: "Who beat?" There could be no moral victory.

"To hell with that—we can beat these guys," he reaffirmed. Chills permeated the room. Steve had challenged all of them, many personally and by name, but while he appeared uncontrollably enraged, every action was measured. He knew precisely whose buttons he could push and how they would respond. He had broken them down and built them back up, and there was light at the end of the tunnel. Leon's long run had restored their confidence, and Mance's last-second catch had them poised to make a comeback. Therefore, instead of becoming discouraged, his fiery halftime rant galvanized their will to win.

"There's just one more thing." They were hanging on Steve's every word. "I'm a Spartan. You're all Giles High School Spartans. You are the masters of the best offense in the country—the single wing. There ain't no way I'm gonna sit on my rear end, feeling sorry for myself, and let a bunch of city boys come down here in my own backyard and take that away from me!" They were at a fever pitch as his speech reached its climax: "By God, go out and WIN this damn ball game!"

At peak enthusiasm, the Spartans prepared to return to action. As Steve left the classroom, he passed Vic Edwards, who had been listening from the hallway. Without stopping, Steve remarked, "You think I got their attention?" and marched toward the outer door. Vic answered in the affirmative, but understood no response was necessary.

Outside, kids with bandanas tied all over them, some as young as three or four years old, lined the fence and watched with admiration as their heroes made their way back to the stadium. Every player was bouncing up and down in anticipation. Leon had finished the first half with 118 yards, while Allen Pinkett had tallied 135, and both backs had averaged over eight yards per carry. Indeed, a duel was shaping up for the second half. With the score 18–14, twenty-four minutes remained to decide a state champion.

Unlike the previous week against Jefferson Forest, Steve instructed Bobby Munsey to boot the ball deep to start the third quarter. The kick was low, took a high bounce over a Park View player, and rolled to a stop at the one-yard line. Pinkett hurried to retrieve the ball and did his best to return it to the fifteen-yard line before the Giles coverage team converged and brought him down. Regardless, it was the worst starting position of the day for the Patriots.

With their lead all but evaporated, Ed Scott knew his team was in a dogfight and encouraged them at halftime to remain composed and focus on what they could control. This became increasingly difficult, however, when Pinkett tested the right side on first down and ran smack-dab into Greg King and Barry Farmer. It was a gain of, at most, one for the junior. "Well, if the first play is any indication, the left side of the defense of Giles made some adjustment there," highlighted Jeff Nichols over the boisterous crowd.

Rocky Coppola carried next on a toss sweep, spinning his way for seven yards before being run down by Cecil Austin, hustling to the perimeter to save a first down. Mark Chapman, playing through pain, helped secure the tackle. Then, on third-and-two, Pinkett went straight ahead but was stuffed short of the marker by an impassioned Greg King, and the Lowlife Defense had forced a three-and-out. It was clear Steve's tactics at intermission were already paying dividends.

Cecil Austin got a decent rush on the resulting Scott Lageman punt, and while it wasn't blocked, the kick was a shank that essentially went straight up and bounced out of bounds near the original line of scrimmage. Once officials sorted it out, the ball was spotted at the twenty-five-yard line. "Whoa, that's a break. Now the Spartans are going to get the ball deep into Park View territory," said Harold Chafin. It was a punt of just one yard, and Giles was in business again.

Looking to cash in on the short field, Steve put the ball back in his top playmaker's hands. Leon took the buck lateral to the edge, and with the ball on the left hash, he had plenty of room to maneuver. The Patriots countered and seemed to have him boxed in, but Leon's fight was unmatched. He eluded defenders, slipping five tackles on his way to nine yards. *Leon King has as good of moves as anybody anywhere.* Two plays later, the Spartans had a fresh set of downs at the Park View fifteen.

Leon then forged ahead on 46, grinding out five tough yards, the picture-perfect blocking scheme honed by hours of repetition under their coach's watchful eye. Steve stayed with six-hole as he sent in the next play but decided on the buck-lateral series instead. Seconds later, Greg King kept on 36 Buck and blasted his way into the end zone for the ten-yard touchdown. With thousands on their feet, videographer Jack Williams panned across the fervent crowd to preserve the moment on 16mm film. "The Spartans are leading for the first time today, and the Spartan crowd is going wild," Harold Chafin reported proudly.

To push the lead to four, Steve elected to go for two. Rolling to his right, Leon found Greg Mance, just as he had on the final score before the half, but this time, Mance could not hold on, and the conversion was waved off—no good. Nevertheless, with 7:26 remaining in the third frame, Giles was on top, 20–18. Jeff Nichols made a fitting observation on WNRV: "This ball game is getting a little bit wild now."

Park View began their next drive on their own twenty-four-yard line. On the first play, John Nettles handed off to Rocky Coppola, but he was leveled almost immediately by Greg King for a two-yard loss. "That was like two trucks running together," Harold Chafin documented for his listeners. "Boy, I tell you, that was a hard lick." Greg continued to play inspired, demonstrating why he was a captain and leader by example. Behind the sticks, Coach Scott took to the air, but after two straight incompletions, it was another three-and-out for the Patriots, their second to start the half. Scott Lageman's punt landed close to midfield and rolled to the Giles forty-three, but the Spartans would again have favorable field position.

Even with the lead and the ball, Steve remained aggressive. Right out of the gate, Leon tried for another explosive play in the passing game, but when he attempted to hit Charlie downfield on a crossing route, the throw was picked off by a leaping Rocky Coppola. Ed Scott and assistant Mike Nunnally waved their arms excitedly as the Park

View outside linebacker returned the interception across the fifty and into Giles territory to the forty-seven-yard line. Despite twenty unanswered points by the Spartans, their fourth turnover suddenly gave their opponents new life.

With momentum teetering, Scott realized the importance of harnessing the opportunity. Revisiting the same quarterback sneak used in the opening quarter, John Nettles took the first-down snap and streaked past unblocked defenders into the secondary before Mark Chapman and Steve Chafin combined for the stop. The strategic one-step draw garnered eleven yards, and the Patriots had something going at the Giles thirty-six.

After notching three on first down, Scott called a speed option play, a design the Spartans had yet to see from the visitors. Attacking down the line to his right, Nettles pitched wide to Allen Pinkett, who cut back toward the middle and, in a flash, knifed through the defense, blazing past the pursuit for a thirty-three-yard touchdown, his fourth. *Pinkett is running crazy.*

At this point, going for two seemed a foregone conclusion. From a power-I set, Pinkett ran a toss sweep around right end, shook off a tackle, and went in standing up for the Patriots' first successful conversion. "This is the most points that's been scored against Giles all year," confirmed Harold Chafin, as with 4:07 left in the third, Park View had retaken the lead, 26–20.

The back-and-forth continued after Greg Mance brought the ensuing kickoff out to his thirty-two-yard line. Together, hauls by Leon and Mance advanced the ball to the forty before Steve ordered the heavy hitter, 44, on third-and-short. Behind a good push up front, Leon carried off-tackle for six and a first down. While it was tough sledding, the run was classic Ragsdale, brash and bare-knuckled, the kind of yardage that made Harry and Steve proud. After the last interception, it also reestablished the Spartans' identity of running the football and controlling the line of scrimmage.

On the next snap, Leon handed to Mance on "21 Reverse," the

outside companion play to their regular wingback counter. Timmy Martin sealed the edge, and Rodney Freeman led Mance into the open field along the home sideline. Terrance Lardy recovered to make the tackle at the Park View forty-five but was flagged for a face mask. It was the game's first penalty and an extra fifteen yards for the Spartans. "The Giles fans up and cheering loudly on that one," Jeff Nichols noted.

Shadows were growing longer as the game neared the fourth quarter. From the thirty-yard line, the Patriots appeared once more to have Leon pinned down, but the wily tailback turned nothing into four yards. Still, after he and brother Greg earned three apiece, Giles was confronted with a fourth-and-inches from just outside the Park View twenty. Steve sent Timmy Martin under center to try to draw the defense offside, but when they didn't jump, he called a time-out, the Spartans' first of the half.

With the decision to go for it never in question, Steve waved Timmy to the sideline to retrieve the directive. As the teams came to the line, Park View's tightly aligned defensive front indicated they were expecting something quick and direct inside, perhaps a wedge or line buck from Greg King. But Steve had other ideas. He called 42 Buck into the boundary, and behind Don Sparks, Leon broke loose up the sideline for ten before being upended by Don Presley inches shy of the ten-yard line. Jeff Nichols marveled at the play call: "Well, I'll tell you, Steve Ragsdale showed some guts there!" Harold Chafin was equally astounded.

Based on the spot, Giles could get another first down inside the one-yard line. Steve came back to the outside reverse, seeking to duplicate the result earlier in the drive. Greg Mance took the handoff from Leon and appeared to have the corner, but Pinkett closed quickly from the secondary, his elite speed helping him limit Mance to a one-yard gain. "Pinkett made some kind of super defensive play to stop Greg Mance," stated Chafin.

The Bandana Express kept pounding, though. On the tenth play of the drive, Greg King faked to Timmy Martin, charged into the line, and steamrolled his way across the goal line on 36 Buck for the nine-yard touchdown. A play not in their single-wing repertoire to start the year, the wide fullback trap was added in preparation for the playoffs and had just produced its second consecutive score to complete an all-important sixty-eight-yard march.

"Championship football at its best," declared Jeff Nichols as Bobby Munsey kicked the extra point, and the Spartans pulled back in front, 27–26. The final twelve seconds ticked away once Pinkett returned Munsey's kickoff to the twenty-five, and the officials wound the clock. After a seesaw third quarter, the game headed to the final stanza with Giles clinging to a one-point advantage.

CHAPTER 22

TICKLED TO DEATH

WHILE KOOL & THE GANG'S hit song "Celebration" was rapidly making its way up the Billboard Hot 100 chart in the first week of December, it would be another nine weeks before it reached number one. In Pearisburg, however, there was set to be a celebration, one way or the other, in just one quarter of play. On the heels of Greg King's second touchdown, the Spartans were ahead 27–26, but Park View was looking to answer, starting at their own twenty-five-yard line.

To begin the drive, the Patriots ran the same option play they had scored with on their last possession. John Nettles worked down the line, but a hard-charging Barry Farmer disrupted his path, causing an early pitch to Terrance Lardy, who was rotating in for Pinkett. With that, Chuck Stone and Greg Mance were able to converge on Lardy and bring him down for a two-yard loss.

Steve was still mixing the defensive fronts, and with Park View in a long yardage situation, he moved from a six-man line to his base 5–2 scheme. Consequently, when Nettles turned to throw on second down, he couldn't find an open receiver and was sandwiched by Barry Farmer and Turd Martin for a sack and a loss of three more. On the sideline, Babette Farmer cheered vigorously for her brother alongside the rest of the Bandanaettes.

On third-and-fifteen, Nettles targeted flanker Dave Bell, but after being flushed from the pocket, the pass was thrown short, and the

Patriots had gone three-and-out in a hurry. Worse yet, Allen Pinkett had not even touched the ball. Scott Lageman's third punt of the half was not fielded by Leon and eventually rolled dead at the Giles forty-three. It was a thirty-seven-yard kick, but the Spartans would have good field position once again with 10:14 left. If ever there was a time for one of the single wing's prolonged and deliberate drives, Steve knew this was it.

After Greg Mance gained two on first down, Leon took flight into opposing territory with nine yards on the buck lateral. To his teammates, Leon's feet were so graceful and acrobatic that he seemed to glide, almost floating on air—like Walter Payton. Off to a promising start, Greg King then churned out six yards of his own. Frank Hughlett nearly stopped him at the line, but Greg kept his feet moving and pinballed his way down to the forty. Striving to stay one step ahead of the defense, Steve followed that up with 47. Leon faked to Mance and scooted up the gut, notching six more, and the drive remained on schedule.

With two first downs, the Bandana Express had moved methodically to the Park View thirty-four-yard line, but that's when circumstances took a turn for the worse. On the next play, Leon slashed off-tackle behind a colossal push from the offensive line, but the Spartans were flagged for holding. It was the first penalty against Giles and a costly one, as holding was still fifteen yards at the high school level. Therefore, the offense was left facing a first-and-twenty-five situation backed up close to midfield. It would take a heroic effort to rebound from this setback.

Greg King got four yards back on first down, but Steve realized they needed a chunk play to have a shot at moving the chains. At which point, Greg King faded back to pass, appearing to look deep before dumping it off to Leon on a screen pass with a convoy of blockers out in front. Mo, Randy Martin, and Barry Farmer escorted Leon down the left hash as he weaved through the Patriots' defense to the twenty-nine-yard line.

While a pickup of sixteen, the Spartans were still short of the sticks with third-and-five upcoming. The catch-and-run did put them in four-down territory, though, and they would need it after Leon advanced the ball just three yards on his next tote, setting up a pivotal fourth-and-two with 6:04 to go in the game.

"This is a big one," stressed Harold Chafin, knowing a first down would enable Giles to continue draining the clock. It would be their third fourth-down conversion attempt of the game. The Spartan players believed in their style of play because, from the time they entered the program, they had heard Steve repeatedly underscore the same idea of toughness, physicality, and attention to detail. Consistent messaging was another lesson he had learned from Harry. So it was no surprise when Turd brought the play call into the huddle: 44.

"Goes to Leon King, right side—he's got it! Cuts inside and gets down to the twenty," broadcast Jeff Nichols. With decisive movement up front, the single wing overwhelmed Park View at the point of attack, and Leon tore off-tackle for six yards. It was his twenty-fifth carry, and he showed no signs of fatigue. More importantly, Giles had overcome the penalty to earn a new set of downs. "That particular series had to really inspire the Spartans and the Spartan faithful," Nichols explained.

Like a machine, Leon added five more on first down, prompting Ed Scott to take a time-out, the Patriots' first of the second half. During the run, Steve watched Don Sparks execute a powerful knockdown block on the six-hole trap and decided to call it again on the next play. Meanwhile, Jeff Nichols was vocalizing the thoughts of everyone in attendance on WNRV: "You don't always get what you expect in these championship games, but today, it's been as advertised."

Out of the time-out, the scoreboard indicated second-and-five at the Park View fifteen-yard line. Leon took the snap on 46 and, following Mo through the hole, artfully sidestepped a defender, skipped outside, and raced toward the pylon. He was met by Allen Pinkett at the end zone, but Leon ran through the attempted tackle, dragging Pinkett across the goal line for the touchdown!

"Leon King made a super move at the flag to go in for the TD, and the Bandana Bunch of Giles High School [are] up on their feet!" Jeff Nichols announced. Leon had gone over two hundred yards rushing on the day and two thousand for the season. The fifteen-yard jaunt was his sixth carry on a ten-play, fifty-seven-yard scoring drive that used over five minutes of clock, and Giles held a seven-point lead, 33–26, with 5:04 remaining.

I want to go for the win right now. With a successful two-point conversion, it would be a two-possession game with time working against the Patriots. But should the gamble fail, Ed Scott's ball club would have a chance to go for the win on a conversion attempt of their own, should they find the end zone in the game's final minutes. *We're going for two to put it out of reach.*

From the three-yard line, Steve wanted to utilize Greg King's power, and with its success in the second half, 36 Buck seemed the logical play call. But the run was stopped short when Dave Bell, who had been inserted at safety, tripped up Greg shy of the goal line, and Park View had life, the score still 33–26. Everyone in attendance, including Steve, knew the door had been left open for the Patriots.

The subsequent kickoff was high and short, and Pinkett took it on the run at the twenty-five. Heading up the middle like a man possessed, Pinkett made it to the Patriots thirty-five before dragging the pile to the thirty-eight-yard line. "That young man makes my all-state team," raved Jeff Nichols.

Terrance Lardy, now playing fullback, slashed off the right side for eight yards on first down before being cut off by Todd Dennis and toppled by Charlie, who was nearing 140 tackles for the season. Steve screamed encouragement to his defense as the clock ticked toward the four-minute mark. On the opposite sideline, Ed Scott considered his next move, opting to revisit 4 Wham, and Pinkett burst across midfield for six, moving the chains to the Giles forty-eight.

After John Nettles advanced the ball three yards on the

quarterback sneak, Ed Scott called Pinkett's number again. This time, the 170-pound running back hit the off-tackle hole and barreled over Greg Mance, coming up from his corner position. Charlie made a shoestring tackle at the thirty-eight-yard line to save the touchdown, but Pinkett continued to gobble up yardage with a gain of seven and another first down.

Greg Mance had played football since the third grade and had never been hit like that. Instead of making a move, Pinkett lowered his shoulder and ran flat over him, stepping on him in the process. Clearing the cobwebs, Greg acknowledged he should not try to square him up again. With under three minutes remaining, Steve called a time-out to settle his defense.

The crowd stood, even during the break, as the tension was building toward an epic finish. On the next play, Nettles faked to Pinkett off-tackle before dropping back on a play-action pass. A quick pump fake and Nettles targeted tight end Joe Boone down the right seam, but the throw was deflected and nearly intercepted by a leaping Mark Chapman. Regardless of Pinkett's exploits on the ground, the Spartans' objective of defending the Park View passing game had been a resounding success, for the Patriots had not completed a pass all afternoon.

On second-and-ten from the Giles thirty-eight, Nettles tossed to Pinkett sweeping left. Mo fought through a double-team to stay outside, but led by Terrance Lardy, Pinkett hit the edge at full throttle. Several Spartans gave chase but to no avail, including Mark Chapman, still hobbled by injury, and Greg Mance, who, like Steve Chafin, learned he could not head him off from across the field, even with a pursuit angle. The Giles coaching staff could only watch as Pinkett blew the doors off the home sideline, motoring untouched for a thirty-eight-yard touchdown.

The Spartan fans could not believe their eyes. Having scored all thirty-two points for Park View, Allen Pinkett had set a new Group AA state playoff record, eclipsing the previous mark set by Mickey

Rogers of Gate City in 1974. Incidentally, his five touchdowns tied another record held by Rogers. More importantly, though, the Patriots had gone sixty-two yards in six plays, and the scoreboard now read 33–32 with 2:45 showing. All that remained was the extra-point decision—kick for the tie or go for two and the lead.

Steve stood with his hands on his hips, peering across at Ed Scott, awaiting the verdict. In the meantime, Mark Chapman left the game, having reaggravated his injured leg, and was replaced at safety by Timmy Martin. Seeing this, Scott decisively signaled for the two-point conversion, just as he had done after the Patriots' three previous scores. Weighing his play call, he held a brief discussion with assistant Mike Nunnally, who doubled as the school's head baseball coach. Nunnally suggested they run the play that had been the most successful, and Scott agreed. Thus, 4 Wham was shuttled into the game with tight end Joe Boone.

Steve sent his defensive unit into their goal-line scheme, which was essentially a 6–5 alignment. *What are they going to do? They've been running Pinkett off-tackle all day long.* Charlie and Mo passionately rallied the troops. They recalled their Thursday-night practice before the Galax game and the eternity of one-on-ones, which finished at the goal line. "Come on, boys, the game's on the line!" the coaches had yelled that night.

With that in mind, Charlie roused the Spartans. "They're not scoring! They're not getting in!"

"Let's go! We're stopping them!" shouted Mo. Within seconds, their message reverberated through the entire defense, their leadership vehemently coursing through the veins of their teammates.

Pinkett surveyed the field as Park View broke the huddle and lined up in the power-I formation. He had been nearly unstoppable, rushing twenty-three times for 224 yards, but the most climactic three yards still lay ahead.

"Nettles . . . gives it to Pinkett," began Jeff Nichols. As soon as the ball was snapped, Chuck Stone crashed inside to collapse the off-tackle opening. Simultaneously, Barry Farmer penetrated inside and, at the last instant, launched his body out toward the hole, the top of his head grazing Pinkett's ankle as he passed. Off balance, Pinkett lunged for the goal line, but as he did so, Charlie arrived, along with Greg King and Greg Mance, to finish him off. Pinkett's helmet lay at the goal line as the officials rushed in to make the call. "He's . . . short of the mark! *Giles holds!*" cried Nichols. The ball had not broken the plane. The Lowlife Defense had stopped Pinkett.

In front 33–32, the legions of bandana backers celebrated wildly. Still, Harold Chafin cautioned everyone when he broke in: "You know, this ball game is far from over . . . There's 2:45 left." With two time-outs, Ed Scott chose not to attempt an onside kick but instead hoped his defense could make a stop and get the ball back. The Spartans would likely need at least two first downs to close it out, and they would start with the ball at their own twenty after the kickoff bounced into the end zone for a touchback.

At this critical juncture, Steve was sure of himself. *There ain't no doubt what I'm going to do—I'm giving the ball to Leon King.* Yet, after consecutive power runs by Leon resulted in two and three yards, respectively, Ed Scott took a time-out. If they could hold on third-and-five, the Patriots and Allen Pinkett would have another opportunity. *If they get it back, I've got my doubts if we can stop them.* Looking on, Harry, too, was concerned.

With 2:02 on the clock, Steve mulled a change of pace. *We've been running off-tackle. Maybe we can trap them and run up the gut.* Intent on staying within the straight series, the play call was 48. On Timmy Martin's signal, Leon caught the snap and headed up the middle, but defensive tackle Tom Locascio had squeezed the trap, and nothing was there. The hole was closed entirely. With nowhere to go, Leon bounced down the line and scooted to the outside. He got past one defender, then another. By the time he evaded a third would-be tackler and picked up the first down, the WNRV broadcast booth was in near hysterics.

"Oh, what a play!" exclaimed Harold Chafin in response to the dazzling eight-yard escape.

"He moves laterally as quickly as anybody I've ever seen," gushed Jeff Nichols. "I didn't think he had a chance in the world of making that first down, and what an important one that is!"

Just amazing. He got past three guys.

Time continued to tick away, and after Leon secured four yards on first down, Ed Scott called his final time-out with 1:27 left. This would be Park View's last gasp. Harry, from his vantage point, understood ball security was paramount.

After the stoppage, Steve called 44 again, and when Leon gained three more, it brought up a third-and-three from the Giles forty with the clock now under one minute. "Not a person has left this stadium," remarked Chafin.

With the game on the line, Steve called his tailback's number for a sixth straight time. Leon started right on 46 and, for a moment, appeared to be stopped. But yet again, he refused to be denied and, on a valiant second effort, dove for the line to gain. "It's going to be very close," said Jeff Nichols. "It all depends on where the officials mark it."

With forty-two seconds remaining, all eyes were on the spot, but for listeners elsewhere, it was the boom of the crowd that let them know he had made it. "They say it's a first down, Harold!" trumpeted Nichols.

"Oh, it is! Oh, what a play!" Chafin interjected. "Seconds ticking off—thirty-nine! We're moving down!" The exhilaration in his voice was unmistakable.

The first down punctuated another career day for Leon, who finished with 229 yards on thirty-three carries. Like Pinkett's failed two-point conversion, his final act was decided by less than a yard. *The margin of victory and defeat.*

After taking the delay-of-game penalty, Greg King downed the ball, and the Bandana Express had done it.

"That's going to be the ball game! The Giles Spartans—the 1980 Group AA state champions for the state of Virginia!" proclaimed Jeff

Nichols. "An undefeated 14–0 season and a tremendous come-from-behind 33–32 victory today!"

"Our boys came through and came through in fine fashion," declared an elated Harold Chafin. "State champions of 19-and-80—the Giles Spartans!"

Disregarding requests to stay clear of the playing surface, fans immediately poured onto the field. Nobody from Giles was willing to miss celebrating with their team.

The scene was magical: Residents from all walks of life joined together. Cheerleader and homecoming queen Ronda Myers was picked up and cradled in the arms of Timmy Martin's older brother, Steve, who had joined the fray. Complete with aviator sunglasses, he reveled in the triumph while she smiled radiantly. *Roanoke Times & World-News* photographer Wayne Deel captured the moment, ideal for the front page of the next day's paper. Martin had called in sick from his job in Roanoke and would surely be fired, but in the present, it was well worth it.

Jim Brewster, principal of Graham High School and member of the VHSL executive committee, presented the state championship trophy to the three captains. Charlie, Mo, and Greg King raised the trophy together, surrounded by a sea of supporters, screaming and raising their index fingers to signal the Spartans' ascension to number one. A grin from Charlie revealed a massive dip of Copenhagen already packed in his lip.

Several players were hoisted aloft and carried around the field, and more than fifteen minutes later, most of the multitude was still in the stadium, waving bandanas and cheering on the newly crowned state champs. It was evident the adoring crowd did not want the celebration to end. Announcer Mullie Mulheren summed it up perfectly over the PA: "What a great day in Giles County! We feel like we're sitting on top of Angel's Rest!"

Bob Whitehead, still station manager at WNRV, joined the radio broadcast, and the topic turned to the significance of the victory. Giles athletic director Gary Clark called the win "the best thing that ever happened to Giles County." The mayor of Pearisburg, Clarence Taylor, later echoed the sentiment, comparing it to the construction of the railroad and the arrival of the Celanese plant. To be sure, what the Bandana Express had accomplished couldn't be measured merely on the gridiron. For the first time since the school opened, players were no longer recognized individually as Pearisburg, Pembroke, Newport, or Eggleston boys. They were now united as Giles Spartans. They had brought a community together.

Finally, amid a throng of followers, the Spartans made their way toward the locker room. There, they were met by Harold Chafin, who had left the press box to conduct on-air interviews. Steve was beaming. His usually gruff presence had melted away. "Congratulations! What a ball game. State champions 1980—how does it feel?" asked Chafin.

Overcome with emotion, Steve responded frankly: "Well, it feels—I don't know what it feels like. It feels fantastic, that's for sure. The kids—I'm so proud of them. I've never been as proud of a bunch of kids in my life. Get down 18–0 like that, right off the bat, and just keep fighting back, and never quit a second—never quit one second—I'm darn proud of them."

After several minutes, Steve was able to corral his players into the gymnasium and talk to them away from all the commotion. Their hearts beat quickly, awaiting his remarks. Despite his young age, Steve was undeniably a father figure, and they sought his approval.

"Boys, nobody has worked any harder than you have," he began. "You've given me everything I have ever asked for. When I wanted a hundred percent out of you, you gave a hundred and ten." They epitomized toughness, and their perseverance had earned his respect. "I want every one of you to look me in the eye—I'm damn proud of you!"

Steve got choked up when he reminisced about the path of his seniors, where they had started, and how far they had come. In many ways, his own journey ran parallel. *I didn't know squat*, he thought, calling to mind the beginning. Indeed, he had learned as much from these boys as they had learned from him, and it had changed him forever. After all the ups and downs, seeing him get sentimental was a powerful image for the players.

Then Steve said something his boys would never forget, something that transcended football. Since his tenure began, the United States and the world had been in a state of unrest. American hostages had been held in Iran for 399 days, and the Soviet Union had invaded Afghanistan, further escalating Cold War tensions. With Vietnam barely in the rearview mirror, the prospect of a reinstated military draft remained on the minds of young men across the country. "If I had to go to war," he said, misty-eyed, "I'd want you right by my side, each and every one of you." American morale had declined in recent years, but in them, Steve saw reason for optimism. "If there are kids in our country like you men here, I feel comfortable in any conflict," he concluded.

Steve didn't shout excessive praise—it wasn't his style—so this meant more than any commendation he had ever given them. In fact, many felt it was the most significant accolade they, or any young man, could earn.

Harry could remember when he, too, had been deeply moved as a coach. In December 1954, 150 of his friends, family, and former players greeted him with a surprise banquet and testimonial dinner to recognize twenty-five years of service to Narrows High School. Modeled after the radio and television program "This Is Your Life," host Brooks Johnson, cocaptain of Harry's first team, traced his career as far back as his college days. His former Lynchburg College mentor, Edward L. Wright, delivered the keynote address. William H. Barrett, his first principal, also spoke. But the finest tribute came from Vic Kreiter, head coach at Pulaski High School, when he said, "Harry Ragsdale is the kind of coach I'd want my own son to play for." It was among his greatest honors in a career worthy of any hall of fame.

Harry had quietly shuffled into the gym to observe Steve's poignant postgame comments. He and his wife, Sarah, had raised Steve with what he termed "fifty percent discipline, fifty percent love," and while his son didn't play high school football, he had lived it all the same. Harry could remember nearly every play of every game he ever coached, but he couldn't recall ever being more proud than he was right then.

Afterward, he told Harold Chafin, "When you spot another team three touchdowns and then come back and win, that's a champion . . . I'm proud of them all. They played a great game, and I'm tickled to death with them." He then made his way around and shook hands with every player, congratulating them on their accomplishment.

The Bandana Express had reached the end of the line for 1980. Fittingly, Queen's "Another One Bites the Dust" played on WNRV. To commemorate their first state championship, Harry tied a red bandana around Steve's neck, a gesture photographed by Jack Williams. It was to be a moment etched in time for Steve Ragsdale. A great start to his coaching career, indeed.

A homemade banner welcomes the Giles Spartans to the 1980 Virginia Group AA state championship game.

Captains Greg King (40), Charlie Mullins (33), and Mike Ratcliffe (64) lead the team out for pregame warm-ups.

With more than ten thousand in attendance, the home stands are packed just prior to kickoff.

Coach Steve Ragsdale gives instructions on the sideline during the first quarter of action.

Allen Pinkett (24) scores his third touchdown as Park View (Sterling) takes an 18–0 lead in the second quarter.

Leon King (43) follows Don Sparks (77) outside on the buck-lateral pitchout late in the first half.

Giles fans display red bandanas in various ways as they cheer on the Bandana Express.

Coach Ragsdale directs Timmy Martin (10) near the sideline ahead of a critical fourth down in the third quarter.

The varsity cheerleaders, known as the "Bandanaettes," watch with anticipation in the second half.

WDBJ Channel 7 (Roanoke) sports reporter Roy Stanley (kneeling) prepares for the next play.

Leon King evades Scott Lageman (56) during his final touchdown run, putting Giles up 33–26 late in the game.

Captains Charlie Mullins, Mike Ratcliffe, and Greg King collectively raise the state championship trophy.

The hometown crowd celebrates the newly crowned state champions following the 33–32 victory.

Coach Ragsdale takes time afterward to answer questions from multiple sportswriters providing coverage.

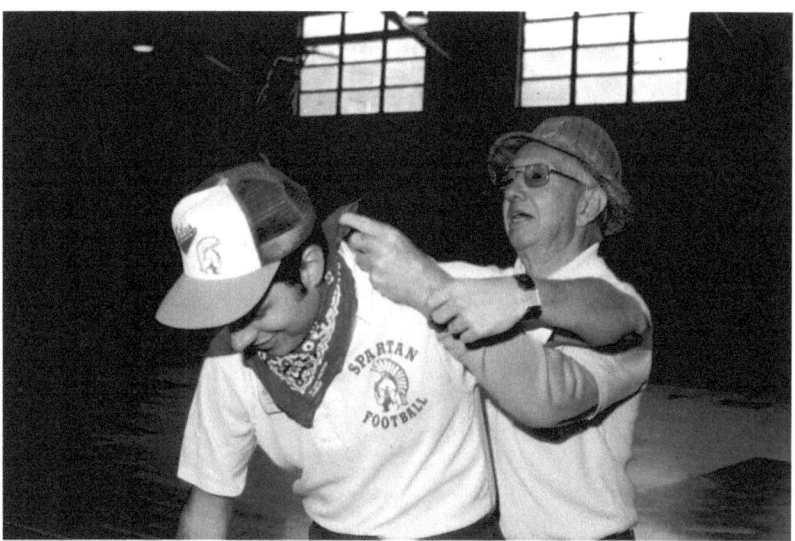

Harry Ragsdale ties a red bandana around his son's neck to commemorate the Spartans' first state title.

The team picture of the 1980 Giles Spartans, the Bandana Express, Virginia Group AA state champions.

NOTES

PROLOGUE

10   *defending state champions:* Mike Judge, "Chargers Old Hands at State," *Bluefield Daily Telegraph* (WV), December 9, 1993.

10   *Steve citing Vince Lombardi:* Lloyd Combs, "Giles Not Slowed by Rain, Mud," *Bluefield Daily Telegraph*, December 6, 1993.

11   *"Every play we run . . .":* Steve Ragsdale, pregame speech, video recording, filmed December 11, 1993.

11   *beloved WDBJ sports reporter Roy Stanley:* Original WDBJ Channel 7 coverage, video recording, aired December 6, 1980.

12   *They had been those kids:* Marty Smith (@MartySmithESPN), "I attended the game. I was four years old," Twitter (now X), February 16, 2023, https://x.com/MartySmithESPN/status/1626262075516370944.

CHAPTER 1

13   *Narrows vs. Blacksburg:* Original 16mm game film, filmed November 10, 1961; "Narrows vs. Blacksburg," original WNRV radio broadcast, aired November 11, 1961; Bill Brill, "Narrows Beats Blacksburg for New River Crown," *Roanoke Times* (VA), November 11, 1961; "Green Wave Champ Again," *Roanoke World-News* (VA), November 11, 1961; "Phlegar Stars in Title Win," *Southwest Times* (Pulaski, VA), November 12, 1961; "Greenies Take 23rd Consecutive Win," *News-Journal* (Radford, VA), November 13, 1961; Marty Horne, "Narrows Adds Another Title," *Roanoke Times*, November 14, 1961; Don Gerald, "Narrows, Minus First Down Til Half, Edges by Indians for League Title," *Montgomery News Messenger* (Christiansburg, VA), November 16, 1961; "Narrows Wins Title, Tops Blacksburg 14–6 in Thriller," *Virginian Leader* (Pearisburg, VA), November 16, 1961.243

13   *When the conditions are right:* "Mountains Give Signs of Weather," *Bluefield Daily Telegraph*, January 17, 1937; "Peters Mountain Termed Truly Unique," *Beckley Post-Herald* (WV), July 6, 1962.

13   *Heavy rain had forced a postponement:* "Rain Plays Havoc with Grid Schedules," *Roanoke Times*, October 21, 1961.

14   *Fans were encouraged to arrive early:* "Big One Friday Night for Wave- Indians," *Virginian Leader*, November 9, 1961.

14   *at Coburn's Department Store: Virginian Leader,* "Narrows Wins Title."

14   *oldest business in town:* Fiftieth Anniversary Historical Committee, *The First Fifty Years: A History of the Town of Narrows 1904–1954* (Giles County Chamber of Commerce, 1956), 20.

14   *rocks on a nearby hillside: Virginian Leader,* "Narrows Wins Title."

14   *the town of 2,500:* US Census Bureau, "1960 Census of Population, General Population Characteristics, Virginia." https://www2.census.gov/library/publications/decennial/1960/population-volume-1/09768066v1p48ch3.pdf.

14   *new sports editor:* "Bill Brill Named Times Sports Editor," *Roanoke Times*, September 10, 1961.

14   *their daytime license:* "History," WNRV The Ridge, New River Interactive Media, LLC, https://millcreek.wnrvbluegrassradio.com/history-html.

14   *held his post longer:* "Narrows High Coach Honored," *Roanoke Times*, December 12, 1954.

14   *Norfolk & Western passenger train:* "Ragsdale Retires: 'Coach' Ends 43 Year Career at Narrows High," *Virginian Leader*, July 18, 1973.

15   *lucky to win two or three games:* "New River District," *Roanoke Times*, September 3, 1961.

15   *a perfect 8-0 record:* "Narrows and Blacksburg in Tonight's Timesland Scholastic Grid Feature," *Roanoke Times*, November 10, 1961.

15   *newly formed in 1960:* "District 6 Splits into Three Groups," *Roanoke Times*, November 3, 1959.244

15   *first locked horns in 1936:* "Narrows Shuts Out Blacksburg, 12 to

	0," *Roanoke Times*, October 24, 1936; "Narrows High Eleven Trims Blacksburg, 12–0," *Bluefield Daily Telegraph*, October 24, 1936.
15	***On that afternoon:*** "Green Wave May See Records Smashed by Martinsville 11," *Narrows News* (VA), September 19, 1940.
16	***he was hired in 1959:*** "Ken Stickley to Coach Football at Blacksburg," *Roanoke Times*, June 5, 1959; "Ken Stickley New Coach for Indians," *Montgomery News Messenger*, June 11, 1959.
16	***made the move to fullback mid-season:*** "Breland, BHS All-State Candidate, So Versatile That It's Hard to Figure Where to Play Him," *Montgomery News Messenger*, October 26, 1961.
16	***most sought-after high school player:*** Ozzie Worley, "Sports Stuff," *Roanoke World-News*, November 11, 1961; Marty Horne, "Sought-After Dan Phlegar Leans Toward Scholarship in Virginia," *Roanoke Times*, December 6, 1961; "Phlegar is State's Best," *Virginian Leader*, December 7, 1961.
17	***the first touchdown the previous year:*** "Narrows Stays Undefeated, 30–6" *Roanoke Times*, October 22, 1960; Rocky Vaught, "Narrows' 30–6 Win Called Poor Effort," *Roanoke World-News*, October 22, 1960; "Narrows Hi Team Clobbers Blacksburg 30–6" *Sunset News-Observer* (Bluefield, WV), October 22, 1960.
18	***at the age of 98:*** Associated Press, "Coach Stagg Says Age 98 Is Good Retirement Time," *Roanoke Times*, September 17, 1960.

CHAPTER 2

22	***Giles vs. Graham (Scrimmage):*** Original 16mm game film, filmed August 26, 1978; Stubby Currence, "Graham, Bluefield Collide Friday," *Bluefield Daily Telegraph*, August 29, 1978.
22	***bench press over 300 pounds:*** "Veteran G-Men Top SWD Pick," *Bluefield Daily Telegraph*, August 27, 1978; Bob Foley, "'What's Up Front' Graham Strong Point," *Bluefield Daily Telegraph*, September 13, 1978.245
22	***just three months earlier:*** "Steve Ragsdale Named Football Coach at GHS," *Virginian Leader*, May 10, 1978.

23	*thirty-two-game winning streak:*	Bob Adams, "Narrows Wallops Dublin by 32–14 for 32nd Victory," *Roanoke Times*, November 13, 1962.
23	*as the town's mayor:*	"3 New Council Are Elected in Narrows," *Bluefield Daily Telegraph*, May 5, 1976.
23	*their thirty-ninth wedding anniversary:*	"Sara Simmons Is Wed Saturday to Harry Ragsdale," *Roanoke Times*, August 27, 1939; "Summer Season Climaxed with Nuptials of Popular Couple Here Saturday Afternoon," *Narrows News*, August 31, 1939.
23	*When Carlock arrived at Graham:*	Ken Clay, "Carlock Named Graham Coach," *Bluefield Daily Telegraph*, May 11, 1973.
24	*So when the G-Men blanked Bluefield:*	Stubby Currence, "G-Men Take 13–0 Win Over Beaver," *Bluefield Daily Telegraph*, September 7, 1974.
24	*both schools had shared since 1936:*	Stubby Currence, "Beavers Cash In on Long Runs and Breaks to Hand Graham 13 to 2 Defeat," *Bluefield Daily Telegraph*, November 12, 1936.
24	*Hall of Famer "Bullet" Bill Dudley:*	"Graham Flogs Princeton 10–7," *Bluefield Daily Telegraph*, November 20, 1937.
24	*Every game we're in:*	"Giles Spartans Face Lean Year," *Bluefield Daily Telegraph*, August 27, 1978.
24	*Third-year southpaw:*	*Bluefield Daily Telegraph*, "Veteran G-Men."
24	*one of ten seniors:*	*Bluefield Daily Telegraph*, "Veteran G-Men."
25	*had won a state title:*	"Bradley Happy to Win Crown but Sorry for Salem," *Bluefield Daily Telegraph*, December 1, 1962.
25	*Even Virgil L. "Stubby" Currence:*	Stubby Currence, "The Press Box," *Bluefield Daily Telegraph*, August 26, 1978.
25	*coined the name "G-Men":*	"The Stubby Currence Project," Melissa Currence, https://stubbycurrence.com; "Graham High School: A Storied History," Tazewell County Public Schools, accessed January 29, 2017, http://ghs.tazewell.k12.

va.us/?PageName=%27AboutTheSchool%27.246

25   *"Games aren't won on paper . . .":* Bluefield Daily Telegraph, "Veteran G-Men."

25   *He also excelled academically:* "Ragsdale Member of Who's Who," *Virginian Leader*, May 9, 1973.

26   *Steve knew his biggest challenge:* Bluefield Daily Telegraph, "Giles Spartans Face Lean Year."

27   *prime collegiate prospects:* Bluefield Daily Telegraph, "Veteran G-Men."

27   *physical and mental toughness:* Bluefield Daily Telegraph, "Giles Spartans Face Lean Year."

28   *best athletes didn't want to play:* Bluefield Daily Telegraph, "Giles Spartans Face Lean Year."

28   *Boys in Narrows grew up:* Marty Horne, *"Winning Football Tradition At High School In Narrows,"* Roanoke Times, October 13, 1961.

CHAPTER 3

30   *Giles vs. Narrows:* Original 16mm game film, filmed September 15, 1978; "Narrows 48, Giles 0," *Roanoke Times & World-News* (VA), September 16, 1978; "Narrows Crushes Spartans, 48–0," *Bluefield Daily Telegraph*, September 16, 1978; Dwight Lucas, "Wave Massacres Giles in 48–0 Rout," *Virginian Leader*, September 20, 1978.

30   *even the buildings in Narrows:* Jerry Ratcliffe, "Game Plan," *Blacksburg Sun* (VA), November 2, 1977.

30   *what he called Formation A:* Glenn Scobey Warner, *Football for Coaches and Players* (Stanford University, 1927), 130-137.

31   *Harry patterned his early offense:* Marty Horne, "Reign Ends for Ragsdale at Narrows," *Roanoke Times*, April 21, 1963.

31   *Naval active duty:* Horne, "Reign Ends for Ragsdale."

31   *head coach at Princeton University:* Charles W. Caldwell, *Modern Single Wing Football* (J.B. Lippincott, 1951).

31   *Narrows ran the Princeton offense:* Horne, "Reign Ends for Ragsdale"; 247 *Virginian Leader*, "Ragsdale Retires."

32   *While some Giles players:* Dave Scarangella, "Giles' Single Wing Double Trouble," *Roanoke Times & World-News*, October 14, 1980.

32   *with a 22–6 victory:* Eddie Sutphin, "Spartans Surprise Fort Chiswell 22–6," *Blacksburg Sun*, September 3, 1978; Thomas Stafford and John Thacker, "Pioneers Lose Opener to Power Laden Giles County Spartans," *Southwest Virginia Enterprise* (Wytheville, VA), September 5, 1978; Dwight Lucas, "Giles Eleven Plows Pioneers Under," *Virginian Leader*, September 6, 1978.

32   *shut out 16–0 by Floyd County:* "Spartans Stunned by Floyd County," *Bluefield Daily Telegraph*, September 9, 1978; "Floyd Co. 16, Giles 0," *Roanoke Times & World-News*, September 9, 1978; "Buffs Bust Spartans in 16–0 Contest Here," *Virginian Leader*, September 13, 1978; "Buffs Blank Giles 16–0," *Floyd Press* (VA), September 14, 1978.

32   *multi-tiered concrete bleachers:* "Narrows Builds School Stadium," *Roanoke Times*, November 3, 1940; "Concrete Stadium Work Is Underway for Local School," *Narrows News*, November 7, 1940.

32   *by the time Harry was commissioned:* "Martinsville and Narrows Will Play," *Roanoke Times*, September 18, 1942; "Prominent Narrowsonian Is Dead," *Virginian Leader*, November 16, 1983.

33   *including lights and fencing:* "Appalachian Directors Increase Limit on Players to 18," *Southwest Times*, May 2, 1946.

33   *Patteson accepted the post:* Dave Scarangella, "Coaches Leaving NRD," *Blacksburg Sun*, July 24, 1977; "Wave's Patteson Tries a New Game," *Blacksburg Sun*, August 28, 1977.

34   *Coach of the Year honors:* "Patteson is Coach of Year in District," *Virginian Leader*, November 30, 1977; "Narrows' Patteson Named Coach of the Year," *Roanoke Times & World-News*, December 13, 1977.

34 *In October of 1930:* "County High School Basket Ball Schedule," *Pearisburg Virginian*, October 16, 1930; *Virginian Leader*, "Ragsdale Retires."

35 *predicted a possible decline:* Rocky Vaught, "Championship Is No Surprise to Fans of Coach Ragsdale," *Roanoke World-News*, November 3, 1960.

35 *Hot Rod had purchased:* Dave Scarangella, "'Green Wave Power' Reigns in Narrows," *Roanoke Times & World-News*, November 6, 1979.

36 *but the 1978 edition:* "Narrows Seeking Repeat of 1977," *Bluefield Daily Telegraph*, August 27, 1978; "Wave Looks for Break," *Blacksburg Sun*, August 27, 1978.

37 *34–0 shutout of Alleghany:* "Narrows Green Wave Rolls to 34–0 Victory," *Bluefield Daily Telegraph*, September 3, 1978.

37 *24–0 blanking of George Wythe:* "Narrows Decisions GW," *Bluefield Daily Telegraph*, September 9, 1978.

CHAPTER 4

39 *Giles vs. Blacksburg:* Original 16mm game film, filmed September 22, 1978; "Blacksburg 10, Giles 0," *Roanoke Times & World-News*, September 23, 1978; Roland Lazenby, "Ailing Blacksburg Struggles with Spartans," *Blacksburg Sun*, September 24, 1978; Dwight Lucas, "Giles Spartans Give Indians a Scare," *Virginian Leader*, September 27, 1978.

40 *thirty-one-year-old Dave Crist:* Quintin Gustin, "New Coach Arrives Just in Time," *Blacksburg Sun*, August 13, 1975.

40 *served as the head coach himself:* "Name Lacy Brown New B'bg Coach," *Montgomery News Messenger*, March 8, 1951.

40 *arrival from East Tennessee State College:* "Savages List 10 Game Schedule to Start Sept. 9," *Montgomery News Messenger*, August 11, 1949.

41 *they slipped past Covington:* Dave Scarangella, "Indians Scalp Cougars on Last Minute Score," *Blacksburg Sun*, November 27, 1977.

41	*defeated Southampton:* Dave Scarangella, "Cinderella Blacksburg Wins State Crown," *Southwest Times*, December 4, 1977.
42	*the most challenging aspect:* "BHS Gets Single-Wing Test," *Blacksburg Sun*, September 20, 1978.
42	*increasingly depleted roster:* Roanoke Times & World-News, "Blacksburg 10, Giles 0."
42	*lost to injury in the preseason:* Roland Lazenby, "Knees Bring Rough Road," *Blacksburg Sun*, September 20, 1978.
43	*Bill Patteson and Bill Brown:* Gary Baker, "Blacksburg Faces Spartans," *Blacksburg Sun*, September 26, 1979.
43	*Steve was thrilled:* Roland Lazenby, "Ragsdale Elated Over Close Game," *Blacksburg Sun*, September 24, 1978.
43	*back to Blacksburg from Texas:* Roland Lazenby, "New Formation Helps Coleman," *Blacksburg Sun*, September 27, 1978.
43	*harder than he had all season:* Lazenby, "Ragsdale Elated."
45	*Thomas and Tabitha Ragsdale:* Virginian Leader, "Prominent Narrowsonian Is Dead"; US Census Bureau, "Virginia, Lunenburg County, 1930 US census, population schedule," accessed June 28, 2011, https://www.ancestry.com.
45	*a tobacco-farming community:* Gay Weeks Neale, *The Lunenburg Legacy* (Luneburg County Historical Society, 2005).
45	*president of the student body:* "Ragsdale, Bell and Austin Nominated," *Critograph* (Lynchburg, VA), September 25, 1929; "With the Seniors: Harry Ragsdale," *Critograph*, March 12, 1930; Lynchburg College, *Argonaut* (Lynchburg, VA: 1930), 41; "Harry Ragsdale Dies; Ex-Coach Mayor in Narrows," *Roanoke Times & World-News*, November 10, 1983; *Virginian Leader*, "Prominent Narrowsonian Is Dead."
45	*lineman for the Hornets:* Lynchburg College, *Argonaut* (Lynchburg, VA: 1930), 94.
45	*"meanest and roughest bunch of boys":* Virginian Leader, "Ragsdale Retires."

46 *at the Virginian Railway power plant:* Sam R. Pennington, "Virginian Railway Feature," *Sam R. Pennington's Feature Stories Magazine*, June 1933.

46 *taken the job sight unseen:* Horne, "Reign Ends for Ragsdale."

46 *for $115 a month: Virginian Leader*, "Ragsdale Retires"; Frank K. Stafford, "A Study of Secondary Education in Giles County" (master's thesis. University of Virginia, 1933), 79.

46 *Chesapeake & Potomac Telephone Company: Roanoke Times & World-News*, "Harry Ragsdale Dies."

46 *"I was scared to death": Virginian Leader*, "Ragsdale Retires."

46 *"I didn't like it at first":* Horne, "Reign Ends for Ragsdale."

46 *"In the first game we played": Virginian Leader*, "Ragsdale Retires."

46 *27–0 win over Eggleston:* "Narrows High Blanks Eggleston Team, 27–0" *Roanoke Times*, October 11, 1931.

46 *"In 1938, Culpeper wouldn't play": Virginian Leader*, "Ragsdale Retires."

47 *even a team without a coach:* "Narrows Rolls Over Blacksburg, 22 to 0," *Roanoke Times*, September 14, 1941.

47 *The 1946 Narrows Green Wave:* "Pearisburg Wins Over Narrows, 25–0," *Roanoke Times*, November 9, 1946.

47 *Bob Lawson's Christiansburg club:* Christiansburg High School, *Demon* (Christiansburg, VA: 1948), 46.

CHAPTER 5

48 *Giles vs. Graham (Scrimmage):* Original 16mm game film, filmed August 24, 1979.

49 *trounced the Narrows Jaycees, 52–0:* "Pembroke Recreation," *Virginian Leader*, October 20, 1976; "Pembroke Wins Football Title with 6–0 Record for the Season," *Virginian Leader*, December 8, 1976.

49 *a 22–20 thriller to Blacksburg:* "Blacksburg Braves Nip Spartans,

22–20," *Blacksburg Sun*, September 25, 1977.

50   *competitive fire:* Dave Scarangella, "Giles' Leon King 'Likes to Do Things His Own Way,'" *Roanoke Times & World-News*, December 4, 1980.

50   *had fallen to Radford, 32–14:* Eddie Sutphin, "Bobcats Overpower Giles Spartans, 32–14," *Blacksburg Sun*, October 1, 1978; Dwight Lucas, "Scrappy Spartans Bow 32–14 to Radford 'Cats," *Virginian Leader*, October 4, 1978.

50   *and George Wythe, 26–6:* "George Wythe 26, Giles 6," *Roanoke Times & World-News*, October 7, 1978; Dwight Lucas, "Maroons Spoil Giles Homecoming 26–6" *Virginian Leader*, October 11, 1978.

50   *Phillip Oliver ran wild:* Christiansburg 26, Giles 6," *Roanoke Times & World-News*, October 14, 1978; Michael Connally, "Oliver Runs Over Giles; Demons Win," *Blacksburg Sun*, October 15, 1978; Dwight Lucas, "Demons' Oliver Runs Wild Over Spartans," *Virginian Leader*, October 18, 1978.

51   *It was October 1932:* Charlie Adair Jr., "Narrows VA," *Bluefield Daily Telegraph*, October 23, 1932; "Locals Lose to Narrows 18 to 6," *Montgomery News Messenger* (Christiansburg, VA), October 26, 1932; Narrows High School, *Narrosonian* (Narrows, VA: 1933).

51   *Lynchburg College teammates, Robert Gerald:* Lynchburg College, *Argonaut* (Lynchburg, VA: 1930), 94; "William R. Gerald Dies at 79; Former Teacher, VA counselor," *News-Journal* (Wilmington, DE), December 27, 1984.

51   *Captain George Pearis:* "Captain George Pearis (1746–1810)," Family Search, https://ancestors.familysearch.org/en/L4HW-MPV/captain-george-pearis-1746-1810.

51   *losing 7–0 to Lane High School:* "Title Contest Is Hard Fought," *Roanoke Times*, December 4, 1927.

51   *the 1933 Narrosonian confirmed:* Narrows High School, *Narrosonian* (Narrows, VA: 1933).

51   *shocked the Bobcats a year earlier:* David J. Bisset, "Narrows

Shocks Unbeaten Radford," *Southwest Times*, November 6, 1977; "Wave Routs Radford for Best Season in Decade," *Virginian Leader*, November 9, 1977.

51 *dispatching the Spartans 34–14:* "Galax 34, Giles 14," *Roanoke Times & World-News*, November 4, 1978; Dwight Lucas, "Spartans Steam Rolled by Maroon Tide 34–14," *Virginian Leader*, November 8, 1978.

52 *Vince Lombardi on Football:* George L. Flynn, ed., *Vince Lombardi on Football* (Wallynn Inc., 1973).

54 *"like climbing a mountain":* "Spartans Hope to Turn Corner," *Blacksburg Sun*, September 2, 1979.

54 *"anywhere from mediocre to poor,":* Dave Scarangella, "Giles Resurgence Surprises Coach," *Roanoke Times & World-News*, October 11, 1979.

54 *"just treading water":* Blacksburg Sun, "Spartans Hope to Turn Corner."

55 *"just not as experienced":* Bob Foley, "Graham Young But Talent-Laden," *Bluefield Daily Telegraph*, September 2, 1979.

55 *district's hundred-yard dash champion:* Craig Nesbit, "Indians Run Away with Track Titles," *Southwest Times*, May 13, 1979.

56 *because he loved it:* Scarangella, "Giles' Leon King."

CHAPTER 6

57 *Giles vs. Narrows:* Original 16mm game film, filmed September 22, 1979; "Cook Leads Narrows to Win," *Roanoke Times & World-News*, September 23, 1979; "Narrows Whips Giles," *Bluefield Daily Telegraph*, September 23, 1979; "Narrows Beats Spartans 28–13, Defense Tough, Cook Runs Hard," *Virginian Leader*, September 26, 1979.

57 *estimated 5.9 magnitude earthquake:* "Shaking Up Ole Virginny," *Roanoke Times*, June 1, 1897; Margaret G. Hopper and G.A. Bollinger, *The Earthquake History of Virginia, 1774–1900* (Dept. of Geological

Sciences, Virginia Polytechnic Institute and State University, 1971), 55– 66; Gil Bollinger, "The Giles County Earthquake of 1897 — Virginia's Largest Temblor," *Smithfield Review* 2 (1998): 65-75; "The 1897 Giles County Earthquake, Virginia," US Geological Survey, US Department of the Interior, https://earthquake.usgs.gov/ earthquakes/eventpage/ ushis334/region-info.

57 *in prime time for NBC:* "1979 Orange Bowl: Oklahoma vs Nebraska," aired on January 1, 1979, on NBC, video recording.

57 ***Lott had gained publicity:*** Berry Tramel, "Switzer Tales: Washington's Silver Shoes, Lott's Bandana," *Oklahoman* (Oklahoma City, OK), May 13, 2010.

58 *the bandana his trademark as well:* Bob Foley, "The Giles Spartans: Call Them the Bandana Bandits," *Bluefield Daily Telegraph*, November 23, 1980.

58 *over Fort Chiswell, 33–8:* "Giles 33, Fort Chiswell 8," *Roanoke Times & World-News*, September 8, 1979; "Spartans Open with 33–8 Win over Visiting Fort Chiswell," *Virginian Leader*, September 12, 1979.

58 *Floyd County, 46–6:* "Giles 46, Floyd 6," *Roanoke Times & World-News*, September 15, 1979; Tom Kane, "Spartans Destroy Buffaloes 46–6, to Up Season Mark to 2–0," *Virginian Leader*, September 19, 1979.

58 *While graduation claimed:* Bob Foley, "Narrows: Tidal Wave on Horizon?" *Bluefield Daily Telegraph*, September 2, 1979; "Wave Hunting Another Title," *Blacksburg Sun*, September 2, 1979; Ken Rakes, "Wave in Running for Grid Title," *Virginian Leader*, September 5, 1979.

58 *"Narrows is big,":* "Fortunes Turn on Breaks, Injuries," *Virginian Leader*, September 5, 1979.

59 *something else was circulating:* Foley, "The Bandana Bandits."

60 *What in the world is going on:* Foley, "The Bandana Bandits."

62 *still echoed the sentiment:* Scarangella, "Green Wave Power."

62 *on a Green Wave victory:* Scarangella, "Green Wave Power."

62   *the Celanese plant:* "Giles Textile Plant Is Nearly Finished," *Roanoke Times*, December 17, 1939; "Celco Process to Start Dec. 26," *Narrows News*, December 21, 1939; *Giles County, Virginia: History – Families* (Giles County Historical Society, 1982), 389.

63   *had their own version:* Foley, "The Bandana Bandits."

66   *why he was being recruited by:* Foley, "Tidal Wave."

CHAPTER 7

67   *Giles vs. Radford:* "Giles Shuts Out Radford 27–0," *Roanoke Times & World-News*, October 6, 1979; "Giles Topples Bobcats," *Bluefield Daily Telegraph*, October 6, 1979; Craig Nesbit, "Spartans Take Advantage of 'Cats Mistakes," *Blacksburg Sun*, October 7, 1979; "Giles Ties Indians for Second Place in NRD Gridiron Standings," *Virginian Leader*, October 10, 1979.

67   *his team's 6–6 tie with Blacksburg:* "Giles Ties Blacksburg 6–6," *Roanoke Times & World-News*, September 30, 1979; "Giles Ties," *Bluefield Daily Telegraph*, September 30, 1979; Jane Kuhn, "Blacksburg, Giles Tie in 6–6 Shocker," *Blacksburg Sun*, September 30, 1979; Tom Kane, "Spartans Tie Up Indians, 6–6 in Tough Defensive Game Here," *Virginian Leader*, October 3, 1979.

67   *He told Bob Foley:* Bob Foley, "Big Night for Wave, Giles," *Bluefield Daily Telegraph*, October 5, 1979.

67   *He went a step further:* Basil Parsell, "Giles High Spartans," *Virginian Leader*, October 3, 1979.

68   *We should have won:* Foley, "Big Night."

68   *called the 6–6 stalemate:* Kuhn, "6–6 Shocker."

68   *"almost pulled off the upset":* Roanoke Times & World-News, "Giles Ties Blacksburg."

68   *"We gave Narrows two touchdowns":* Foley, "Big Night."

69   *had penned the headline:* David J. Bisset, "Bobcats Entertain Red, Bandana Spartans," *News-Journal*, October 5, 1979.

70 *November of 1934:* "Narrows Trims Radford High School, 18 to 6," *Roanoke Times*, November 11, 1934.

70 *Kenneth Hall had first suggested:* David J. Bisset, "'33 Team Enjoys Homecoming," *News-Journal*, October 30, 1983.

70 *captain of the 1934 eleven:* "Narrows, VA," *Bluefield Daily Telegraph*, September 16, 1934.

70 *infamously branded the "Dust Bowl":* "Athletic Field Called All-American Dust Bowl," *News-Journal*, November 17, 1964; Ralph Berrier, "Stadium Had Good Start at Goal," *News-Journal*, February 23, 1992; David J. Bisset, "RHS Athletic Boosters Are Making a Difference," *News-Journal*, March 20, 1999.255

70 *new stadium opened in 1967:* "New Coach, Offense, Stadium Greet Team," *News-Journal*, October 13, 1967.

70 *the new superintendent:* "Harold Absher Named New Superintendent," *Virginian Leader*, August 29, 1979.

70 *championships in 1971 and 1972:* David J. Bisset, "Happiness Is Being #1!" *News-Journal*, December 6, 1971; David J. Bisset, "Bobcats Crush Southampton Indians 41–20 to Capture 2nd Straight State Championship," *News-Journal*, December 11, 1972.

71 *turned the job down:* David J. Bisset, "Lineburg Says No to Salem," *News- Journal*, May 30, 1979.

71 *tragedy struck:* David J. Bisset, "RHS Youth Dies After Track Injury," *News- Journal*, April 11, 1979.

71 *victory over Carroll County, 19–15:* David J. Bisset, "Key Plays Lift Cats," *News-Journal*, September 30, 1979.

71 *had not had a losing season:* "Tradition: Bobcat Success Stems from Dedication, Pride," *Blacksburg Sun*, September 2, 1979.

71 *Bobcats' 0–10 season of 1962:* "Giles County Upends Bobcats 14–12 in Season's Last Game," *News-Journal*, November 14, 1962.

71 *By Friday, Steve had decided:* Bisset, "Bandana Spartans."

71 *Steve emphasized readiness:* Parsell, "Giles High Spartans,"

October 3, 1979.

74   *We've got so far to go:* Scarangella, "Giles Resurgence."

CHAPTER 8

75   *Giles vs. George Wythe:* "George Wythe Edges Giles County," *Roanoke Times & World-News*, October 13, 1979; "Wythe Nips Spartans," *Bluefield Daily Telegraph*, October 13, 1979; "Maroons' DuPuis Stops Spartans," *Blacksburg Sun*, October 14, 1979; "Maroons Trip Spartans in Homecoming Win," *Southwest Virginia Enterprise*, October 16, 1979; Tom Kane, "George Wythe Edges Giles, 7–6, Spartans Drop to 5th Place," *Virginian Leader*, October 17, 1979.256

75   *"Giles is this year's surprise team":* Bob Foley, "G-Men Face Tough Test at VHS," *Bluefield Daily Telegraph*, October 12, 1979.

77   *a feature by a young sportswriter:* Scarangella, "Giles Resurgence."

77   *if we met them this week:* Scarangella, "Giles Resurgence."

77   *don't know how we'll do:* Scarangella, "Giles Resurgence."

77   *into the Timesland Top 10:* "Northside Leads Prep Poll," *Roanoke Times & World-News*, October 12, 1979.

78   *Spartans took Pendleton Field:* "The New Stadium Will Be the Star," *Southwest Virginia Enterprise*, September 5, 1978.

78   *6–0 and 21–20 losses to Blacksburg and Radford:* Roland Lazenby, "Indians Nip George Wythe in Mud Bath." *Blacksburg Sun*, October 15, 1978; David J. Bisset, "Bobcats Escape Scare, Edge Maroons," *Blacksburg Sun*, October 22, 1978.

78   *all that prevented the Maroons:* Bob Foley, "Few Numbers a Big Problem for GW Team," *Bluefield Daily Telegraph*, September 2, 1979.

79   *a school-record 240 yards against Giles:* "'Good Moves' Boost Woods," *Roanoke Times & World-News*, October 10, 1978.

79   *good nucleus of returning starters:* "George Wythe to Steamroll Enemy," *Blacksburg Sun*, September 2, 1979.

79   *Head coach Chet Brown:* Bob Johnson, "Brown Has Good Record

at Wytheville," *Roanoke Times*, September 25, 1940.

79 *first met Narrows in 1937:* "Narrows Beaten by Wytheville in Late Rally," *Roanoke Times*, November 6, 1937; "Narrows Nosed Out by Wytheville Eleven 12–7 in Exciting Engagement," *Bluefield Daily Telegraph*, November 7, 1937; "W.H.S. Downs Narrows Team by Score of 12–7," *Southwest Virginia Enterprise*, November 9, 1937.

79 *arrived from Hopewell in 1946:* "Wytheville Meets Narrows Tonight," *Roanoke Times*, September 20, 1946.

79 *added two District Six titles:* "Maroons Find Success Under Leslie Parson," *Roanoke Times*, November 20, 1951.

79 *was built in 1951:* Raymond Colley, "Wytheville Grid Prospects Cheery While Marion Hopes for the Best," *Roanoke Times*, September 1, 1951; "GWHS History," George Wythe High School, Wythe County Public Schools, https://gwhs.wythe.k12.va.us/about_g_w_h_s/g_w_h_s_history.

79 *be ready before it starts:* Basil Parsell, "Giles High Spartans," *Virginian Leader*, October 17, 1979.

79 *to be excellent against misdirection:* *Blacksburg Sun*, "George Wythe to Steamroll."

80 *when you're not ready to play:* Parsell, "Giles High Spartans," October 17, 1979.

81 *in a position of winning before:* Parsell, "Giles High Spartans," October 17, 1979.

82 *a 39–14 loss to Dublin:* "Dublin Subdues Narrows, 39–14" *Roanoke Times*, October 10, 1959.

83 *a high school All-American:* Associated Press, "Dan Phlegar on All-Star Grid Team," *Roanoke Times*, January 12, 1962; "Area Boys on All-Star Grid Squad," *Roanoke Times*, January 12, 1962.

CHAPTER 9

85 *up the country music:* Gary Trust, "Rewinding the Country Charts: 35 Years Ago, Waylon Jennings' 'Dukes' Theme Sped to No. 1," *Billboard*, November 1, 2015, https://www.billboard.com/

pro/rewinding-the-country-charts-35-years-ago-waylon-jennings-dukes.

85   *Billboard Hot 100 charts:* "Waylon Jennings | Biography, Music & News," Billboard, https://www.billboard.com/artist/waylon-jennings.

85   *one of the oldest in the world:* "New River," Virginia Department of Wildlife Resources, Commonwealth of Virginia, https://dwr.virginia.gov/waterbody/new-river.

87   *this was their year:* Bob Foley, "Good Season Expected at Giles," *Bluefield Daily Telegraph,* August 31, 1980.

87   *Christiansburg, 28–6:* Randy King, "Giles Destroys Christiansburg's Hopes for Title," *Roanoke Times & World-News,* October 20, 1979; John Freeman, "Giles Capitalizes on Mistakes," *Blacksburg Sun,* October 21, 1979.

87   *Lord Botetourt, 6–0:* Dave Scarangella, "No Moral Win for Botetourt," *Roanoke Times & World-News,* October 27, 1979; "Giles Edges Lord Botetourt," *Bluefield Daily Telegraph,* October 27, 1979.

87   *Galax, 48–20:* "Giles 48, Galax 20," *Roanoke Times & World-News,* November 10, 1979; "Giles Downs Galax 48–20," *Blacksburg Sun,* November 11, 1979.

88   *a 13–0 loss to Carroll County:* "Carroll County 13, Giles 0," *Roanoke Times & World-News,* November 3, 1979; "Gillespie Explodes as CC Whips Spartans 13–0 in a Mild Upset," *Virginian Leader,* November 7, 1979.

88   *New River District Coach of the Year:* David J. Bisset, "Houska, Cook, Ragsdale Lead All-District Team," *Blacksburg Sun,* November 28, 1979; "NRD Grid Honors Are Announced," *Virginian Leader,* November 28, 1979.

88   *All-Region IV pick:* "Abingdon Coach Best in Region IV," *Roanoke Times & World-News,* December 3, 1979; Craig Nesbit, "Indians Place Five on All-Regional," *Blacksburg Sun,* December 5, 1979.

88   *All-Group AA:* "Narrows' Oney, Giles' Woods, RHS' Lakey on All-State Team," *Bluefield Daily Telegraph,* December 28, 1979; "Houska,

Polan Get All-State Honors," *Blacksburg Sun*, December 30, 1979.

88 ***offensive and defensive lines:*** Dave Scarangella, "Christiansburg the Early Pick," *Roanoke Times & World-News*, August 31, 1980.

88 ***the Princeton system:*** Caldwell, *Modern Single Wing Football*.

88 ***as the primary puller:*** "Giles: Spartans Have Backfield Speed, Outside Shot at Title," *Blacksburg Sun*, August 31, 1980.

89 ***Duck was injured:*** Foley, "Good Season Expected"; *Blacksburg Sun*, "Spartans Have Backfield Speed."

90 ***was behind on renovations:*** "Citizens Campaign Raises Funds to Sod Grundy Athletic Field," *Virginia Mountaineer* (Grundy, VA), August 7, 1980; "Wave Opens with Lebanon," *Virginia Mountaineer*, September 4, 1980.

91 ***second-generation football coach:*** Robert Anderson, "Larry Bradley Has Good Tutor in Father Burrhead," *Bristol Herald Courier* (VA), August 27, 1978.

91 ***often seen with a cigar:*** Robert Anderson, "Bradley Inherits Fire from Granddad," *Roanoke Times*, September 22, 2006.

91 ***rumored to have pulled out a hatchet:*** Anderson, "Bradley Inherits Fire."

91 ***more laid back than his father:*** Ben Cates, "Heritage's Brad Bradley Eyes Third State Title This Weekend," *News & Advance* (Lynchburg, VA), December 6, 2017.

91 ***played for at Graham:*** Anderson, "Good Tutor in Father Burrhead."

91 ***first state championship in wrestling:*** "Wave Wrestlers Win State AA Crown," *Virginia Mountaineer*, February 23, 1978; "Wave Wrestlers Open Season," *Virginia Mountaineer*, November 30, 1978.

91 ***a basketball title in 1956:*** "Graham Cops Virginia State Crown with 48–41 Win Over James Monroe," *Bluefield Daily Telegraph*, March 11, 1956; "Coach 'Burrhead' Bradley," *Bluefield Daily Telegraph*, May 26, 1998.

91 ***his father and grandfather's footsteps:*** Cates, "Heritage's Brad Bradley."

91 *in the finals, 6–2:* "Clover High School Wins Championship," *Roanoke Times*, June 4, 1933.

91 *best in the area in 1936:* Stubby Currence, "Narrows High School Team Wins International Field Meet Held Here Yesterday," *Bluefield Daily Telegraph*, May 3, 1936; "Narrows Romps Off with Track Meet," *Pearisburg Virginian*, May 7, 1936.

92 *52–39 in the state semifinals:* "Clintwood in Finals with 45-Game Streak," *Richmond News Leader*, March 10, 1951.

92 *upwards of five hundred contests:* "Saturday Night Was All Ragsdale," *Valley Leader & Narrows News* (Pearisburg, VA), December 16, 1954.

92 *Van Meter informed his coach:* Bob Foley, "Grundy's Football Season: The Impossible Dream," *Bluefield Daily Telegraph*, November 14, 1980.

92 *leadership and stability:* Tom Wall, "'Facelift' Season Ahead for the Golden Wave," *Bluefield Daily Telegraph*, August 31, 1980.

92 *four up front that size or larger:* Robert Pilk, "Grundy Facing Problems," *Bristol Herald Courier*, August 24, 1980; Wall, "'Facelift' Season"; *Virginia Mountaineer*, "Wave Opens with Lebanon"; Bob Foley, "Giles Looking for 'Icing on the Cake' Friday Night," *Bluefield Daily Telegraph*, November 12, 1980.

92 *powerful tailback Ralph Coleman:* Wall, "'Facelift' Season"; "Grundy Star, Volunteer Player Take Weekly Honor," *Bristol Herald Courier*, November 11, 1980.

92 *31–6 romp over Virginia High:* "Grundy Rolls Past Bristol, VA 31–6," *Bluefield Daily Telegraph*, September 21, 1963.

93 *Barry Farmer and Alvin Martin:* Foley, "Good Season Expected."

93 *"Passing is a dirty word":* Wall, "'Facelift' Season."

94 *two three-hundred-pounders:* *Virginia Mountaineer*, "Wave Opens with Lebanon."

94 *Steve began to wonder:* Dave Scarangella, "Giles, Narrows Want

Better Results in Playoffs," *Roanoke Times & World-News*, November 13, 1980.

94 ***We looked awful:*** Dave Scarangella, "Goode, Thomas Head All-Timesland Team," *Roanoke Times & World-News*, December 16, 1980.

CHAPTER 10

95 ***Giles vs. Parry McCluer:*** Original 16mm game film, filmed August 29, 1980; Dave Scarangella, "Giles Upends Defending State Champ," *Roanoke Times & World-News*, August 30, 1980; "Giles Wins," *Bluefield Daily Telegraph*, August 30, 1980; Randy Bare, "Blues Lose Heartbreaker 16–15," *Buena Vista News* (VA), September 3, 1980; "Giles Over PM, 16–15," *News-Gazette* (Lexington, VA), September 3, 1980; "Spartans Trip A State Champs 16–15 in Hard Fought Grid Opener," *Virginian Leader*, September 3, 1980.

95 ***Foreigner concert in Roanoke:*** Dan Smith, "The Tip-Off: A Guide to Weekend Events," *Roanoke Times & World-News*, December 7, 1979.

95 ***defeat Jefferson Forest, 14–0:*** Dave Scarangella, "Southampton Wins Again," *Roanoke Times & World-News*, December 9, 1979; "Southampton Cops AA, 14–0," *Bluefield Daily Telegraph*, December 9, 1979.

95 ***Washington & Lee (Montross) 20–6:*** Dave Scarangella, "Timmy Jones Leads Parry McCluer to Group A Title," *Roanoke Times & World-News*, December 9, 1979; "Parry McCluer Takes Single A," *Blacksburg Sun*, December 9, 1979.

96 ***attract the coaches' attention:*** Bob Foley, "Mark Chapman, Greg Mance Big Surprises for Spartans," *Bluefield Daily Telegraph*, November 18, 1980.

96 ***sidelined with a broken hand:*** Foley, "Good Season Expected."

96 ***"blocking that concerns us":*** *Blacksburg Sun*, "Spartans Have Backfield Speed."

96 ***Our season depends on blocking:*** *Blacksburg Sun*, "Spartans Have Backfield Speed."

97 *worked at the Celanese:* "Chafin Accepts Position with First National," *Virginian Leader*, October 5, 1966.

97 *Chafin was now the president:* Jeff Byrd, "Football Fever: Giles County Residents Have Football on the Brain," *Roanoke Times & World-News*, November 14, 1980.

98 *third in the New River District:* Scarangella, "Christiansburg the Early Pick."

98 *"bully boys of small schools":* "Area Prep Teams Gear Up Tonight," *Bluefield Daily Telegraph*, August 29, 1980.

98 *community of 6,700:* US Census Bureau, "1980 Census of Population, General Population Characteristics, Virginia" https://www2.census.gov/prod2/decennial/documents/1980/1980censusofpopu80148uns_bw.pdf.

98 *more a state of mind:* Robert Anderson, "Blues Coaching Icon Williams Dies," *Roanoke Times*, November 4, 2005.

98 *devotion to the Fighting Blues:* Garrett Turner, "'Because It's tradition': A Window into Parry McCluer Football," *WDBJ7*, August 25, 2016, https://www.wdbj7.com/content/news/Because-its-tradition-Parry-McCluer-Football-391255331.html.

98 *1958 Parry McCluer graduate:* "Forty-Five Seniors Graduate as School Closes on June 2nd," *Buena Vista News*, May 29, 1958; Parry McCluer High School, *Parrimac* (Buena Vista, VA: 1958), 21.

98 *to his alma mater in 1974:* "Williams, Robert Ernest," *Roanoke Times*, November 4, 2005.

99 *legendary coach Pete Brewbaker:* Mark Boorman, "Monster Defense?" *Roanoke Times & World-News*, November 8, 1977; Anderson, "Williams Dies."

99 *state titles in 1977 and 1979:* Mark Boorman and Tony Stamus, "Blacksburg Wins It All, Blues Are Champs, Too," *Roanoke Times & World-News*, December 4, 1977; Dave Scarangella, "Timmy Jones Leads Parry McCluer to Group A Title," *Roanoke Times & World-News*, December 9, 1979; "Parry McCluer Takes Single A,"

Blacksburg Sun, December 9, 1979.

99 ***the 1980 edition:*** Jim Bowen, "Blues Seek Fifth Title," *News-Gazette*, August 27, 1980.

100 ***for games like this:*** Scarangella, "Giles Upends Defending State Champ."

100 ***announcer Clayton Camden:*** "Camden, Randolph Clayton," *Roanoke Times & World-News*, February 10, 1993; "'Here Come the Blues,'" *News-Gazette*, September 11, 2013.

100 ***traditional navy-blue uniforms:*** Turner, "A Window into Parry McCluer Football."

100 ***interception in the state finals:*** Scarangella, "Timmy Jones Leads Parry McCluer."

101 ***a broad skill set:*** Foley, "Mark Chapman, Greg Mance Big Surprises."

101 ***a 5–2 Monster:*** Boorman, "Monster Defense?"

103 ***all-state candidate:*** "Two Blues Named All-State by AP," *News-Gazette*, December 30, 1980.

103 ***another all-state candidate:*** *News-Gazette,* "Two Blues Named All-State."

103 ***experiencing severe leg cramps:*** Scarangella, "Giles Upends Defending State Champ."

104 ***1979 state semifinals:*** Randy King, "Parry McCluer Gets Revenge in Playoffs," *Roanoke Times & World-News*, December 2, 1979.

104 ***thought about a field goal:*** Scarangella, "Giles Upends Defending State Champ."

104 ***could see him coming:*** Scarangella, "Giles Upends Defending State Champ."

CHAPTER 11

106 ***Giles vs. Narrows:*** Original 16mm game film, filmed September 19, 1980; Jeff Byrd, "Giles Shuts Out Narrows 16–0," *Roanoke Times &*

World-News, September 20, 1980; "Giles Defeats Wave," *Bluefield Daily Telegraph*, September 20, 1980; "Spartans Win 16–0 over Wave; Giles Dominates Second Half," *Virginian Leader*, September 24, 1980.

107 ***at the age of forty-seven:*** "Giles High Assistant Principal Dies Suddenly," *Virginian Leader*, September 3, 1980; "Charles E. Harris," *Bluefield Daily Telegraph*, September 3, 1980.

107 ***of the varsity cheerleaders:*** Giles High School, *Shield* (Pearisburg, VA: 1981), 18.

107 ***James River at home, 35–7:*** Original 16mm game film, filmed September 5, 1980; "Giles 35, James River 7," *Roanoke Times & World-News*, September 6, 1980; "Giles Spartans Coast," *Bluefield Daily Telegraph*, September 6, 1980; "James River Knights Lose, 35–7, to Newcomer Giles Friday Night," *Botetourt County News & Fincastle Herald* (VA), September 11, 1980; "Spartans Roll in Like the Fog to Defeat James River 35–7," *Virginian Leader*, September 10, 1980.

107 ***Vietnam on April 6, 1968:*** "Sparks' Death Reported," *Virginian Leader*, April 24, 1968.

108 ***the days before the railroad:*** Fiftieth Anniversary Historical Committee, *The First Fifty Years: A History of the Town of Narrows 1904-1954* (Giles County Chamber of Commerce, 1956), 20.

109 ***replacing sixteen starters:*** "Narrows Pursuing 3rd District Title," *Virginian Leader*, August 27, 1980; Bob Foley, "Narrows Green Wave Tough Again," *Bluefield Daily Telegraph*, August 31, 1980; "Narrows: Youth Movement Begins for Green Wave," *Blacksburg Sun*, August 31, 1980.

109 ***7–0 by Tazewell:*** "Tazewell 7, Narrows 0," *Roanoke Times & World-New*, August 30, 1980; Tom Wall, "Tazewell Stuns Narrows," *Bluefield Daily Telegraph*, August 30, 1980; "Wave Loses Football Opener 7–0 to Tazewell at Narrows," *Virginian Leader*, September 3, 1980.

109 ***16–0 by George Wythe:*** "George Wythe Blanks Narrows," *Roanoke Times & World-News*, September 13, 1980; Tom Borrelli, "George

Wythe Maroons Manhandle Green Wave," *Bluefield Daily Telegraph*, September 13, 1980; "Narrows Plays Best of Season but No Match for GW Maroons," *Virginian Leader*, September 17, 1980.

109　*21–6 road loss to Alleghany:* "Alleghany 21, Narrows 6," *Roanoke Times & World-News*, September 6, 1980; "Green Wave Defeated," *Bluefield Daily Telegraph*, September 6, 1980; "Inexperience Said the Main Cause for Wave Gridiron Loss," *Virginian Leader*, September 10, 1980.

109　*would require knee surgery: Virginian Leader,* "Narrows Plays Best of Season."

109　*all-district performer a year later: Blacksburg Sun,* "Houska, Cook, Ragsdale"; *Virginian Leader,* "NRD Grid Honors."

109　*48–0 and 28–13 victories: Roanoke Times & World-News,* "Narrows 48, Giles 0"; *Roanoke Times & World-News,* "Cook Leads Narrows."

109　*one of only three veterans:* Foley, "Wave Tough Again."

110　*"one step short of berserk":* Foley, "Wave Tough Again."

110　*surprised the Soviet Union 4–3:* Associated Press, "Final: United States 4, Soviet Union 3," *Roanoke Times & World-News*, February 23, 1980.

110　*"between Pearisburg and Narrows":* "Pearisburg vs. Narrows," *Pearisburg Virginian*, November 21, 1935.

110　*shocked the undefeated Green Wave:* "Pearisburg Trips Narrows Hi, 7 to 0," *Roanoke Times*, November 23, 1935; Pearisburg Trips Narrows Hi, 7 to 0," *Pearisburg Virginian*, November 28, 1935.

111　*The pep rally:* Leslie Lucas et al., "We've Got It All Together," *Spartonian* (Giles High School), October 1980.

113　*at 255 and 260 pounds:* Foley, "Wave Tough Again."

CHAPTER 12

117　*Giles vs. Blacksburg:* Original 16mm game film, filmed September 26, 1980; Steve Woodward, "Giles Roughs Up Blacksburg 27–7,"

Roanoke Times & World-News, September 27, 1980; "Giles Wins Big NRD Game," *Bluefield Daily Telegraph*, September 27, 1980; Jon Cummings, "Giles' Rushing and 'D' Shuts Down Blacksburg," *Blacksburg Sun*, September 28, 1980; "Spartans Massacre Tribe 27–7; Vault to NR Grid Standings Top," *Virginian Leader*, October 1, 1980.

117 **handwritten in soap:** J. Michael Head, "Giles Ready for Forest Invasion," *News* (Lynchburg, VA), November 25, 1980.

120 **still the underdog:** Foley, "Icing on the Cake."

120 **Indians were ranked eleventh:** "Indians Move to 11th in Poll," *Blacksburg Sun*, September 24, 1980.

120 **Group AAA Salem, 6–0:** Bob Teitlebaum, "Blacksburg Downs Salem on Disputed Fumble," *Roanoke Times & World-News*, September 6, 1980; "Indians Edge Past Spartans on Fumble Return," *Blacksburg Sun*, September 7, 1980.

120 **and Radford, 34–7:** "Indians Humble Radford," *Roanoke Times & World- News*, September 20, 1980; David J. Bisset, "Indians Manhandle 'Cats, 34–7," *Blacksburg Sun*, September 21, 1980.

120 **tie against Christiansburg, 27–27:** Jeff Byrd, "Christiansburg, Blacksburg Tie," *Roanoke Times & World-News*, September 13, 1980; Bill Mason, "Indians, Demons' Battle Ends in 27–27 Tie," *Blacksburg Sun*, September 14, 1980.

120 **winning twenty-seven straight:** "Braves Blast Dublin," *Blacksburg Sun*, October 19, 1977; Craig Nesbit, "Shockley Is Big Winner," *Blacksburg Sun*, October 11, 1978.

120 **current junior and senior classes:** Jim McDonald, "Middle School Wins, Future Bright," *Blacksburg Sun*, September 26, 1976; "Blacksburg Braves Nip Spartans, 22–20," *Blacksburg Sun*, September 25, 1977.

120 **"stop the running attack":** David J. Bisset, "Blacksburg Must Stop Giles' Single Wing," *Blacksburg Sun*, September 24, 1980.

120 **Greg Keys was the leading rusher:** "Keys Is Top Rusher," *Blacksburg*

Sun, September 21, 1980.

121 *won the 220-yard dash:* "District Track: NRD Results," *News-Journal*, May 9, 1980.

121 *hosted the high-powered Terriers:* "Byrd High Will Meet Unbeaten Narrows Today," *Roanoke Times*, November 7, 1938.

121 *later serve as superintendent:* "Ahalt Resigns, Dunn Named His Successor," *Virginian Leader*, June 5, 1974; "The Ahalt Years: An Era of Progress," *Virginian Leader*, July 17, 1974.

121 *leading scorer in the state:* Howard Hammersley, "Shirley Crowder Continues to Lead Scoring, Alex Lasch Second," *Roanoke Times*, November 8, 1938; Narrows High School, *Narrosonian* (Narrows, VA: 1939), 26.

121 *led by Junior "Toar" Skeens:* Narrows High School, *Narrosonian* (Narrows, VA: 1939), 12.

121 *Greenies dispatched the visitors:* "Narrows Beats Vinton, 20 to 6," *Roanoke Times*, November 8, 1938.

121 *defensive units with catchy nicknames*: Ryan Vooris, "The Best NFL Defensive Unit Nicknames," *Bleacher Report*, August 7, 2010, https:// bleacherreport.com/articles/431194-the-best-nfl-defensive-unit-nicknames.

122 *Alvin Martin caught his eye:* Steve Ragsdale, motivational speech, filmed September 17, 2021, video recording.

124 *"he can run forever":* Woodward, "Giles Roughs Up Blacksburg."

124 *turning point for the Spartans:* Foley, "Icing on the Cake."

124 *over the Radford Bobcats, 35–0:* Original 16mm game film, filmed October 3, 1980; "Giles Takes First with 35–0 Victory," *Roanoke Times & World- News*, October 4, 1980; "Giles Rips Radford," *Bluefield Daily Telegraph*, October 4, 1980; David J. Bisset, "Spartans Too Quick for 'Cats," *News- Journal*, October 5, 1980; "Giles Number 1 in NRD; Spartans Bomb Cats," *Virginian Leader*, October 8, 1980.

124 *named homecoming queen:* "Maroons Attempt Spoiler's Role but

Giles Scores a Big 27–0 Win," *Virginian Leader*, October 15, 1980.

124 *Using this adjustment:* Original 16mm game film, filmed October 10, 1980.

124 *prevailing 27–0:* Original 16mm game film, filmed October 10, 1980; "Giles Topples Wythe 27–0," *Roanoke Times & World-News*, October 11, 1980; Tom Wall, "Unbeaten Giles Spartans Steamroll George Wythe," *Bluefield Daily Telegraph*, October 11, 1980; Marty Gordon, " Maroons Fade in Second Half in Loss to Giles," *Southwest Virginia Enterprise*, October 14, 1980; *Virginian Leader*, "Maroons Attempt Spoiler's Role."

CHAPTER 13

126 *Giles vs. Christiansburg:* Original 16mm game film, filmed October 17, 1980; Steve Woodward, "Giles Remains Undefeated," *Roanoke Times & World-News*, October 18, 1980; Tom Borrelli, "Spartans Defeat Demons," *Bluefield Daily Telegraph*, October 18, 1980; "Passing Game a Bright Spot in Demons' Loss," *Blacksburg Sun*, October 19, 1980; Bill Mason, "Spartans Sink Blue Demons," *News Messenger (*Christiansburg, VA), October 20, 1980; "Giles Tightens Hold on Top Spot, Defeat Demons 28–20 in Thriller," *Virginian Leader*, October 22, 1980.

127 *"won the state championship?":* Dave Scarangella, "Perfect Season Ends with a State Crown," *Roanoke Times & World-News*, December 7, 1980.

127 *"if we won it this year?":* Scarangella, "Perfect Season."

128 *nearly folded in 1939:* "Varsity Football May Be Dropped," *Montgomery News Messenger*, November 29, 1939; "C.H.S. Reverses Grid Decision," *Montgomery News Messenger*, December 6, 1939.

128 *A new coach:* "Pick New Coach for Local School," *Montgomery News Messenger*, August 28, 1940.

128 *Notre Dame monogram winner:* "Recapitulation of 1939 Football Season," University of Notre Dame, https://fightingirish.com/wp-content/ uploads/2022/10/NDFB_1939_Final_Stats.pdf.

128 *revived the sport:* "Demons Win Initial Game in Five Years," *Roanoke Times*, October 12, 1940; Jesse Chapman, "Christiansburg High Gets Results from New Policy," October 15, 1940.

128 *his alma mater, Covington:* "Coach Albert to Accept New Post," *Montgomery News Messenger*, May 14, 1941.

128 *for thirty-three years:* "Boodie Albert Dies Suddenly," *News-Journal*, July 17, 1974.

128 *embraced the challenge:* Dave Scarangella, "Coach Discusses Goals," *Blacksburg Sun*, August 3, 1977.

128 *continued to stress the phrase:* Dave Scarangella, "Coach Gets Spirit Going," *Blacksburg Sun*, September 4, 1977.

128 *edged George Wythe 14–7:* Dave Scarangella, "Christiansburg Beats George Wythe," *Blacksburg Sun*, September 4, 1977.

128 *so had the community:* Scarangella, "Coach Gets Spirit Going."

128 *had been picked to win:* "Coaches' Choice," *Blacksburg Sun*, August 31, 1980; Scarangella, "Christiansburg the Early Pick."

128 *resulted in a roster:* "Christiansburg: Blue Demons Aim for Crown in Tight NRD Race," *Blacksburg Sun*, August 31, 1980.

128 *thirty-eight points per game:* Dave Scarangella, "Christiansburg Has No Trouble Making Points," *Roanoke Times & World-News*, October 14, 1980.

129 *"best we've faced all year":* Virginian Leader, "Maroons Attempt Spoiler's Role."

129 *close to eight hundred yards:* "New River District Stats," *News-Journal*, October 17, 1980.

129 *led the league in passing:* Blacksburg Sun, "Blue Demons Aim for Crown."

129 *nearly 60 percent of his throws:* Scarangella, "Christiansburg, Giles Highlight Prep Slate."

129 *All-Region IV selection: Roanoke Times & World-News*, "Best in

Region IV." 269

129 **UPI Group AA Top 10:** "Giles Moves into Top 10," *Blacksburg Sun*, October 15, 1980.

130 **number one song in America:** Kevin Rutherford, "Rewinding the Charts: In 1980, Another One Topped the Chart for Queen," *Billboard*, October 4, 2019, https://www.billboard.com/pro/queen-another-one-bites-the-dust-rewinding-the-charts.

131 **same $3.10 an hour:** US Department of Labor, "History of Federal Minimum Wage Rates Under the Fair Labor Standards Act, 1938-2009," https://www.dol.gov/agencies/whd/minimum-wage/history/chart.

131 **fifty-two American hostages:** Britannica, "Iran Hostage Crisis," last updated February 15, 2025, https://www.britannica.com/event/Iran-hostage-crisis.

131 **they had last lost 39–14:** *Roanoke Times*, "Dublin Subdues Narrows."

131 **a new electronic scoreboard:** "Dublin Athletic Field Undergoes Facelifting," *Roanoke Times*, September 7, 1961; "Dukes' Field Gets Modern Scoreboard," *Southwest Times*, September 10, 1961.

132 **whipped the Dukes, 34–0:** Howard Jennings, "Dublin Dukes Walloped 34–0 by Green Wave," *Southwest Times*, November 5, 1961.

132 **was inadequate to host:** Nancy Musgrove, "No Seats for Fans, Officials Say," *Blacksburg Sun*, November 2, 1980.

132 **the outdoor basketball goals**: Musgrove, "No Seats for Fans."

134 **"a tournament chess player":** Mason, "Spartans Sink Blue Demons."

CHAPTER 14

138 **overwhelmed the Celtics, 34–6:** Steve Woodward, "Mance's Three TDs Help Beat Catholic," *Roanoke Times & World-News*, October 25, 1980; "Spartans Smack Celtics," *Bluefield Daily Telegraph*, October 25, 1980; "Giles Has Easy Time in 34–6 Victory over Roanoke Catholic," *Virginian Leader*, October 29, 1980.

138 *over the winless Cavaliers, 38-7:* Original 16mm game film, filmed October 30, 1980; "Giles Captures NRD Title," *Bluefield Daily Telegraph*, October 31, 1980; "Giles Takes First Title," *Roanoke Times & World-News*, November 1, 1980; "Giles Spartans Win Football Mantle in New River District," *Virginian Leader*, November 5, 1980; "Carroll Falls Again," *Carroll News* (VA), November 6, 1980.

139 *third in the state:* United Press International, "Virginia Coaches Football Poll," *News Messenger*, November 5, 1980.

139 *Ronald Reagan was elected:* "Reagan Wins Big," *Roanoke Times & World- News*, November 5, 1980; Associated Press, "Reagan Scores Sweeping Victory," *Bluefield Daily Telegraph*, November 5, 1980.

139 *Walter Cronkite apprised the nation:* Ellen Goodman, "And That's the Way It Is – Or Is It?" *Washington Post*, June 16, 1980.

142 *even considered daytime games:* Susan Loving, "Football Teams Possibly Facing Games on Saturday," *Blacksburg Sun*, September 6, 1978.

144 *Kenneth French: Virginian Leader*, "Ragsdale Retires."

144 *1941 Narrows eleven:* "French and Bayles Captains for Coming Football Season," *Narrows News*, January 23, 1941.

144 *University of Georgia:* Robert Anderson, "Service Defined Life of Former Colonels Coach," *Roanoke Times*, June 16, 2007.

144 *William Fleming in Roanoke:* William Fleming High School, *Colonel* (Roanoke, VA: 1981), 148.

145 *walloped Galax 51-14:* Original 16mm game film, filmed November 7, 1980; "Giles Rips Galax, goes 10-0," *Roanoke Times & World-News*, November 8, 1980; "Giles Rips Galax, 51-14," *Bluefield Daily Telegraph*, November 8, 1980; "Spartans Play Taps for Galax; 10-0 for Season with 51-14 Win," *Virginian Leader*, November 12, 1980.

145 *like Bo Derek:* "10," Rotten Tomatoes, accessed October 6, 2020, https:// www.rottentomatoes.com/m/10.

145 *Southwest District runner-up:* Dave Scarangella, "Giles to Play

Grundy; Narrows Meets Abingdon," *Roanoke Times & World-News*, November 9, 1980; Bob Foley, "'Combination' Puts Grundy in Playoffs," *Bluefield Daily Telegraph*, November 9, 1980.

145 *over rival Broad Run, 11–10:* Michael Martz, "Grammo Lifts Pats to Title," *Loudoun Times-Mirror* (Leesburg, VA), November 13, 1980.

CHAPTER 15

146 *Giles vs. Grundy:* Original 16mm game film, filmed November 14, 1980; Doug Doughty, "Spartans Eliminate Grundy," *Roanoke Times & World- News*, November 15, 1980; Bob Foley, "Unbeaten Giles Murders Grundy," *Bluefield Daily Telegraph*, November 15, 1980; Bill Evans, "Giles Too Strong in 31–0 Decision," *Bristol Herald Courier*, November 15, 1980; Gary Reed, "Giles Stops Grundy, Face Abingdon," *News Messenger*, November 16, 1980; "Giles Routs Grundy, 31–0," *News- Journal*, November 16, 1980; "Spartans Reduce Golden Tide to Little Ripples," *Virginian Leader*, November 19, 1980; "Wave Falls in Playoffs to Powerhouse Giles," *Virginia Mountaineer*, November 20, 1980.

146 *"district's premier linemen":* Foley, "Icing on the Cake."

147 *gave Grundy the nod:* Scarangella, "Giles to Play Grundy."

147 *triumph over Abingdon:* "Golden Wave Upsets District Leaders 14–7," *Virginia Mountaineer*, October 16, 1980.

147 *first winning season:* Foley, "The Impossible Dream."

147 *"The Year of the Wave":* Foley, "The Impossible Dream"; Grundy Senior High School, *Wave* (Grundy, VA: 1981), 136.

147 *two students were killed:* Roland Lazenby, "Grundy High Students Die in Car Wreck," *Roanoke Times & World-News*, October 20, 1980; "Grundy Mishap Kills 2 High School Students," *Bluefield Daily Telegraph*, October 20, 1980.

148 *told several newspapers:* Lazenby, "Grundy High Students Die"; *Bluefield Daily Telegraph*, "Grundy Mishap Kills 2."

148 *the rest of their season:* Bob Foley, "Golden Wave Faces Its Biggest

Challenge," *Bluefield Daily Telegraph*, October 24, 1980.

148 *"We learned a lot":* Evans, "Giles Too Strong."

148 *"a lot of improvement":* Coy Bays, "Grundy to Face Single Wing Against Giles County," *Bristol Herald Courier*, November 14, 1980.272

148 *sure to remind them:* Evans, "Giles Too Strong."

148 *Golden Wave's size advantage:* Foley, "Icing on the Cake."

148 *"no razzle-dazzle":* "Golden Tide Is Best Spartans Have Faced," *Virginian Leader*, November 12, 1980.

148 *Grundy's "Mr. Football":* Grundy Senior High School, *Wave* (Grundy, VA: 1981), 140.

148 *rushed for 1,550 yards:* Foley, "The Impossible Dream"; Scarangella, "Giles, Narrows Want Better Results."

148 *in all ten games:* Evans, "Giles Too Strong"; Reed, "Giles Stops Grundy."

148 *tops in the Southwest District:* Foley, "The Impossible Dream."

148 *"best high school running back":* "Grundy Star, Volunteer Player Take Weekly Honor," *Bristol Herald Courier*, November 11, 1980.

148 *We have to keep them:* Bays, "Grundy to Face Single Wing."

148 *final NRD rankings:* "1980 New River District Final Football Stats," *News-Journal*, November 14, 1980.

149 *the backfield stable:* Scarangella, "Giles, Narrows Want Better Results."

149 *Single wing's deception:* Foley, "Icing on the Cake"; Bays, "Grundy to Face Single Wing."

149 *Single wing is our tradition:* Foley, "Icing on the Cake."

149 *"It's a beautiful offense":* Bob Foley, "The Ancient Single Wing Presents Problems Galore," *Bluefield Daily Telegraph*, November 14, 1980.

149 *Sports Hall of Fame:* "Lotito, Tony Sr.," *Roanoke Times & World-News*, February 11, 1994; "Antonio 'Tony' Lotito," Emory & Henry College Sports Hall of Fame, https://hof.ehc.edu/members/antonio-tony-lotito.

149 *Bluefield College in 1941:* Brian Woodson, "Football Return Pleases Lotito," *Bluefield Daily Telegraph*, July 21, 2010.

150 *"used a six-man line":* Foley, "Ancient Single Wing."

150 *late October 1932:* "Narrows High Loses to Pocahontas, 20–0," *Roanoke Times*, October 30, 1932; Narrows High School, *Narrosonian* (Narrows, VA: 1933).

150 *in his second season:* "Tony Lotito Making Good Coaching Record at Poca," *Bluefield Daily Telegraph*, November 6, 1931.

150 *all-district linebacker:* "Hall, Heldreth Among SWD Honorees," *Bluefield Daily Telegraph*, December 2, 1979.

150 *just sixty-four points:* Bob Foley, "Golden Wave Offense, Defense Come Together," *Bluefield Daily Telegraph*, November 11, 1980.

150 *"That buck lateral":* Foley, "Golden Wave Offense, Defense."

150 *closed the regular season:* United Press International, "Virginia Coaches Football Poll," *News Messenger*, November 12, 1980.

150 *received a boost midweek:* Foley, "The Impossible Dream."

151 *let the game be moved:* Byrd, "Football Fever."

151 *$5,800 barrier:* Byrd, "Football Fever."

152 *proclaimed "Bandana Day":* Byrd, "Football Fever."

152 *since 1946:* Robert Freis, "Mayor: 47 Years Will Do," *Roanoke Times & World-News*, March 11, 1993.

152 *bustling with talk:* Byrd, "Football Fever."

153 *feel the pace quicken:* Foley, "Giles Murders Grundy."

155 *a hundred-yard rusher:* Reed, "Giles Stops Grundy."

156 *Abingdon–Narrows game:* Doughty, "Spartans Eliminate Grundy."

157   *"one of the best teams":* Doughty, "Spartans Eliminate Grundy."

157   *27–7 winners over Narrows:* Original 16mm game film, filmed November 14, 1980; Bob Teitlebaum, "Narrows Falls to Abingdon," *Roanoke Times & World-News*, November 15, 1980; Tom Wall, "Abingdon Smashes Green Wave, 27–7," *Bluefield Daily Telegraph*, November 15, 1980; Steve Bawden, "Falcons Fly High Against Narrows," *Bristol Herald Courier*, November 15, 1980; "Wave Ends Successful Season on 27–7 Loss," *Virginian Leader*, November 19, 1980.

CHAPTER 16

158   *Giles vs. Abingdon:* Original 16mm game film, filmed November 21, 1980; Bob Teitlebaum, "Giles Tops Abingdon for Region IV Crown," *Roanoke Times & World-News*, November 22, 1980; Tom Borrelli, "Giles Whips Abingdon, Advances," *Bluefield Daily Telegraph*, November 22, 1980; Bill Evans, "Giles 'Wings' Abingdon in Regional Final," *Bristol Herald Courier*, November 22, 1980; Gary Reed, "Spartans Claim Region IV Title," *News Messenger*, November 23, 1980; "Spartan Fans Flock to Abingdon as Giles Wins Region," *Virginian Leader*, November 26, 1980.

158   *full moon:* Borrelli, "Giles Whips Abingdon"; "Moon Phases 1980 – Lunar Calendar for Abingdon, Virginia, USA," Time and Date AS, accessed October 26, 2020, https://www.timeanddate.com/moon/phases/@4743815?year=1980.

158   *the prime-time drama Dallas:* United Press International, "'Kristen Shephard Dunnit,'" *Southwest Times*, November 23, 1980; "Millions Tune In to Find Out Who Shot J.R.," History, last updated November 19, 2024, https://www.history.com/this-day-in-history/millions-tune-in-to-find-out-who-shot-j-r.

159   *renaming the stretch of road: Virginian Leader,* "Spartan Fans Flock to Abingdon."

159   *defeated Narrows, 21–0:* Dave Scarangella, "Abingdon Eliminates Narrows 21–0," *Roanoke Times & World-News*, November 24, 1979; Bob Foley, "Abingdon Makes Up for Last Year, Decisions Wave

21–0," *Bluefield Daily Telegraph*, November 24, 1979; Craig Nesbit, "Abingdon Blanks Narrows for Title," *Blacksburg Sun*, November 25, 1979; "Green Wave Bows 21–0 to the Abingdon Falcons," *Virginian Leader*, November 28, 1979.

159 *at Jefferson Forest, 10–7:* "Jefferson Forest Wins, Will Play Southampton for State Championship," *Roanoke Times & World-News*, December 2, 1979; "Abingdon Bows to Cavaliers," *Bluefield Daily Telegraph*, December 2, 1979.

159 *Bob Buchanan resigned:* "Bob Buchanan Leaving AHS," *Bluefield Daily Telegraph*, January 12, 1980.

159 *decided to take the job:* Bill Evans, "Curtis Burkett Hoping to Keep Falcons Flying," *Bristol Herald Courier*, August 24, 1980; Bill Evans, "Burkett Retained Pride at Abingdon," *Bristol Herald Courier*, November 20, 1980.

159 *Coach of the Year:* "NRD, SWD All-Star Teams Are Chosen," *Bluefield Daily Telegraph*, November 27, 1980.

159 *New in 1978:* Bill Evans, "Abingdon May Find Good Things in '78," *Bristol Herald Courier*, August 27, 1978.

159 *replaced Latture Field:* Evans, "Abingdon May Find Good Things"; Tim Hayes, "Abingdon Falcons Go Back to the Future at Latture for VHSL Benefit Game," *Bristol Herald Courier*, August 21, 2019.

159 *had told his team:* Robert Pilk, "Blue Bubble Bursts For AHS," *Bristol Herald Courier*, November 22, 1980.

159 *Negative thirteen degrees Fahrenheit:* "December 31, 1967: Weather During the Ice Bowl," National Weather Service, US Department of Commerce, https://www.weather.gov/grb/123167_Icebowl.

159 *Ray Nitschke's frostbitten toes:* United Press International, "3 Dallas Cowboys Suffer Frostbite," *Madera Tribune* (CA), January 5, 1968.

160 *They're the best team:* Dave Scarangella, "Redemption?" *Roanoke Times & World-News*, November 19, 1980.

160 *out of a pro set:* Evans, "Curtis Burkett Hoping"; "Falcons Rated Best

in Southwestern Area," *Virginian Leader*, November 19, 1980.

160   *Offensive Back of the Year: Bluefield Daily Telegraph*, "NRD, SWD All- Star Teams."

160   *both school records:* "Abingdon High School Athletic Records," Washington County Public Schools, accessed October 19, 2020, https://ahs.wcs. k12.va.us/o/abingdon/documents/athletics/athletic-records/439134.

160   *eleven touchdown passes:* Evans, "Burkett Retained Pride"; "Luv That Blue," *Bristol Herald Courier*, November 21, 1980.

160   *All-Group AA wide receiver: Bluefield Daily Telegraph*, "All-State Team."

160   *sixteen catches for 511 yards:* Evans, "Burkett Retained Pride"; *Bristol Herald Courier*, "Luv That Blue."

160   *another school record:* "Abingdon High School Athletic Records."

160   *eighth in all-time:* Marshall Johnson, "Individual Records – Receiving Touchdowns," *VirginiaPreps*, July 31, 2005, https://virginiapreps.rivals. com/news/individual-records-receiving-touchdowns.

160   *clocked in at 4.5:* Evans, "Curtis Burkett Hoping"; *Virginian Leader*, "Falcons Rated Best."

160   *on almost any play:* Scarangella, "Redemption?"

160   *termed a "40 scheme":* Evans, "Curtis Burkett Hoping."

160   *only forty-three points: Bristol Herald Courier*, "Luv That Blue."

161   *all-staters Steve Knight: Bluefield Daily Telegraph*, "All-State Team"; Tim Hayes, "History with Hayes: Knight Was a Nightmare for Foes at Abingdon, UT," *Bristol Herald Courier*, October 7, 2016.

161   *a defensive pair:* Evans, "Curtis Burkett Hoping"; Evans, "Burkett Retained Pride."

161   *all-region selection:* "21 Land All-Regional Spots," *Bluefield Daily Telegraph*, December 9, 1979.

161 *second consecutive season:* Bluefield Daily Telegraph, "SWD Honorees"; Bluefield Daily Telegraph, "NRD, SWD All-Star Teams."

161 *technique and determination:* Hayes, "Knight Was a Nightmare."

161 *was naturally concerned:* Bill Evans, "Falcons Meet Giles for Region IV Title," Bristol Herald Courier, November 21, 1980.

161 *sixty-five receiving yards:* Doughty, "Spartans Eliminate Grundy."

161 *including Larry Bradley:* Foley, "Golden Wave Offense, Defense."

161 *"go for the home run":* Evans, "Falcons Meet Giles."277

162 *in late November:* "Narrows Pounds Pulaski, 35 to 6," Roanoke Times, November 19, 1939; "Narrows' Unbeaten Green Wave Rolls Over Oriole Eleven," Southwest Times, November 19, 1939; "Narrows' Unbeaten Green Wave Rolls Over Oriole Eleven," Narrows News, November 23, 1939.

162 *a national record:* "Narrows High Claims Two Football Records," Bluefield Daily Telegraph, November 19, 1939.

162 *serving in World War II:* "Johnson, VPI's Blocking Back, Wouldn't Change," Roanoke Times, November 19, 1946; "Tech Names 32 Sun Bowlers; Scrimmages Start," Roanoke Times, December 20, 1946; Jack Carper, "Cincinnati Outclasses Tech in Sun Bowl 18–6," Roanoke Times, January 2, 1947; Donna Alvis-Banks, "WW II Vet Helped Tech Earn Its First Bowl Bid," Roanoke Times, July 14, 2002.

168 *in the first half:* Reed, "Spartans Claim Region IV Title."

169 *"until the horn blew":* Evans, "Giles 'Wings' Abingdon."

169 *"It sure wasn't easy":* Borrelli, "Giles Whips Abingdon."

169 *We played too cautious:* Reed, "Spartans Claim Region IV Title."

170 *"guy from Green Bay":* Pilk, "Blue Bubble Bursts."

CHAPTER 17

171 *Giles vs. Jefferson Forest:* Original 16mm game film, filmed November 29, 1980; "Giles vs. Jefferson Forest," Original WNRV

radio broadcast, aired November 29, 1980; Bob Teitlebaum, "Giles Wins to Gain Group AA final," *Roanoke Times & World-News*, November 30, 1980; Bob Foley, "Spartans Roll Into State Finals," *Bluefield Daily Telegraph*, November 30, 1980; Bob Foley, "Steve Ragsdale: Call Him The Gambler," *Bluefield Daily Telegraph*, November 30, 1980; Mike Ashley, "Spartans Stop Cavaliers, 30–21," *News Messenger*, November 30, 1980; Tony Mitchell, "Giles Semi-Final Strategy: Throw Caution to the Wind," *News & Daily Advance* (Lynchburg, VA), November 30, 1980; J. Michael Head, "Forest Got 'Snow Job,'" *News & Daily Advance*, November 30, 1980; Mike Williams, "Giles Earns Shot at Title with Win," *Southwest Times*, November 30, 1980; David J. Bisset, "King Leads Giles to State," *News-Journal*, November 30, 1980; "Spartans Beat Cavs; Move into Finals," *Virginian Leader*, December 3, 1980.

171 *the powerful leg:* Foley, "Call Him The Gambler."

172 *"with an onside kick":* Teitlebaum, "Giles Wins."

172 *a hot new tune:* Jeff Byrd, "'Spartan Fever' Now a Hit Song," *Roanoke Times & World-News*, December 3, 1980.

172 *He felt his team:* Reed, "Spartans Claim Region IV Title."

172 *12–0 champions:* J. Michael Head, "Cavs Need Two Bricks for Load," *Daily Advance* (Lynchburg, VA), November 29, 1980.

172 *caution to the wind:* Foley, "Call Him The Gambler"; Mitchell, "Throw Caution to the Wind."

172 *opened in 1972:* "About Us," Jefferson Forest High School, Bedford County Public Schools, accessed December 31, 2017, https://bedfordjfhs.sharpschool.net/about_us.

172 *since the beginning:* Jefferson Forest High School, *Selvetta* (Forest, VA: 1973), 25.

173 *head coach Lou Holtz:* William Barry Furlong, "Secrets of a Turnaround Coach," *New York Times*, December 12, 1976.

173 *Steve likened them:* Bob Foley, "Giles Faces Cavaliers in State Semis," *Bluefield Daily Telegraph*, November 29, 1980.

173 **All-state running back:** *Bluefield Daily Telegraph*, "All-State Team."

173 **had graduated:** Tony Mitchell, "Jefferson Forest Favored Again," *Daily Advance*, August 27, 1980.

173 **dose of inside running:** Mitchell, "Jefferson Forest Favored Again."

173 **Back of the Year:** J. Michael Head, "Cavaliers, Generals Dominate All-Seminole District Team," *News*, November 22, 1980; Tony Mitchell, "Fuqua, Thompson, Cox Garner Seminole Awards," *News*, November 22, 1980; Jefferson Forest High School, *Sabre* (Forest, VA: 1981), 8.

173 **just under six feet tall:** Randy King and Mike Head, "Cavaliers Dominate All-Area Football Team," *Daily Advance*, November 27, 1980.279

173 **twenty touchdowns:** Head, "Cavs Need Two Bricks."

173 **top offensive lineman:** Head, "All-Seminole District Team"; Mitchell, "Seminole Awards"; Jefferson Forest High School, *Sabre*, 8.

173 **six-foot-five tight end:** King and Head, "All-Area Football Team."

173 **eighteen yards per catch:** Mitchell, "Seminole Awards."

173 **over Martinsville, 21–0:** J. Michael Head, "Cavs Must Stop Colts' Campbell," *News*, November 21, 1980; Jefferson Forest High School, *Sabre*, 9.

173 **Alleghany, 24–7:** Doug Doughty, "Jefferson Forest in Group AA Semifinals," *Roanoke Times & World-News*, November 22, 1980; J. Michael Head, "Forest Fire: Cavs, 24–7," *News & Daily Advance*, November 22, 1980; Tony Mitchell, "Forest Point Spread Deceiving," *News & Daily Advance*, November 22, 1980.

173 **defense and kicking game:** Foley, "Giles Faces Cavaliers."

173 **players like Jeff Calloway:** Mitchell, "Jefferson Forest Favored Again."

173 **all-region defensive lineman:** Jefferson Forest High School, *Sabre*, 68.

173 *eighty-one points:* Head, "Cavs Need Two Bricks"; Jefferson Forest High School, *Sabre,* 9.

173 *linebacker David Allen:* Mitchell, "Jefferson Forest Favored Again"; Head, "Cavs Need Two Bricks."

173 *state-champion wrestler:* Jefferson Forest High School, *Sabre,* 94.

173 *fifty-six takeaways:* Head, "Cavs Must Stop Colts' Campbell."

173 *thirty-four interceptions:* Head, "Cavs Must Stop Colts' Campbell"; Head, "Cavs Need Two Bricks."

173 *week of practice:* Tony Mitchell, "At Giles: Son of Single Wing," *Daily Advance,* November 27, 1980.

173 *expected multiple looks:* Foley, "Giles Faces Cavaliers"; Dave Scarangella, "Jefferson Forest Hasn't Been Able to Find a Giles Weakness," *Roanoke Times & World-News,* November 27, 1980.280

173 *featured Mickey Stinnett:* Mitchell, "Jefferson Forest Favored Again."

173 *All-Group AA selection:* Bluefield Daily Telegraph, "All-State Team."

174 *the past two seasons:* Bill Evans, "Jefferson Forest FG Edges Falcons, 10–7," *Bristol Herald Courier,* December 2, 1979; Head, "Cavs Need Two Bricks."

174 *past Abingdon, 10–7:* "Jefferson Forest Wins, Will Play Southampton for State Championship," *Roanoke Times & World-News,* December 2, 1979; "Abingdon Bows to Cavaliers," *Bluefield Daily Telegraph,* December 2, 1979; Evans, "Jefferson Forest FG Edges Falcons."

174 *newly opened:* Jefferson Forest High School, *Sabre,* 118–119.

174 *in the number one spot:* United Press International, "Virginia Coaches Football Poll," *News Messenger,* November 12, 1980.

175 *three hours before:* "Giles-Jefferson Forest Game Could Attract 10,000 Fans," *Roanoke Times & World-News,* November 26, 1980.

175 *crowd was massive:* Mitchell, "Throw Caution to the Wind."

175 *to heavy blankets:* Teitlebaum, "Giles Wins."

176 *twenty degrees warmer:* Jefferson Forest High School, *Sabre*, 10.

176 *the Bedford Otters:* Sherrill Coleman, *The Otters* (B&B Printing, 1991).

176 *for a 25–6 victory:* "Narrows Wallops Bedford, 25 to 6," *Roanoke Times*, December 3. 1939; "Bedford High Otters Defeated by Narrows Team," *Bedford Democrat* (VA), December 7, 1939; "Narrows High Claims State Grid Honors As Easterners Refuse to Play Green Wave," *Narrows News*, December 7, 1939.

176 *refused to play:* "Narrows Claims State C Diadem," *Roanoke Times*, December 6, 1939; *Narrows News*, "Narrows High Claims State Grid Honors."

176 *twenty-one-game:* Thornton Tice, "Narrows High School Has Set Great Mark with 21 Straight," *Roanoke Times*, December 10, 1939.

177 *all-district linemen:* Head, "All-Seminole District Team."

177 *a 13–12 triumph:* Scarangella, "Giles Weakness."

178 *regional playoff record:* Virginia High School League, "Group AA Regional Records," *Official Program: 1980 Football Playoffs*; Bisset, "King Leads Giles to State."

178 *Dempsey's NFL record:* Alaa Abdeldaiem, "What Is the Longest Field Goal Kick in NFL History?" *Sports Illustrated*, February 3, 2019, https:// www.si.com/nfl/2019/02/03/longest-field-goal-nfl-history-matt-prater-broncos.

178 *He almost made it:* Foley, "Call Him The Gambler."

181 *a 1978 hit song:* Paul Grein, "Kenny Rogers: He Was Even Bigger Than You Realize," *Billboard*, March 21, 2020, https:// www.billboard.com/music/ awards/kenny-rogers-biggest-star-1980-9340122; *Britannica*, "Kenny Rogers," last updated February 11, 2025, https://www.britannica.com/ biography/ Kenny-Rogers-American-singer-songwriter.

181 *"The Gambler":* Foley, "Call Him The Gambler."

182 *If we can neutralize:* Teitlebaum, "Giles Wins."

182 *the chagrin of Styles:* Head, "Forest Got 'Snow Job.'"

183 *heck of a game:* Foley, "Call Him The Gambler."

183 *kickoff did for them:* Mitchell, "Throw Caution to the Wind."

184 *state playoff record:* Virginia High School League, "Group AA State Records," *Official Program: 1981 Football Playoffs*; Head, "Forest Got 'Snow Job.'"

184 *"keep me busy":* Head, "Forest Got 'Snow Job.'"

184 *"I said at halftime":* Ashley, "Spartans Stop Cavaliers."

184 *"riverboat gamblers born":* Foley, "Call Him The Gambler."

184 *"more nerve than I do":* "Giles vs. Park View," Original WNRV radio broadcast, aired December 6, 1980.

184 *14–13 winners over Tabb:* Sean Adams, "Patriots Nip Tabb Saturday," *Loudoun Times-Mirror*, December 4, 1980.

CHAPTER 18

185 *Richard Charlton:* "Narrows Downs Pearisburg, 19–0," *Roanoke Times*, November 21, 1936.

185 *Jim Johnson:* "Captains Chosen at Narrows High," *Roanoke Times*, March 23, 1940; "Jim Johnson Is Unanimously Selected on Times Grid Squad," *Narrows News*, December 19, 1940.

186 *an ideal candidate:* Bob Foley, "Giles' Randy Martin 'Center of Attention,'" *Bluefield Daily Telegraph*, November 20, 1980.

186 *an essential cog:* Foley, "Center of Attention."

186 *"Dandy Randy":* Foley, "Center of Attention."

187 *his first ten games:* "Loudoun Dominates All-District Football Teams," *Loudoun Times-Mirror*, November 27, 1980.

187 *His other statistics:* Tom Borrelli, "Spartans' Title Game Foe Has Climbed the Ladder," *Bluefield Daily Telegraph*, December 2, 1980

187 *"one of the best backs":* Michael Martz, "Patriots Slip By Osbourn,"

Loudoun Times-Mirror, October 2, 1980.

187 **Patriots won 7–6:** Michael Martz, "Patriots Edge James Monroe," *Loudoun Times-Mirror*, November 20, 1980.

188 **Blue Streaks, 29–19:** Michael Martz, "Patriots Defeat Streaks, 29–19, for Regional Title," *Loudoun Times-Mirror*, November 27, 1980.

188 **two years prior:** Bob Morgan, "Streaks Top Patriots with Passing Game," *Daily News-Record* (Harrisonburg, VA), November 13, 1978.

188 **Osbourn and Broad Run:** Martz, "Grammo Lifts Pats to Title"; Martz, "Patriots Slip By Osbourn."

188 **a 14–13 triumph:** Adams, "Patriots Nip Tabb."

189 **Early-season losses:** "County, Broad Run Look to Tough Games, Park View and Valley Regroup," *Loudoun Times-Mirror*, September 11, 1980; Michael Martz, "Vikings Flatten Patriots," *Loudoun Times-Mirror*, October 16, 1980.

189 **"get behind early":** Scarangella, "Giles' Leon King."

189 **at full strength:** Adams, "Patriots Nip Tabb."

190 **"make some adjustments":** Borrelli, "Spartans' Title Game Foe."

190 **eighty-five stops:** *Loudoun Times-Mirror*, "Loudoun Dominates All-District."

190 **top defensive tackles:** Associated Press, "Several Spartans Make AA Team," *Bluefield Daily Telegraph*, December 23, 1980.

190 **eighty-four tackles:** *Loudoun Times-Mirror*, "Loudoun Dominates All- District."

190 **All-Suburban First Team:** Borrelli, "Spartans' Title Game Foe."

190 **all-district selection:** *Loudoun Times-Mirror*, "Loudoun Dominates All- District."

191 **particularly up front:** Borrelli, "Spartans' Title Game Foe"; "Park View Is Not Big – But They're Quick and Like to Hit," *Virginian Leader*, December 3, 1980.

191 *"It scares me":* "State AA Crown Is on Line," *Loudoun Times-Mirror*, December 4, 1980.

191 *final send-off:* Michael Martz, "Football: Serious Business," *Loudoun Times-Mirror*, December 11, 1980.

191 *"After you win":* Martz, "Football: Serious Business."

191 **Sterling Park:** "Sterling Park, VA Community Profile," HomeTownLocator, accessed April 28, 2012, https://virginia.hometownlocator.com/va/ loudoun/sterling-park.cfm.

191 *in all the hullabaloo:* Dave Scarangella, "Giles Fans Ready for Game," *Roanoke Times & World-News*, December 6, 1980.

192 *impromptu bandana parade:* "Giles vs. Park View," Original WNRV radio broadcast, aired December 6, 1980 "Spartan Fever Turns to Bandana Delirium, Giles Wins It All," *Virginian Leader*, December 10, 1980.

192 *madhouse up here:* Scarangella, "Giles Fans Ready."

192 *glowing proudly:* Cheryl Downey-Laskowitz, "Christmas Star in Pearisburg Salutes Team," *Roanoke Times & World-News*, December 10, 1980; "Star Has Winner's Look," *Virginian Leader*, December 10, 1980.284

193 *largest of its kind:* N. A. Turkheimer, "World's Biggest Electric Star Will Make Debut on Mill Mountain Nov. 23," *Roanoke Times*, November 6, 1949.

193 *Fourteen years later:* "Pearis Chamber Committees Appointed," *Virginian Leader*, October 9, 1963.

193 *intended to be temporary:* Downey-Laskowitz, "Christmas Star in Pearisburg."

193 *Mayor Clarence Taylor:* *Virginian Leader*, "Star Has Winner's Look."

193 *"Noel" spelled backward:* "In Remembrance of the Fallen Rivals of the 1980 Giles High School Spartans," Unpublished poem.

CHAPTER 19

194 *Giles vs. Park View:* Original 16mm game film, filmed December 6, 1980; "Giles vs. Park View," Original WNRV radio broadcast, aired December 6, 1980; Dave Scarangella, "Giles Wins State Title in Football," *Roanoke Times & World-News,* December 7, 1980; Scarangella, "Perfect Season"; Tom Borrelli, "Giles Wins Virginia Championship," *Bluefield Daily Telegraph,* December 7, 1980; Skip Major, "Park View Bows to Giles, 33–32," *The Washington Post,* December 7, 1980; David J. Bisset, "Giles Wins Group AA State Title," *News Messenger,* December 7, 1980; Mike Williams, "Giles Sowns Park View, 33–32 for AA State Title," *Southwest Times,* December 7, 1980; Associated Press, "Park View Nipped; Pinkett Sets Record," *Winchester Star* (VA), December 8, 1980; *Virginian Leader,* "Spartan Fever Turns to Bandana Delirium"; "Giles Spartans Win State Championship," *Virginian Leader,* December 10, 1980; Michael Martz, "Giles Nips Patriots in Thriller," *Loudoun Times-Mirror,* December 11, 1980; Martz, "Football: Serious Business."

195 *"Bandana Country":* Martz, "Football: Serious Business."

195 *Hilltop Grocery:* Martz, "Football: Serious Business."

195 *Fairchild Incorporated:* Martz, "Football: Serious Business."

195 *names of fifteen Spartans:* Martz, "Football: Serious Business."

197 *climbed the towers:* Scarangella, "Giles Wins State Title."285

197 *Melvin Grubb:* Samantha Perry and Charles Boothe, "'He Was One of a Kind': Renowned Photographer, Beloved Community Member Mel Grubb Dies at 93," *Bluefield Daily Telegraph,* February 15, 2018.

197 *the following day:* Borrelli, "Giles Wins Virginia Championship."

198 *All-district kicker: Loudoun Times-Mirror,* "Loudoun Dominates All- District."

200 *behind a touchdown:* "Giles vs. Park View," Original WNRV radio broadcast, aired December 6, 1980.

200 *win convincingly: Bluefield Daily Telegraph,* "Giles Captures NRD Title"; *Roanoke Times & World-News,* "Giles Takes First Title"; *Virginian Leader,* "Spartans Win Football Mantle"; *Carroll News,*

"Carroll Falls Again."

200 **fourth miss all season:** *Loudoun Times-Mirror*, "Loudoun Dominates All- District."

200 **all-district selection:** *Loudoun Times-Mirror*, "Loudoun Dominates All- District."

200 **tight as a banjo string:** Scarangella, "Perfect Season"; Bisset, "Giles Wins Group AA State Title"; Martz, "Giles Nips Patriots in Thriller."

201 **victory over Handley:** Michael Martz, "Patriots Assume Lead in District Standings," *Loudoun Times-Mirror*, October 30, 1980.

203 **worried plenty:** "Giles vs. Park View," Original WNRV radio broadcast, aired December 6, 1980 audio recording.

CHAPTER 20

205 **will be the game:** Scarangella, "Perfect Season."

205 ***It'll be over:*** Martz, "Giles Nips Patriots in Thriller."

205 **to a state title:** George Stone, "Abingdon Shot Down in AA Finals," *Bristol Herald Courier*, June 3, 1984; Donald Huff, "Park View Builds Athletic Dominance," *Washington Post*, June 7, 1984.

206 **going to get buried:** Borrelli, "Giles Wins Virginia Championship."286

208 **state playoff record:** Virginia High School League, "Group AA State Records," *Official Program: 1981 Football Playoffs*.

210 **"in five seconds":** Scarangella, "Giles Wins State Title."

211 **seemed plain scared:** Borrelli, "Giles Wins Virginia Championship."

210 **consensus All-American:** Newton Spencer, "Coaches' Decision Helped Breland Make All-America," *Roanoke Times*, December 9, 1966.

212 **get them fired up:** Bisset, "Giles Wins Group AA State Title."

CHAPTER 21

215 *how Princeton blocked:* Caldwell, *Modern Single Wing Football,* 61–73.

CHAPTER 22

222 *it reached No. 1:* "Kool & the Gang | Biography, Music & News," Billboard, https://www.billboard.com/artist/kool-the-gang.

225 *two thousand for the season:* Associated Press, "Several Spartans Make AA Team."

225 *go for the win:* Borrelli, "Giles Wins Virginia Championship."

226 *state playoff record:* Virginia High School League, "Group AA State Records," *Official Program: 1981 Football Playoffs.*

228 *was concerned:* "Giles vs. Park View," Original WNRV radio broadcast, aired December 6, 1980.

229 *Just amazing:* Borrelli, "Giles Wins Virginia Championship."

229 *Harry, from his vantage point, understood:* "Giles vs. Park View," Original WNRV radio broadcast, aired December 6, 1980.

230 *the front page:* Scarangella, "Giles Wins State Title."

231 *echoed the sentiment: Virginian Leader,* "Star Has Winner's Look."

232 *a surprise banquet: Roanoke Times,* "Narrows High Coach Honored"; Bob Roemer, "Time For Sports," *Roanoke Times,* December 12, 1954; *Valley Leader & Narrows News,* "Saturday Night Was All Ragsdale."

BIBLIOGRAPHY

Baker, Rick. "Four Seasons Football." Historical High School Football Results for Central Appalachia. https://fourseasonsfootball.com.

Caldwell, Charles W. *Modern Single Wing Football.* J.B. Lippincott, 1951.

Christiansburg High School. *Demon.* 1948.

Coleman, Sherrill. *The Otters.* B&B Printing, 1991.

Edwards, Vic. *Winging It: Spartan Football 1961–2001.* Published by the author, 2001.

Fiftieth Anniversary Historical Committee. *The First Fifty Years: A History of the Town of Narrows 1904–1954.* Giles County Chamber of Commerce, 1956.

Flynn, George L., ed. *Vince Lombardi on Football.* Wallynn Inc., 1973.

Giles County, Virginia: History – Families. Giles County Historical Society, 1982.

Giles High School. *Shield.* 1981.

Grundy Senior High School. *Wave.* 1981.

Hopper, Margaret G., and G.A. Bollinger. *The Earthquake History of Virginia, 1774–1900.* Dept. of Geological Sciences, Virginia Polytechnic Institute and State University, 1971.

Jefferson Forest High School. *Selvetta.* 1973.

Jefferson Forest High School. *Sabre.* 1980.

Jefferson Forest High School. *Sabre.* 1981.

Lynchburg College. *Argonaut.* 1930.

Narrows High School. *Narrosonian.* 1933.

Narrows High School, *Narrosonian*. 1939.

Neale, Gay Weeks. *The Lunenburg Legacy*. Luneburg County Historical Society, 2005.

Nelson, David M. *The Anatomy of a Game*. University of Delaware Press, 1994.

Parry McCluer High School. *Parrimac*. 1958.

Perkins, Mark. *Football History of Narrows High School*. Volume 1 (1931–1962), 1995. Video recording.

Stafford, Frank K. "A Study of Secondary Education in Giles County." Master's thesis, University of Virginia, 1933.

Warner, Glenn Scobey. *Football for Coaches and Players*. Stanford University, 1927.

William Fleming High School. *Colonel*. 1981.

www.ingramcontent.com/pod-product-compliance
Lightning Source LLC
LaVergne TN
LVHW041750060526
838201LV00046B/962